Spies and Spymasters
of
The Civil War

Spies
and
Spymasters
of
The Civil War

Donald E. Markle

HIPPOCRENE BOOKS
New York

For information, address
HIPPOCRENE BOOKS
171 Madison Avenue
New York, NY 10016

Cataloging in Publication Data

Markle, Donald E.
     Spies and spymasters of the Civil War / Donald E. Markle.
         p.   cm.
     Includes bibliographical references and index.
     ISBN 0-7818-0227-X
     1. United States—History—Civil War, 1861–1865—Secret service.
     2. Spies—United States—History—19th century.   3. Spies—United
     States—Biography.   4. Intelligence service—United States—
     History—19th century.   I. Title.
     E608.M345   1993
     973.7'85—dc20   93-36068
                                                              CIP

Printed in the United States of America.

Contents

Acknowledgments

This book would not have been written had it not been for the Gettysburg Elderhostel Program sponsored by the Gettysburg YWCA. Their confidence in me as a teacher of Civil War courses was the inception of this project. In addition, the reaction of the Elderhostel students, when I discussed Civil War spies—"you should write a book about them"—gave me the impetus to follow through.

My research was aided in no small way by the efforts of Tem Tipton, reference librarian at the Adams County Library (Gettysburg), who made full use of the state-wide inter-library loan system to acquire books on the subject of Civil War spies for me. I could not have done it without her help. In addition, Louise Arnold-Friend, historian with the Military History Institute at Carlisle Barracks introduced me to the extensive Civil War holdings of the Institute. Her introduction opened a reservoir of original texts relating to spies of the Civil War.

Many historical and civic organizations were responsive to my queries regarding specific events and/or persons from their areas. Without exception the organizations responded quickly and were most helpful with their input. They include: Commissioners of Charles County Maryland; Congressional Research Service; Historical Book Section; Gettysburg College Library; International Museum of Photography; Iowa State Historical Society; Kentucky Military History Museum; Maryland Historical Society, Moorland-

Spingarn Research Center, Howard University; Museum of the Confederacy; New York State Historical Society; State Archives of Iowa; Surratt House Museum; Texas Department of Criminal Justice; United States Army Military History Library; United States Supreme Court and the Virginia Historical Society.

Deserving special mention is Dr. Gabor Boritt, Civil War Professor, Gettysburg College. Dr. Boritt was extremely helpful in guiding this first time writer though the maze of writing, approaching publishers and publication. Although a very busy man he was always patient and responsive to my queries.

Like most writers, I must say that my family was very supportive throughout the endeavor. My children never doubted that I would finish the project, and that gave me a great deal of incentive to continue. My wife was patient and at the same time served as my disciplinarian. Her positive attitude was infectious and greatly assisted me in finishing the project.

There were many other librarians, research personnel and friends who were supportive of the project, and I do thank them for their support and assistance.

And finally, I am indebted to Hippocrene Books for the publication of my book. I am well aware of the risks involved with first time writers and I hope that the finished project will do all of us proud.

Donald E. Markle
Gettysburg, Pennsylvania
1993

Introduction

Spying is often called the "second oldest profession" and historically speaking it well may be. European nations, for example, living in close contact with other nations, have had spy organizations since records have been kept. The British have always been highly respected for their espionage efforts, which in many ways contributed to their continued survival. In the United States, however, the picture is entirely different, for until 1884 the United States spying efforts were unorganized, event-driven, and sporadic at best.

During the Revolutionary War, the newly formed government was blessed with a spymaster who also served as the General of the Army, General George Washington. Without exception, histories of espionage contain Washington's name and rank him near the top of all time great spymasters. After the war, with his guidance, however, the newly formed United States made a conscious effort not to get entangled in the problems of Europe and the art of spying in the new country faded away. U.S. ambassadors abroad probably had staff members who kept their ears and eyes open for news of value, if that can be called spying, but nothing was done on an organized scale.

Later, in the War of 1812 and the Mexican War, spies were again used. In the Mexican War, General Winfield Scott organized "spy companies" composed of native Mexican men who went among the local Mexican population to develop intelligence. This was a move of necessity as General Scott could not utilize his English speaking Regular Army personnel. With the peace treaty, the necessity disappeared, and the spy companies were immediately disbanded. Spying remained dormant in the U.S. military until the beginning of the Civil War.

Spying during the Civil War was incredibly easy for both sides. The enemies were the same nationality (American), they spoke the same language (with dialects), had the same moral codes and backgrounds, had been under the same government, and knew each other's geography well, a situation unknown in other countries of the world. Then, as now, to be an effective spy in a foreign land requires years of extensive training in the nuances of the language, customs and manners of the country, such as eating with the fork in a certain hand, dress, personality traits, etc. These were not issues for a Civil War spy, Union or Confederate, but one had to be willing, brave and intelligent to avoid capture. Amateurs were welcome and became the core of both the Union and Confederate spy systems.

To understand spying during the Civil War readers must enter a "time warp" and take a good look at the 1860s. Passions ran high in support of both the Union and the Confederacy with very little middle ground. The Union was split between the abolitonists who demanded an end to slavery and the "peaceniks" who wanted peace at any price. The Confederacy had a dis-unified front—one group believed strongly in the issue of states rights, another fought for the continuation of slavery, and a third consisting of "Unionists" believed the war to be wrong. All of these causes led to spying for and against all efforts.

Documentation proves the American Civil War was a war of amateurs, particularly in the military sense. Less than 50 percent of the general officers who served in either army were West Point graduates, the remainder were volunteers and political appointees—amateurs in the art of warfare. It is easy to understand why both sides readily took to amateur spies. Being amateurs themselves, it was natural that their spies would be amateurs as well. The only Union Military Intelligence Unit during the Civil War belonged to the Adjutant General who had sole responsibility for answering questions from families concerning family members in the War. With no professional intelligence arm in the military or government, there was no choice but to accept the many volunteer spies that enlisted. Some of the recruits were loyal, others double agents, an easy position to obtain with the lax recruiting procedures of both armies.

At the onset of the war there is no doubt that the Confederacy had the upper hand in the world of spying for many reasons:

• The Union government had organized departments and established functions, where the Confederacy could place agents as employees and recruit those already in place with Southern sympathies. The Union did not initially have a government to target by location or by name.
• The Confederacy, prior to secession, began to develop espionage rings in Washington. For example, Rose O'Neal Greenhow and Benjamin F. Stringfellow started their activities prior to the onset of the hostilities. There is no evidence that the Union had any spy operation in place within the Confederacy. The earliest known ring is that of Elizabeth Van Lew in Richmond which was started on her own initiative. The Union spent the first few years playing "catch up."
• The Confederacy gained much strategic intelligence from the Union military officers and U.S. Government workers who "went south" after the secession. The Union, in contrast, gained little as the movement to the North was minimal.
• With the exception of General Robert E. Lee's two invasions of the North, General Braxton Bragg's advance into Kentucky and occasional raids, Union spies who went behind the Confederate lines were entering hostile territory and had few "safe houses" where Union sympathizers would assist their efforts. The Confederacy on the other hand had an established network of safe houses and courier lines, such as the Doctor's Line, which was established early in the war by Confederate sympathizers who remained in the North, predominately in the Southern Maryland area.

Technology impacted on the spying activities of the Civil War. The telegraph was used effectively for military and governmental messages, but the Civil War spy could not utilize the telegraph in enemy territory—and radio was yet to appear. But telegraph did aid the mission of the spy by providing a method of moving information in a rapid manner once the information got to a telegraphic outpost. The military could receive reports in a more timely manner, but the major newspapers acquired reports often as rapidly as the military commander. Therefore enemy newspapers became important to the spy in enemy territory. There are many examples of spies collecting newspapers and having them couriered to their governments, or else performing a clipping service whereby articles of interest were clipped and either couriered or signaled back to their governments. In addition, telegraphic spies listened in on enemy communications either by tapping telegraphic lines or by acting as a telegrapher for the enemy. They were rare, but most effective.

The rapid movement of information may be credited for the high number of female agents in the Union and the Confederacy. For the first time during a war, the civilian population received timely news of their armies, their losses, their victories and their problems. Patriotic females with a deep-seated desire to assist their governments, in areas other than nursing, were fed by the daily reports from the battlefields—a totally new experience that could well have led to an adventurous female undertaking the role of spy for her government.

Another technological development that came into its own about this time was photography. Both sides were fascinated by personal and historic pictures, but there were also enterprising photographers who served the Union and the Confederacy as photographic spies. For the Confederacy, A.D. Lytle photographed Union encampments in the Louisiana area, placing particular emphasis on the weapons and number of troops. For the Union, Alexander Gardner was employed as a photographic covert operator by Allan Pinkerton, head of the Secret Service for General George McClellan. Gardner photographed areas of geographic interest to the field commanders for use in producing maps for military use. General Sherman also made use of photographers to produce maps while on his Atlanta and March to the Sea campaigns. Few individual spies employed photography for their missions as it had not yet come into public use.

One final point of warning regarding the spy activities of both the Union and Confederate spies of the Civil War—their information was not always accurate. One example of bad information reported by a spy was in the fall of 1862 when the Confederate Generals Van Dorn and Price were considering an attack on Corinth in Mississippi. General Van Dorn had a female spy located in Corinth who unfortunately provided him with faulty information. Based on her input General Van Dorn grossly underestimated the number of Federal troops he faced. This miscalculation lead to a Confederate rout with a loss of over 5,000 of his 25,000 troops.

The study of individual spies teaches a great deal about the intelligence operations during the Civil War. All of the spies included in this book represent a unique facet of spying—particular styles, superior intellects, opportunities that arose, and unique methods of spying that could only be productive in that era.

I have attempted to relate individual impacts on the outcome of the Civil War, on the modern world of intelligence, and on the individual techniques developed to counter problems such as movement of intelligence, establishment of credibility within services and methods of establishing confidence with the enemy. I have also tried to carry each story beyond the Civil War. It is often difficult for a person who has served as a spy to return to normal life—some of our spies did and some did not.

Chapter 1

Civil War "Spy Chiefs"

The intelligence efforts for both the Union and the Confederate governments during the first two to three years of the Civil War can be characterized by the phrase "too many Indians and not enough chiefs." Neither side had an organized intelligence department and both lacked central control. The Services depended on individual spies who on their own, sometimes as a lark, decided to spy for their government. Elizabeth Van Lew for the Union and Belle Boyd for the Confederacy were self-appointed intelligence gatherers in the early years. By 1863, the Union military had an effective organized regional intelligence service, due basically to the initiative of General U.S. Grant. Evidence shows that the Confederacy was still struggling with proposals for organizing military intelligence at the close of the war.

When hostilities broke out in April of 1861, it is valid to say that the Confederacy had by far the better of the two intelligence networks. Why? First and foremost, they had a functioning organized government and military to target (the United States) while

1

the Union had only a phantom to counter. In contrast, initially no one knew where the Confederate government would locate, what its structure would be, or who would be its civilian and military leaders.

There were Confederate sympathizers in positions of trust in the U.S. Government at the beginning of the war and many of them, particularly the ones strategically placed, were convinced they should stay in those positions during the entire conflict. Both Rose O'Neal Greenhow and Thomas Conrad, Confederate spy leaders in Washington, had ring members working in the War Department and relaying information to them. The Union could not duplicate this in the early stages of the Confederacy.

A good example of the early Confederate foresight in this area is the work that Colonel Thomas Jordan did in establishing the Confederate spy operations in Washington in conjunction with Rose O'Neal Greenhow. Colonel Jordan served as a U.S. Army officer prior to the fall of Fort Sumter in South Carolina, and had the distinction of being the West Point roommate of General Sherman. He was stationed in Washington in 1861 and quietly went about establishing Confederate espionage rings in the city. When the war effort turned earnest, Colonel Jordan gave up his secret endeavors and became a Cavalry colonel serving under General Pierre Beauregard. The Washington network he established was flourishing and paid off handsomely. Mrs. Greenhow was able to supply information to the Confederacy prior to the first Battle of Bull Run in Virginia, which gave the Confederacy their first victory. Colonel Jordan, using the name of Thomas J. Rayford in his intelligence endeavors, never spoke of his work in Washington, and left no written accounts of his activities or of the people involved. He remained silent on this phase of his military career throughout his lifetime—the true mark of a professional intelligence operative!

Colonel Thomas Jordan's counterpart, and eventual replacement in Richmond, was Major William Norris. Prior to the war he had graduated from Yale and was practicing law in New Orleans. His Richmond organization grew to at least 60 personnel including 10 captains, 20 lieutenants and 30 sergeants, as well as scores of enlisted men, all of whom were more interested in maintaining the courier links with the North and supplying intelligence to the Richmond government than the day-to-day intelligence required for a functioning army. Norris' organization's philosophy may have come about through the action of General Robert E. Lee. Prior to General Joseph Hooker's troops crossing the Rappahannock on April 12, 1863, Norris provided him with the following information:

- General Hooker had 150,000 troops with him.
- There were 10,000 reinforcements on the way.

General Hooker actually had 130,000 men and 9,000 reinforcements but Norris was not too far off. However, General Lee dismissed the report as having no validity. Disbelief of intelligence information is indeed disheartening to an intelligence officer.

Prior to November 30, 1864, when the Confederacy established an official Secret Service, the only intelligence unit of the Confederate military was the General Intelligence Office, headed by Chaplain William A. Crocker, established by General Order 45, January 26, 1862. The sole function of this department, like that of the Union, was "to collect information regarding the sick and wounded."

Probably the most knowledgeable Confederate general on the use of intelligence was Stonewall Jackson, who succinctly stated his requirements as:

- Position of enemy forces
- Number of troops and their movements
- Generals in command and in their headquarters
- Location of the headquarters of the commanding general

Jackson felt this was all the information he needed to counter the enemy.

Like his counterpart Colonel Thomas Jordan, Major William Norris was an extremely private man who never talked or wrote of his experiences after the war. The only possible source of information of value, his private papers, were destroyed in a house fire in 1890.

The self-imposed silence of Colonel Jordan and Major Norris, along with the Confederate burning of the city of Richmond, makes it difficult for contemporary scholars to learn much about the Confederate intelligence organizations. Bits and pieces survive, enough to lead to a great deal of what-if speculation. There is no evidence to suggest that the Richmond-based intelligence service had any impact on day-to-day operations of the Confederate military—that information appears to have been supplied by scouts and spies assigned to the individual armies. Generals who believed in intelligence used their spies and scouts and those who did not understand the value of field intelligence were remiss in this area. This is easily understood when one realizes that no senior officers were assigned the role of military intelligence.

In addition to the Confederate spymasters there was also a Confederate spycatcher by the name of General John Henry Winder, who operated in Richmond and was the head of a group known as the Safety Committee that searched for Union spies throughout the Confederacy. General Winder, although credited with the capture of Timothy Webster, was actually ineffective in his spy catching efforts. He was a man who understood the meaning of graft and enjoyed the practice throughout his career. One Union spy reported that he was given a travel pass for the Confederacy by making a generous contribution towards a new dress uniform for General Winder. Union spies routinely got the travel pass for a contribution of $100. General Winder was totally ignorant of the world of espionage and did virtually nothing to correct the situation. He was not in the same league as his Union counterparts, Pinkerton and Baker.

The Union picture is much clearer, but initially haphazard in nature. When the Civil War began there had been no intelligence element in the United States Army since General Winfield Scott's spy companies in the Mexican War. The last spymaster had been the superb General George Washington. The institutional Secret Service was established in 1860 by the Department of the Treasury but only for counterfeiters, and in 1901 for the protection of senior government officials. This organization did not have an official head until July 5, 1865.

The first step in establishing a military intelligence service came with the assumption of command of the Army of the Potomac by General George McClellan who brought with him Allan Pinkerton, the well-known railroad detective. Prior to his re-entry into the U.S. Army, George McClellan had been associated with the railroads in Chicago, and had utilized Pinkerton as a detective. He was well aware that he needed such a man with him in the Army. Like McClellan's appointment, this turned out to be a disaster.

The initial staff for Pinkerton's Secret Service consisted mainly of the core of his male and female detectives who worked for him in his private business, a total of 16 to 18 agents. The most famous of this group was Timothy Webster, a capable spy, who was hanged in Richmond in 1861. Most of Pinkerton's staff continued to work in the detective mode rather than the spy mode, and many left the secret service when Pinkerton returned to civilian life. One Pinkerton endeavor that did prove successful was the interrogation of runaway slaves as they came into Union lines; they often had valuable information potentially useful to the Union forces. If the agents found a Negro that could read and write and appeared to be intelligent, they made every effort to have that person "turned around" and sent back into the South as a spy. John Scobell was the most successful of the Negro spies that were recruited by Pinkerton's operation.

Pinkerton's main shortcoming was that he lived in awe of General McClellan, not only in his personal life but as chief of his Intelligence Service, and that fact was his downfall. Any successful intelligence chief must be unbiased, must develop accurate intelligence, must not slant the results to any particular individual's desire and should report his results as a tool to his superior. Pinkerton did none of this! He knew that McClellan was reporting exaggerated Confederate troop figures to Washington, but rather than stick to the reality that his agents reported to him, he allowed the figures to be inflated in order to please his boss (for example, Pinkerton estimated that General Lee had over 200,000 men when in actuality he had only 80,000). He also knew General McClellan's thinking about the Confederacy and he instructed his agents to find the facts that supported the McClellan position, rather than gathering the facts to produce a current intelligence evaluation of the Confederacy, independent of any senior's pre-conceived position. This type of performance is not uncommon when the intelligence chief is under the influence of his superior, but it was detrimental to the Union effort at that time; and it remains detrimental to intelligence efforts today.

Despite his efforts to collect tactical intelligence for General McClellan, Pinkerton never understood the perishability factor of tactical information. What might be of value to a general *now* may be totally useless in *ten minutes*. Pinkerton sent his agents on their missions with no clear instructions for reporting their information. Much of it arrived too late to be of any value and many Civil War historians believe that to be true throughout the war. But with the arrival of General Grenville Dodge in the West and General George Sharpe in the East, the situation changed. They were military men who clearly understood the value of timely intelligence—a problem for any army in the field, even in the 20th century.

There was also an administrative problem associated with the assignment of Pinkerton as head of the Secret Service for General Mc-Clellan. He was charged with supplying intelligence to General McClellan but also was charged with the personal security of the President. While McClellan was marching and training his troops in the Washington area, this was no real problem. However, when McClellan went into the field and Pinkerton went with him the problems arose. How could he be a competent tactical intelligence provider while at the same time be responsible for the personal security of the President of the United States? It spread him so thin that he did neither job very well. It should be noted, in his defense, that without his security efforts on behalf of the President there would have been none. Hard to believe in our modern age, but very true in the Civil War Days!

Later, Pinkerton wrote a book about his intelligence experiences in the Civil War, probably in an attempt to enhance his reputation, and that is all that survives of Pinkerton's war efforts. The entire file of the Pinkerton Secret Service Civil War records burned in the Chicago fire, and once again there are virtually no records for the modern historian to research. Pinkerton's reputation remains as a famous detective, but his intelligence services during the Civil War are clouded by his absolute devotion to the man he served, General George McClellan.

About the same time that McClellan hired Pinkerton, General Winfield Scott, the Senior Union Army officer on active duty, realized that he too needed an intelligence officer. He hired Lafayette Baker, who was given the same title that Pinkerton had—Head of the Secret Service—an unofficial title. This organizational nightmare led to confusion within the government, and within the two Secret Services as well. It was not uncommon for one of the Union Secret Services to arrest an agent of the other as a Confederate spy! There was no coordination or interaction between the two agencies but there was competition!

When Pinkerton went to the field with McClellan, Lafayette Baker had free rein in Washington, D.C., and he relished it! His organization was transferred to the War Department with an annual budget of $65,000 and about 40 agents. He had gone into the Confederacy on a spy mission for General Scott, disguised as an itinerant photographer (it took him three tries to make it behind enemy lines), but he later confined his work to Washington, basically in the area of counter-intelligence and uncovering government fraud. Baker was unrelenting in his efforts and did reasonably well, until late in the war when he fingered a certain Washington lady who was selling presidential pardons. Baker, believing he had an excellent case reported it to President Lincoln, who in fact was signing the pardons for her clients. The President ordered Baker to cease and desist his investigation of the pardon selling operation but he refused, causing a permanent rift between Baker and the President.

When Pinkerton returned to civilian life and a profitable detective business, it became the duty of Baker's Secret Service to protect the President. He was not as conscientious as Pinkerton had been and on April 14, 1865, he got into real trouble. A man from Baker's Secret Service was assigned to guard the presidential box at Ford's Theater! Lafayette Baker never successfully accounted for the whereabouts of his man during that terrible night.

Like Pinkerton, Baker wrote a book about his life in the Secret Service and, like Pinkerton, used his book to justify his actions, a practice used today by some of our international intelligence leaders.

While Baker was busy with his Secret Service in Washington— which was absolutely of no value to the Union military forces— General Grant was building his own military intelligence organization that would serve him throughout the war. Initially, Grant's efforts began in the West in October of 1862, with the assignment of General Grenville Dodge to a dual role, that of Grant's intelligence chief for Western Operations and that of a regimental combat commander.

General Dodge was an engineer who, after the war, became famous as the builder of the Union Pacific Railroad. He entered the Union Army as a colonel in charge of the newly formed 4th Iowa Infantry Regiment. Dodge saw considerable military action with this unit in the West. In addition to his combat role and that of building railroads for the military, he was in charge of General Grant's intelligence operations in the West. Although untrained in this area, he became a proficient spymaster and was of great value to the campaigns of General Grant, and those of General William T. Sherman. General Dodge was quick to adopt excellent spy tradecraft and continued to practice it throughout the war. Some of his techniques included:

• Given the command of the 1st Tennessee Cavalry, a unit of Southern Unionists, Dodge realized the asset he had (they all spoke "Dixie") and enlisted many of them to serve in his spy organization.
• Dodge developed a large cadre of scouts, headed by William F. Harrison, whose activities served as cover for the concurrent spy operations.
• His spies, numbering about 117, were known only by numbers (not names) and no one knew who the other spies were.
• He told his spies never to sellout the Union if captured, but to say enough to save their skins. No spy ever sold out during the entire war. However, even with these instructions about 50 percent of his spies were captured or killed during the war.
• His agents were paid about $750 to spend three months in the South and about $300 to check on troop movements requiring a shorter time in the field.
• He was the first known general to use spies to run down rumors—make them truth or kill the rumors—which were dangerous in an army.
• When spies went on long missions they took couriers with them, so that vital information could be sent back immediately to the Union Army. He frequently used females as couriers because they had a better chance of getting through the Confederate lines.
• Females were regularly employed by General Dodge as spies. Two of his favorites were Jane Featherstone and Molly Malone, who was totally illiterate but very successful as a spy. Molly Malone was Dodge's favorite agent and between May and July of 1863 she was paid $750 for three trips to Meridan, Columbus, Jackson, Okolona and Selma.
• He never revealed the spies in any area to the general in charge of

that area. On one occasion General Stephen Hurlbut demanded to know the agents in his area. Dodge refused. Hurlbut went to General Grant who backed General Dodge in his refusal.

• He frequently used Negro personnel for both spy and courier duties. He organized escaping Negro slaves into the 1st Alabama Colored Infantry and 1st Alabama Colored Cavalry Regiments. He sent the intelligent and willing Negroes south as spies and to establish Negro spy networks throughout the Southern areas. They frequently used their relatives as couriers when in the South.

• He developed a technique to estimate the size of an enemy army by calculating how much space they occupied on a road. This technique proved particularly accurate when time was of the essence.

• General Dodge had a keen interest in maps and topography. His walls were covered with maps of the area and as the spies reported, the maps were updated and corrected. They proved to be useful to General Grant when planning a future campaign.

• When running short of money to operate his intelligence network, he devised a self-paying plan: selling the cotton the Union troops had captured and using the money to finance his operations. General Dodge loved this scheme as he felt that the Confederacy was financing his spy operations against them.

• Late in the War, about 1865, when transferred to the West, he successfully used friendly Indians, half-breeds and Indian wives of white men, as spies against the Indian tribes that harassed the construction of the new railroad.

One of General Dodge's favorite methods of collecting data was to send his Chief of Staff, Captain George Spencer, behind enemy lines under a flag of truce with a message to be delivered personally to the Confederate commander. Spencer was quite adept at convincing the enemy picket officer of his mission and normally succeeded in passing through to the commander. Once, having asked to see General Philip Roddey, the general was furious at his picket officer for bringing the Union officer to his headquarters. The information that Spencer collected resulted in the following message to Major General Richard Oglesby in Jackson:

My. A.A.G. Captain George E. Spencer has just returned from Tuscumbia; succeeded in getting through all of the enemy's camps and obtaining valuable information. The forces are posted as follows: Colonel Bibrell, 900 men at Tuscumbia Landing; Colonel Josiah Patterson, 1,000 at Florence; Colonel M.W. Hannon 1,800 at Tuscumbia; Colonel Roddey's old regiment, 800, at Tuscumbia Landing; Baxter Smith, 350, ten miles this side; Colonel Hampton, 300 at same place; W.R. Juilian, 300, at Grey's, six miles this side; and Smith, 100 at Big Bear. The above all cavalry. Between Courtland and Tuscumbia, one brigade of Infantry, under Colonel Wood, as follows: Colonel A. H. Helvenston, 300; Colonel J.B. Bibb, 500; Colonel W.B. Wood, Sixteenth Alabama, 400. The 1st brigade, and one brigade of cavalry, under General Roddey, arrived at Tuscumbia last week. This more than doubles their force. They have also five pieces of artillery at Florence and six pieces at Tuscumbia.

G.M. Dodge,
Brigadier General

But with all this tradecraft what did Dodge's network accomplish? The entire story will never be told as General Dodge did not write or speak at any length of his intelligence experiences after the war, but there are examples of his success:

• In Missouri his agents reported the advance of troops led by Generals Earl Van Dorn and Sterling Price, thereby saving the Army of the Southwest from ruin.
• General Dodge's spies warned the Union forces of the rapid advance of a strong Confederate force (March 1862) and saved the Union from defeat at Pea Ridge, Arkansas.
• His organization reported that the Confederacy's boast of General Albert S. Johnston's having 60,000 men to assail General Grant's rear was false. Dodge said it was nearer 30,000 and he was correct.
• One of his spies named Sanburn on May 16, 1863, correctly assessed the strength of General Pemberton's forces at Champion Hill (near Vicksburg, Mississippi) and stated that General Johnston could not come to the aid of General Pemberton if attacked by the Union. With this information Grant turned on Champion Hill and defeated Pemberton's forces.
• His most famous spy Henson, a Union sympathizer from Mississippi, actually got inside Vicksburg before the Battle of Vicksburg and was able to relay to Dodge all the vital information about the

10

health, well being, arms, and supplies of the Confederate forces inside the Vicksburg fortifications.

• Prior to the Battle of Atlanta, Georgia, he had two spies in Atlanta that sent information to him on a daily basis.

• One of Dodge's spies in Atlanta came to him with an Atlanta newspaper that carried the headline of General John B. Hood replacing General Joseph Johnston. When told of this fact, General Sherman, who knew General Hood, stated that this change of command meant that the Confederates would attack within 48 hours. Hood did in fact attack within that time and his army was repulsed—Sherman was ready for him.

• A General Dodge spy, actually working on the staff of Confederate General Johnston, informed General Dodge of the exact number of Confederate soldiers fit for duty in the battle for Atlanta, as well as the names of all of the division, brigade and regimental commanders. (Name recognition of opposing officers often helped in planning a strategy.).

General Dodge was a dedicated officer who knew his role and how to accomplish it. He astutely directed the large scale intelligence operations for the Union Western armies and left local intelligence to the subordinate units.

Although his spy tradecraft was excellent, he did get into difficulties with General Grant and President Lincoln for his over zealous action regarding captured spies. On at least two occasions, captured spies were summarily tried and executed prior to the forwarding of paperwork for approval to execute. His hasty actions almost cost him a promotion.

With the end of hostilities he ceased as a spymaster and went on to become a world famous railroad engineer. General Dodge is generally known by Civil War students for combat and railroad building roles, but not as the Western front intelligence chief. His own written works after the war are not explicit about the spymaster role he played, but he was effective and of great value to General Grant during the Union Western campaigns.

When General Grant came east, as the general of the Army, Dodge remained to continue his work for the Western armies. He had to find an eastern intelligence chief, but the task was easy as there was a general operating an intelligence network already. He was George H. Sharpe, who was on the staff of General Meade. General Marsena Patrick, the provost marshal for General Hooker, had recently been ordered to set up an intelligence operation for the entire Union army and he had chosen General Sharpe to handle the tactical intelligence operation. Grant agreed with this move and quickly transferred Sharpe from Meade's staff to his own, where he served for the remainder of the war.

Prior to the war George H. Sharpe had been a successful New York attorney who entered the Union Army as a colonel with the 120th New York Volunteers. He soon became interested in the world of intelligence and was shortly named the first head of the newly formed Union Bureau of Military Information. In the early days of the war his work was not appreciated by his generals who tended to ignore his assessments. However, by mid-1863 the Sharpe organization was the most professional spy organization in the U.S. military since the days of George Washington. By this time, the Union Army had finally surpassed the Confederacy in knowledge of the opposing forces, largely due to the efforts of General Sharpe. His grasp of the importance of intelligence is clearly stated in a letter he wrote to a citizen in Gettysburg who had forwarded information to him. The letter states:

Middleburg, June 29, 1863
7 P.M.

D. McConaughy Esq
Gettysburg

My dear Sir

The General directs me to thank you for yours of today. You have grasped the information so well in its directness & minuteness, that it is very valuable. I hope our friends understand that in the great game that is now being played, everything in the way of advantage depends upon which side gets the best information. . . .

The names of the Generals (& number of forces if possible) are very important to us, as they enable us to guage the reports with exactness. The General begs, if in your power, that you make such arrangements with intelligent friends in the country beyond you to this effect, and that you continue your attention to us, as much as your convenience will permit.

Hoping at some day to have the pleasure of meeting you.
I am Dear Sir
Yours very truly
George H. Sharpe

By the end of the war Sharpe had approximately 200 agents throughout the entire Confederacy. Like General Dodge, his counterpart in the West, General Sharpe never revealed the names of his agents. In his daily reports written to the Provost Marshal, Sharpe referred only to "our agent" and on some occasions he gave a location of operation, but never a name. In the later stages of the war, it was General Sharpe's organization that received the communications from Miss Van Lew in Richmond. The closest one can get to identifying her communications is when General Sharpe refers to receiving a message in code—Miss Van Lew used a code.

General Sharpe continued Pinkerton's practice of using special ethnic groups for spying, in this case the Pamunkey Indians of Southern Virginia. These Indians were a mixture of Negroes intermarried with local Indians and very knowledgeable of the Virginia area. In addition, when the Confederacy began to think of recruiting Negroes as soldiers, Sharpe proposed that the Union send loyal Negroes into the South to infiltrate the Confederate Negro units to cause unrest and win the troops over to the Union cause. General Sharpe wrote in one of his daily reports that "The Negroes are an eminently secretive people; they have a system of mutual understanding amounting almost to free masonry among themselves."

The Provost at the time, General Marsena Patrick, always ensured that the Secret Service men of Lafayette Baker were excluded from the work of General Sharpe. His mission of tactical intelligence was something that was unknown to Baker and his man and General Patrick wanted to keep it that way.

General Sharpe understood the value of rapid transmission of data, much like General Dodge, and he was constantly experimenting with new and novel ideas to increase the speed. One of his ideas was the hot air balloon which did increase the speed of transmission of data but proved highly susceptible to the new rifled weaponry. Finally on December 4, 1864, General Sharpe wrote, "We think we have perfected an arrangement to have immediate information of the movement of the enemy." What General Sharpe was referring to was the following: Each night he would send scouts to the outskirts of Richmond where they would rendezvous with the agents, or their couriers, from Richmond. The information would be in General Sharpe's hands by early morning, which was rapid for that time.

Prior to the Battle of Gettysburg, July 1863, when General Sharpe was assigned to General Joseph Hooker, his organization attempted to alert the General Staff of the impending movement of the Confederate troops. These efforts included:

• Informing General Hooker that the Confederate troops, serving under General Robert E. Lee, were under long marching orders. This report was filed on 27 May 1863.
• As the Confederate troops moved north they were under continual observation of General Sharpe's men and the reports were given to General Hooker's staff.

During the actual Battle of Gettysburg, Sharpe and his capable assistant John Babcock were able to ascertain the following:
• A message had been captured from a courier of President Jefferson Davis to General Lee that no possibility existed for any reinforcements.
• By the morning of July 2, Sharpe's organization had determined that the entire Army of Northern Virginia was present at Gettysburg with the exception of one division, and that every brigade present had been in the fight.
• Later on July 2 and prior to the council of war with General Meade, the Sharpe organization had determined that the missing division of the Army of Northern Virginia had arrived, that it was commanded by General Pickett and that it could be expected to see action on 3 July.
• At that same council of war, General Sharp informed General Meade that he estimated a manpower advantage to the Union of 6 to 1 in fresh troops.

After the final battle at Gettysburg, July 3, 1863, General Sharpe gave General George G. Meade an up-to-date report from his top agent, Babcock, which stated that the Confederacy would not attack again on 4 July as General Lee's army was now too weak. It further recommended that General Meade attack General Lee before he had a chance to retreat. (The lack of action on this report remained a sore point with General Sharpe the rest of his life).

In contrast to the troop estimates supplied by Pinkerton to McClellan, General Sharpe prior to the Battle at Chancellorsville, Virginia, estimated the strength of the Confederate Army to within one-quarter of one percent.

During the entire Civil War General Sharpe used the codename Colonel Streight for all correspondence addressed to him by his agents. Many of them did not know who they actually worked for, then or later. For just as General Dodge referred only vaguely to his intelligence experiences so did General Sharpe. It is a real mark of distinction for these two men, neither trained in intelligence operations, that they were so successful during the war and yet secure enough in their own right that they did not have to dwell on their achievements for the rest of their lives.

After the war George Sharpe became the surveyor of the Port of New York and maintained an interest in New York State politics. He remained a close friend of General Grant throughout the remainder of his life.

In conclusion, it is obvious that neither side in the Civil War had a totally effective intelligence organization. Much was left to the individual efforts and too little thought was given to the transmission of the data for rapid use in the military environment. Generals Dodge and Sharpe did amazingly well considering what they had to work with and their efforts did in fact pay dividends for the Union Army—how many no one but these two men know.

As a point of interest the reader might like to know that it was not until 1885 that the military services formally organized their own intelligence services. The initial army effort was known as the Military Information Division and was part of the Adjutant General's Office. Today that Division has grown within the Department of Defense into a Military Intelligence Department for each service (Army, Navy, Air Force and Marines) a Defense Intelligence Agency and other joint service activities. Generals Dodge and Sharpe were on the right track!

Chapter 2

Intelligence Courier Systems

Report! was a word that caused anxiety for both Union and Confederate spies during the Civil War. Once they had acquired information of use to their superiors, how were they to transmit the data in time to make it of value? This was particularly important if the information was of a military nature and could in fact impact ongoing operations. While many of the spymasters failed to grasp this point, some spies, both Confederate or Union, were aware of the perishable nature of their information and they independently derived many unique ways to pass the data—in some cases even making mad dashes through enemy lines to deliver intelligence in person (ala Belle Boyd).

The first Union spymaster, Allan Pinkerton, had virtually no appreciation of the time sensitive nature of a military intelligence operation. His previous experience was detective work for the railroads. His detectives worked on specific cases until they had enough data to bring about the arrest, then returned home and reported their findings which hopefully led to the prosecution of a perpetrator (not an efficient way to handle military intelligence). Pinkerton's agents such as Timothy Webster and George Curtis were very efficient in penetrating the Confederacy and obtaining valuable strategic intelligence, but both relied upon returning to the Union to pass on their information—neither utilized couriers to perform this function. Not only were they delaying the arrival of potentially time sensitive information but they were increasing their own danger factor by making frequent trips back to the North. (The most efficient spy stays in place and develops his own methods of getting the data to his government without casting any suspicion on himself.)

Later in the war, Negro underground organizations, such as the Legal League, served unofficially as Union couriers, particularly for Union Negro spies such as John Scobell. In addition, Union sympathizers had secret organizations in the Confederacy such as the Order of the Heroes, the Peace Society and the Peace and Constitution Society, with members who served as couriers in cases of emergency. All of these underground organizations were unorganized and strictly a "hit or miss" proposition with untrained personnel.

It was not until the Union military instituted its own military intelligence organizations with specific officers designated as chiefs of Intelligence that the system changed appreciably for the Union. General Grenville Dodge in the West and General George Sharpe in the East both clearly understood the value of the early receipt of military intelligence, and their organizations included a cadre of couriers for the express purpose of transmitting data in a timely manner. In many recorded instances the couriers used by both Generals Dodge and Sharpe were females, since they had a much better chance of crossing enemy lines "to see their boyfriend or a brother, etc." Frequently the spies would take a courier with them to return with the data—if in fact the information potentially had an impact on operations.

One self-appointed Union agent, Elizabeth Van Lew, operating out of Richmond, clearly understood the value of timely intelligence. On her own, with no instructions from the Union, she established five safe houses along a route to Union territory north of Richmond. She had her servants man the houses and serve as courier relay points to carry the intelligence derived by Miss Van Lew to the Union side. Her system was so efficient that when General U.S.

Grant was opposing General Robert E. Lee above Richmond, Miss Van Lew had fresh flowers delivered for his table every day, frequently with an encrypted message inside. Her courier system was very efficient!

The methods utilized by the couriers of the Confederacy were from the very start much more efficient than that of the Union, probably because the Confederacy had an active intelligence network in Washington, D.C., several months before the war began. The earliest Confederate courier line was called the Doctor's Line since it consisted of both real and bogus doctors operating in the Washington and Southern Maryland areas. Doctors were frequently called out at night and other irregular times and they always carried a black bag—which was a great place to hide couriered material. One of the early doctors on this line was Doctor Stowton Dent who moved with ease and was never challenged.

The most famous early couriers for the Confederacy were those used by Rose O'Neal Greenhow who ran an espionage ring in Washington even before President Lincoln came to the White House. Her couriers were very effective and were never caught by the Union.

Mrs. Greenhow used two females, Betty Duvall and Lillie Mac-Kall, in Washington, and one, Antonia Ford, in Manassas, to courier her intelligence to the Confederacy. Just prior to the Battle of Bull Run in Virginia, Mrs. Greenhow had obtained very useful information regarding the size of the Union Army that would be going south, the route of the march, the attempt to cut off General Joseph E. Johnston's troops and the actual order given by General Irvin McDowell to his troops. To pass this information to General Pierre Beauregard she used her courier Betty Duvall.

Miss Duvall had jet black hair which she normally wore in braids. Mrs. Greenhow enciphered her message, folded it as small as she could and then placed the messages in a tiny black silk pouch. The pouch was woven into Miss Duvall's braid in such a manner that it was totally hidden. Miss Duvall then rode south and delivered the packet to an amazed General Beauregard who stood there and watched as Miss Duvall unbraided her hair! This particular packet of information was instrumental in the Confederacy victory in the First Battle of Bull Run.

Later that year when Mrs. Greenhow was arrested by Pinkerton (in her home—a huge counter-intelligence mistake—one never arrests a spy at home) she was very concerned about the incriminating information she had in her bedroom. She feigned a heat attack and asked to be allowed to change her clothes (knowing that Pinkerton did not have a female agent in the group), and was finally allowed to go to her bedroom. At that moment Lillie MacKall, another one of her couriers arrived and also went to the bedroom. After much discussion, Lillie lowered her silk stockings, wrapped her legs with the incriminating evidence, stuffed her shoes with more and then waddled out of the Greenhow house carrying all the evidence that Pinkerton was looking for and never found.

The Confederacy had an established courier route that ran down along the Southern side of the Potomac River in Maryland. On this route was the now famous Surratt House, in Clinton, Maryland, which was used as a safe house for couriers throughout the war. In addition, a farmer by the name of Thomas Jones had a farm right on the point of the Maryland side of the Potomac River directly across from the permanently established Confederate relay station on the southern shore. Mr. Jones served as a lookout for the Union picket boats that patrolled the river searching for illegal river crossings. Jones also provided the boats for Confederate agents to cross the river to and from the Confederate side of the Potomac River. In September of 1861, Mr. Jones was arrested and jailed for his anti-Union actions. During his prison stay his wife died and he became even more embittered against the Union. When he was released several months later he immediately returned to his operations as before.

In addition to the courier line there existed in southern Maryland another line known by Lafayette Baker of the Union Secret Service as the Postmaster Line. Many of the postmasters of southern Maryland had strong Southern sympathies and used their postal offices to facilitate the passing of information to their Southern friends. It was said that the proceedings of a Lincoln Cabinet meeting would be in Richmond within 24 hours of the meeting by using the Postmaster Line. Lafayette Baker finally took troops into southern Maryland and arrested many of the local postmasters in an effort to put an end to their very efficient avenue of communications. In several cases the postmasters' wives very efficiently took over for their husbands and the operation continued.

Newspapers in those days were excellent sources of tactical as well as strategic information and both sides used them effectively. Confederate agents would buy both the Washington and the New York papers in Washington and then have them couriered south via the Paper Route, which consisted of:

- Horseback from Washington to Pope's Creek in southern Maryland
- Ferry across the Potomac at Pope's Creek
- Horseback from southern shore of Potomac to Port Royal on the Rappahannock
- Ferry across the Rappahannock at Port Royal
- Horseback for the last 18 miles to Richmond

This could often be done in less than 24 hours.

A recently discovered Confederate Secret Service document defines the courier routes used for the passing of communications to and from agents in the North. The correspondence says:

> Under the control of this Bureau there are three lines of communications with the United States—two communicating with Washington City—and one with Fortress Monroe. Furnishing information is no part of the duty assigned us—what has been done is voluntary and incidental. We are only required to keep open lines by which Agents, Scouts, etc. can forward letters, papers, and light packages to the Depts. The lines are as follows:
>
> 1. Mathias Point, King George Co Va—Lt C.H. Cawood Commanding, via Allen's Fresh, Newport, Bryan Town, Surratt's Tavern and to Washington.
> 2. Pope's Creek, Westmoreland Co. (near Colonial Beach) Va—Sgt H.H. Brogden Commanding
>   via Marborough, T.B. to Washington.
> 3. Burwell Bay, Isle of Wight Co, Va—Sgt Jon F. Moore Commanding
>   via Williamsburg, Yorktown, Hampton to Fortress Monroe.

The Confederate Government made several serious mistakes regarding couriers. The Union spies Timothy Webster and George Curtis, both posing as Union merchants who wanted to trade in contraband with the Confederacy, became close associates of the Confederate Secretary of War Judah Benjamin. Attempting to communicate with his agents operating in the Union, Benjamin gave both Webster and Curtis correspondence to deliver to Confederate agents in the Union. This proved to be an intelligence service's dream-come-true for the Union as all of the correspondence was read in Washington prior to delivery to the agent. The information in the correspondence led to the discovery of several Confederate agents as well as specific espionage operations in the North. To prevent exposure of the Union operation, identical stationery was purchased from the London stationery shop supplying Benjamin in order that the agent would not know the envelope had been opened.

In addition, in 1864 a young man named Richard Montgomery, who was employed as a government clerk in Washington, volunteered to the War Department that he would like to work as a spy. He was recruited, had his name changed to James Thompson, and was sent to Richmond. There he convinced Captain Norris, of the Confederate Secret Service, that he would be an excellent candidate to carry messages between Richmond and the Confederate operations in Canada at Catharines. He continued to make the round trip for the remainder of the war, always stopping first in Washington prior to delivery. His services provided the Union with the initial knowledge of:

- The Confederate plan to raid a bank in Vermont
- Planned raids against Buffalo and Rochester to cause unrest
- The Confederate plan to burn major buildings in New York City

The Vermont raid could not be prevented as the specific town was not known; the planned raids on Buffalo and Rochester were prevented; and the burning of New York was minimized, all based on the work of the young courier Richard Montgomery, aka James Thompson.

Couriers played a significant role in the Confederate Armies of Tennessee and the West and several of them are worth mentioning, specifically Sam Davis, Adam Johnson and an unknown Union hero. Sam Davis served as the courier for a notorious Confederate spy named Shaw who used the name "Coleman" for his spying activities. He frequently traveled with Coleman between his courier duties and on one occasion both he and Coleman were captured in a sweeping series of raids by Union forces. Upon arriving at the Union place of imprisonment Davis learned that C.E. Coleman was also a prisoner, but his true identity was not known to the Union.

When Davis' saddlebags were searched incriminating papers were found to include:

- Details of the strength and location of Federal troops in middle Tennessee
- Details of the plan to reinforce the army at Chattanooga
- Accurate maps, descriptions and troop dispositions of fortifications at several important locations in Tennessee
- Gifts from the agent Shaw to General Bragg

The information was so accurate that General Dodge concluded that it could only have been obtained from a traitor on his staff and probably given to his nemesis, the Confederate agent Shaw, aka C.E. Coleman. As a result Davis was subjected to severe questioning about the identification of the notorious spy Coleman. He never wavered in his loyalty to both Coleman and the Confederacy. Tried and sentenced to hang he continued to deny any knowledge of the identity of the spy Coleman, who was at that time still being held by the Union; finally Sam Davis was hanged. After the war a monument was erected to him in Knoxville, Tennessee, and he is known today as the "Nathan Hale of the South." Interestingly enough General Dodge, the Union head of intelligence in the West (and the man who condemned him to death) sent a contribution towards the cost of the monument after the war. By this time Dodge was a millionaire (his contribution consisted of ten dollars).

Another Confederate courier in the West was Adam R. Johnson, who served as a courier for General Nathan Forrest. In 1862 Johnson was ordered to memorize an encrypted message letter for letter. General Nathan B. Forrest considered it too important to be sent via telegraph (where it could be intercepted and probably read). After General Forrest was assured that Johnson knew the message thoroughly he was sent to deliver it personally to the governor of Texas, Francis Lubbock. The governor of Texas, while delighted to receive the message, never told Johnson what specific information he had in fact delivered.

The unknown Union hero was a man serving as a Confederate courier between Generals Johnston and Pemberton just prior to the Battle of Vicksburg. In May of 1863, General Johnston sent General Pemberton a message suggesting that he would attack the rear of the Union forces that were threatening Jackson, Mississippi. The courier, prior to delivering the message to General Pemberton, took it to General Grant. Thus General Grant had a good idea of the situation of the opponent's forces.

The movement of intelligence in a timely manner was a major problem throughout the Civil War (as it remains today). Some of the operatives such as Miss Van Lew and Generals Dodge and Sharpe were aware of this shortcoming and did some ingenious maneuvering to increase the speed of delivery. The problem was never solved completely during the Civil War and is one of the major reasons that much of the intelligence garnered during the war did not have the full impact of its potential. Researchers today look at the data and often wonder why it was not utilized by the general involved. The simple answer is that much of it did not arrive in time—a familiar problem even in today's intelligence organizations.

Chapter 3

Secret Organizations

Within the Union and the Confederacy there arose secret organizations that served to hinder the working of their own governments. In the North the organizations were predominantly interested in an early peace at any cost, although some actually espoused the secession of the Northwest from the Union. In the Confederacy, most of the organizations were composed of Unionists who opposed secession from the Union and used their organizations to harm the Confederacy whenever and wherever possible.

For the Union and the Confederate governments these organizations were a worry, but at the same time they served as fertile ground for the spies, Union and Confederate. The organizations served not only as eyes and ears for the spies but also provided safe houses when they were in the area and in some cases, members served as couriers in order to rapidly deliver intelligence to the proper authorities. The spies in return made sure that the organizations, particularly the ones in the South, were recognized by the Union government and that their services to the government(s) would not go unnoticed.

For the Union, the main counter-intelligence efforts against the secret organizations in the North were handled first by Allan Pinkerton and later by Lafayette Baker. Initially, it was Pinkerton's agents who aided and abetted the secret organizations located within the Confederacy; later in the war, both General Grenville Dodge and General George Sharpe understood the importance of these groups and their agents maintained close contact with the groups, using their facilities when in the area and encouraging them to continue their work.

Northern Sympathizers in the South

There were many secret societies composed of Union sympathizers in the Confederacy. In all cases the Societies' active membership was composed not only of the civilian populace but members of the Confederate Army. Four of the more major societies were:

Order of the Heroes
Peace Society
Peace and Constitution Society
The Order in Gainesville, Texas

The general role of these societies was to:

• Aid any member in distress
• Assist Union agents in the area
• Encourage desertion and protect deserters
• Advocate joining the Union forces
• Support the Union forces in the area
• Destroy railroads, telegraph lines and bridges, and to serve as guides when spies were in the area and when the Union troops arrived

Order of Heroes (1864)

This society operated mainly in North Carolina, Tennessee, Virginia and South Carolina. It was composed almost exclusively of strong-minded Unionists. The society was encouraged by the Union to the extent that both President Abraham Lincoln and General U.S. Grant were initiated into the society.

To anyone who joined the Society, the Union (aka President Lincoln) guaranteed the following:

- Exemption from military service in Union
- Protection for your family and property from Union harm when territory was occupied
- After the war, during the Reconstruction period, first choice of captured real estate

With President Lincoln and General Grant as members of the Order of Heroes one would not doubt the validity of the guarantees made. Unfortunately President Lincoln died before they could be put into effect.

Peace Society (1862)

This society operated predominantly in northern Alabama and also in Florida, Mississippi and Georgia. Initially this society was formed in the eastern part of Tennessee (within the Federal lines) and was encouraged by the Union to become active in the Confederacy. It had basically the same objectives as the other societies and was actively involved in breaking down the Confederate government. It was strong enough in Alabama that in the 1863 elections members engineered the election of both State and Confederate officials that were peace candidates.

Peace and Constitution Society (1861)

Oldest of the three major societies, it operated predominately in the state of Arkansas. Membership was estimated at approximately

700 Unionist members. Goals were the same as those of the other two societies and members were very successful in their state.

The Order (1861)

A secret organization in Texas, the Order was pro-Union. Membership was extensive and included both civilian and military members. The organization maintained regular correspondence with members in the Northern army, keeping them informed of their numbers, plans, goals and the strength of the Confederate units in the area. They had been informed that the Yankees would invade Texas from Galveston and Gainesville, where the society was expected to pave the way, and link up at Austin, the state capital. There, either Jim Lane of Kansas or Sam Houston (who had been removed as governor for his pro-Union stand when Texas seceded) would be appointed governor.

The Order was organized initially to resist the Confederate conscript law and other Confederate laws not to the liking of Texas. The Order's main goals were to keep members from fighting for the Confederacy, drive pro-Southerners out of north Texas, seize property, and help restore the Union.

When it became obvious that the Union was not going to invade Texas, the Order, with the blessing of the Union, aligned itself with a number of tribes in Indian territory hostile to the Texas government—that of the Comanches, Caddos, Anadarkos and Kickapoos. They incited the Indians to attack Fort Cobb and thereby caused the withdrawal of the Confederate Chickasaw Battalion to Fort Arbuckle. The Order planned to join the Indians at this point but the tribes settled down and quietly went their way—taking away the Order's chance to further the attack.

In October 1862 hundreds of Order members were arrested and at least 48 executed by a people's court and lynch mobs.

The words of the man who defended the Order members, Dr. Thomas Barrett, are inscribed on a fitting memorial to the episode:

Poor human nature, when acting under great excitement, is to be pitied. I have heard men say when the War Between the States came up, and they went into it, and got the war excitement up, they did things they could not have believed that they ever would have done, but war excitement mastered them.

In addition to the above fairly well organized societies, there was the Legal League loosely organized by the Negroes in the South. The League assisted escaped Union prisoners, acted as couriers for Union spies, conducted independent spying and provided safe housing for Negro spies when they were in the South.

An example of the Negro efforts regarding escaped Union prisoners of war is the following report written by Capt. B. Reed and 1st Lieutenant L.B. Stevenson, both of the 3rd Ohio Infantry, and both captured near Rome, Georgia, in May 1864:

. . . Escaped from Charleston on the way from the cars to the prison, went to negro's quarters, staid in the yard until dark, then made ourselves known to the negroes, who hid us away and took us to the wharf. We could not get away that night. The negores then kept us, Thursday, Friday, Saturday, Sunday and Monday until Monday night when we got a boat at Clark's Wharf. The wind was so high that we could not make way against it, and at 3 o'clock A.M. we were left on the flats.

We then went back to the town and some fisherman kept us till night (Tuesday) while there two shots from Gregg came within 400 yards of us. The negroes took us off at 10 o'clock, having prepared a boat and we started for Morris Island. Met our Picket Boats at 10 O'Clock between Gregg and Lumpler.

The negroes gave us good and reliable information, although they are almost starving themselves, yet they would always give us enough, an old negro woman got us something to eat, I told her we had no money, she said "The Lord God will pay me if you only get through. Those who depend upon the darkies will be safe, in attempting to escape."

Southern Sympathizers in the North

Prior to the Civil War there were at least two secret societies operating predominantly in the North but also in the South. They were known as "Know Nothings" because when asked anything about the societies they "knew nothing." The two main ones were the Order of United Americans and the Order of the Star Spangled Banner. The main beliefs of the organization were:

- Only native American Protestants could be elected to office
- They were anti-Immigrant-Catholic-Liquor
- They opposed the Nebraska Kansas Act

The societies collapsed after 1854 over the slavery issue. The Northern anti-slave Know Nothings went into the Republican Party.

Societies in the North during the Civil War were all grouped together under the general title of Copperheads. The main ones were:

Knights of the Golden Circle
Order of American Knights
Sons of Liberty
Knights of Liberty (Baltimore)

The main purpose of these societies was to sue for peace as soon as possible and at whatever cost. They did not necessarily want the Confederate States back in the Union. Many of the Copperhead societies also nurtured thoughts of active rebellion in the North for two purposes (often independent of each other):

- An active rebellion would force peace negotiations.
- A Northwest Confederacy of their own would also break away from the Union.

These thoughts known to the Confederacy led to a desperate, expensive operation on the part of their side. They had spies operating out of Toronto, Canada, who worked closely with the Union Copperhead societies in an attempt to ferment an uprising in the Northwest and possible secession. The plot was known to the Union and although a worry, it proved to be little more, mainly because the Union had spies not only in the Copperhead societies but also inside the Toronto operation.

Early in the war, the Baltimore Society the Knights of Liberty, after failing to assassinate President Lincoln on his way to Washington, maintained communications with the Confederacy and was actively pursuing an attack on Washington from the North concurrent with a Confederate attack from the South. The organization was infiltrated by Pinkerton's men and the leaders were put into jail. This ended the Knights of Liberty in Maryland—and represents one of Pinkerton's true successes in the Civil War.

The main Copperhead leader was a man named Clement Vallandigham, an Ohio's preacher's son married to a Maryland planter's daughter. He was arrested, tried, found guilty of treason, and sentenced to prison. He eventually made his way to Canada, by blockade runner, where he continued to create problems for the Union, such as running for governor in absentia.

When Vallandigham returned to the U.S., President Lincoln would not arrest him as he felt that would only cause trouble with the Copperheads. He eventually went to the Confederacy for the duration of the war.

While the Northern societies were a constant worry to the government, it appears that the Southern societies were more successful in their mission. No one is really sure how many Confederate soldiers they convinced to desert with the promise that they would protect them for the duration of the war. We do know, however, that desertion was a major problem for the Confederate Army late in the war. Letters from the societies' members no doubt helped this effort.

We also know that the Southern societies were successful in assisting the Union Army by destroying railroads and other sabotage efforts to prevent the Confederate Army from moving supplies and troops easily. They also were always available to assist Union spies that traveled in their area and successfully prevented the arrest of more than a few Union agents.

After the war, the secret societies of both the Union and the Confederacy basically disappeared, only to be replaced by such new organizations as the Ku Klux Klan with General Nathan B. Forrest as the first Grand High Priest.

Chapter 4

Technology Assists in Civil War Spying

The Civil War saw the arrival on the military and espionage scene of new technologies that were utilized with varying degrees of success by the spies of the Union and the Confederacy. These technical advances were photography—used for mapping as well as stroking egos (as everyone liked to have a portrait taken)—the telegraph—which allowed for rapid transmission of data as well as the opportunity for the enemy to listen in on the opposing force's telegraphic communications, and the hot air balloon for aerial observation. Both photography and telegraphy did impact on the espionage efforts of both sides, but the hot air balloon proved too good a target for the new rifled muskets; although of reconnaissance value it was abandoned in early 1863.

Photography dates back to the 16th century, but it did not become a viable technology until 1826 when the first real photograph was made. The technique spread rapidly and by the time of the Civil War it was a well established technique for preserving history. When the war started, it was the actions of independent photographers that spurred both the Union and the Confederacy to use photography as a new spy tool. Both sides had successes with pho-

33

tography but it appears that the Union had the definite advantage in the use of photography for military purposes—mainly due to two men—Alexander Gardner and General William T. Sherman.

Alexander Gardner was the manager of Matthew Brady's Washington studio when hostilities broke out in 1861. He soon left the studio and joined Allan Pinkerton's force as a overt/covert photographer. His efforts were twofold: he worked with topographic engineers, producing photographs of important terrain for military purposes—photos that were then turned into much needed maps (often these photographs were of future battle sites). In return he was given access to a battle area after the battle, and his photographs form a major part of the photographic history of the Civil War.

In addition, Gardner took group photographs of the various Union units. This procedure, while stroking the egos of the unit members, proved to be an excellent way to pick out Confederate infiltrators of the units. The commander would look at the photograph and pick out the men he did not recognize as being members of his unit. The technique was so successful that Confederates attempting to infiltrate a unit were advised to never appear in any photographs.

Gardner's work was well received and proved to be extremely useful to topographic engineers. However, when General George McClellan left the Union Army so did Gardner. The techniques he had developed remained with the Union Army and were further expanded by General Sherman during his March to Atlanta, Georgia.

General Sherman was hampered by a lack of geographic data and maps of the southern areas he was moving through on his way to Atlanta. To solve the problem, he used what were called "dark wagons," in fact photographic developing rooms on wheels. General Sherman sent his engineers and scouts out ahead of the march to photograph areas the army would be moving through. Photographic plates were then given to the crews in the dark wagons, under the command of Colonel O.M. Poe of the Engineer Corps. There the plates were developed and photo maps made for the various commanders. It should be remembered that the negatives had to be processed within a specific time limit after exposure— no mean feat in the field. However, the technique was highly successful and General Sherman's commanders were usually well informed of the geographic obstacles ahead of them.

The Confederacy had its own enterprising photographers in the world of espionage. A.D. Lytle, a Confederate photographer, was very adept at entering the Union camps, especially in the Louisiana area, and conducting photographic reconnaissance. He was particularly interested in items such as number of supply wagons, strength of artillery forces, number of troops and their leaders. He used his camera to record as much information as he could and then would return to his studio and develop the photographs. Then, as now, military commanders tended to believe a photograph more than the spoken word.

It is fair to say that one of the best ways to send a spy either north or south into enemy territory was to arm him with a camera (It did not have to work!). Photographing was so new, to the average man at that time that everyone wanted a picture taken to send home. Lafayette Baker took a broken camera with him on his trip south. He was only suspected when no one received photographs after he had taken them. Not many officers or enlisted men realized the real intelligence value of the camera and its importance to the other side.

Late in the war Confederates reportedly used an advanced from of photography to prepare their messages for courier movement to Richmond.

United States Consulate
Toronto Prv Jany 3, 1865

Honorable W. H. Seward
  Secretary of State
  Washington, D. C.

Sir—The following facts having been given to me:
The Rebels in this city have a quick and successful communications with Jeff Davis and the authorities in Richmond, in the following manner. Having plenty of money at their command, they employ British subjects, who are provided with British passports, and also with passports from Col—(probably, Jacob Thompson) which are plainly written; name and date of issue on fine silk and are ingeniously secreted in the lining of the coat. They carry dispatches, which are made and carried in the same manner. **These messengers, wear metal buttons, which, upon the inside, dispatches are**

most minutely photographed, not perceptable to the naked eye, but are easily read by the aid of a powerful lens.

This information is reliable, from a person who has *seen* the dispatches, and has personal knowledge of the facts. . . .

Your Obedient Servant
R. J. Kimball

What Consular Kimball was reporting is in fact known today as microfilm! The technique had been developed by a Frenchman Rene Prudent Dagron in 1860. The images were on a 2 × 2 mm. diameter glass plate, and could be viewed using a lens developed by Lord Stanhope around 1750.

The telegraph was another new piece of technology for the average soldier, so new in fact that the Union forces had to post guards along the telegraph lines, not only to protect the line from sabotage, but also from the Union soldiers who kept cutting the line to send a piece home as a war souvenir.

But how did the telegraph affect the spies? First and foremost, particularly in the North where an extensive telegraphic network existed, it provided a rapid way to move intelligence. If a Union spy could get his information to one of the Union telegraph outposts, it could be transmitted not only locally but all the way to Washington, D.C. It took some time for all elements to understand this factor but under General U.S. Grant the telegraph and its full potential for moving intelligence was fully realized. The Confederacy did not have the extensive telegraph network (due mainly to lack of wire), but they too understood its value.

Secondly, the telegraph provided an excellent opportunity to "listen in" on the enemy's communications. One could either have a telegraph operator infiltrate the enemy's communications organization, where he read the communications passing through his transmitting station (such as J.O. Kerbey for the Union and the unidentified Confederate operator that worked for General Grant) or the line could be "tapped." Tapping the line meant that a bypass was inserted in the line whereby the communications passing on the line were readable without disturbing the transmission route. Both sides did in fact tap enemy lines, with varying degrees of success. While the Union could and did read the Confederate cipher messages, the Confederacy was never successful in deciphering any of the Union messages from the Grant-to-Lincoln tapped line.

In addition to tapping the lines, other covert uses could be made of the telegraphic lines. By breaking into the line, it was possible to send bogus orders and information to the intended recipient. This was done by both Union and Confederate forces, normally at the local army level where ciphers were not employed. It tended to make commanders wary of unenciphered messages received during a military operation.

While the technologies of photography and telegraphy proved useful to the espionage efforts of the Union and Confederacy, the technology of hot air balloons did not prove to be an asset. Hot air balloons had been around since 1783 and had been used successfully by the French military in 1794. The potential of using balloons is very tempting; an experienced scout in a balloon has the ability to visually assess what the enemy is doing in the field. The problem is that between 1794 and 1861 there was another invention that impacted on the use of balloons—the rifled musket and the rifle. While the French could hoist a balloon knowing that the muskets of the day could only be accurate to about 100 yards—thereby being ineffective against the balloon—Union and Confederate forces had a different problem. In the Civil War there were rifled muskets that were accurate to between 400 and 500 yards—making them excellent weapons to down a tethered balloon.

Professor Thaddeus Lowe believed strongly in the military value of hot air balloons. On June 18, 1861, he conducted a hot air balloon experiment for President Lincoln. He ascended above Washington, D.C., in a balloon with a telegraphic keying device on board and the telegraphic wire hanging out of the balloon to a ground station. He succeeded that day in transmitting the first air-to-ground telegraphic communication. Cumbersome but workable. His message read:

To the President of the United States:
This point of observation commands an area near fifty miles in diameter. The city, with its girdle of encampments presents a superb scene. I have pleasure in sending you this first dispatch ever telegraphed from an aerial station, and in acknowledging indebtedness to your en-

couragement, for the opportunity of demonstrating the availability of the science of aeronautics in the military service of the country.

T. S. C. Lowe

Professor Lowe is also credited with taking the first aerial photograph, again from one of his balloons.

These successes so impressed Lincoln as to the potential of the balloons that he made Professor Lowe the head of the Union Balloon Corps. The Union found that while the balloons did give the scouts a real advantage, not only were they regularly shot down (as they ascended or descended) but the balloons tended to spin in the air—making the scout on board very air sick. The Union Balloon Corps was officially disbanded in May of 1863.

The Confederacy, while envious of the Union efforts in the area of ballooning, made only one balloon attempt in the entire war. That effort is best described in the words of General James Longstreet:

> While we were longing for the balloons that poverty denied us, a genius arose . . . and suggested we . . . gather silk dresses and make a balloon. It was done, and we soon had a great patchwork ship. . . . One day it was on a steamer down on the James River, when the tide went out and left the vessel and balloon high and dry on a bar. The Federals gathered it in, and with it the last silk dresses in the Confederacy.

The result was that while both the Union and the Confederacy were interested in the use of the hot air balloon, reality soon set in and both sides abandoned the projects.

The Civil War is often called the first modern war and the use of the new technologies for espionage purposes serves as a good example. All of the new technologies used by the Union and Confederate forces have been developed into active modern combat tools very much in use in today's army. Today, these technologies are known as photographic intelligence (photography), signals intelligence (telegraph) and aerial reconnaissance (balloons and other aircraft). All of these techniques play a very active role in the military forces of today and will for the foreseeable future.

Chapter 5

Intelligence Gathering by Cryptology

Armies have used the art of cryptology since time immemorial to make their own communications unreadable to an enemy and secondly to have the ability to read the enciphered communications of their enemy thereby gaining very useful intelligence. The science of cryptology was very much a part of early American history as the British systematically read the messages sent to U.S. diplomats in England prior to their delivery. Not much changed until the advent of the Civil War when the world of cryptology with one invention was completely changed—that invention was the telegraph.

With the invention of the telegraph the military had a rapid means of communicating with their forces without having to worry about couriers being captured by the enemy or actually delivering messages to the enemy, or having the enemy read the newly developed wigwag flag system. But it soon became apparent that telegraph lines could be tapped thereby giving the unintended recipient a wealth of information. Therefore the texts had to be enciphered or encoded and these messages represent the first use of electronically transmitted enciphered or encoded messages by the military in time of war. The system was all new and while mistakes were made, the telegraph, and the intelligence gained from it (both friendly and enemy), played a major role in the development of the battles of the Civil War.

Just prior to the beginning of the war, the governor of Ohio, William Dennison, aware that his governmental messages were being read by unintended recipients, asked Anson Stager, the general manager of Western Union, to devise a method of encoding his communications. Stager developed an encoding system, and when George McClellan entered the Union Army he recruited Stager as his communications chief and adopted the Stager system for the command communications of the Union Army. The particular system known as a route cipher system (see Example 1 on page 44) was never read by the Confederacy during the entire course of the war. They got so desperate that Union messages were printed in various Southern newspapers seeking public assistance in breaking them—to no known avail!

As an indication of the use the Union Army made of this route system, an estimated 6,500,000 messages were sent, using the route system during the course of the war. Not one of them was read by the enemy.

In addition, understanding the sensitivity of communications, the Union War Department maintained complete control of the matter of regulating the telegraph and determined how it should be used, and who, and who alone, should have the ciphers. The operators controlling the ciphers and the ciphers themselves were for all practical purposes independent of the commanders under whom they served. They reported directly to the War Department through General Stager giving daily logs of the messages they had sent, including the names of the recipient and the sender.

In contrast to the signals efficiency of the Union, the Confederate signals plan was a dismal failure. Rather than having one high level system of protecting their messages, each group had their own and the systems were not very secure. The main Confederate government system was Virgenere Square (see Example 2 on page 46) that was routinely read by the Union cryptographers (not easily, however, as an average message required about 12 hours of work—there were no computers). One such Confederate message, when broken, gave the name and address of an engraver/printer in New York who was printing Confederate money. The man was arrested, the presses broken and the plates confiscated.

To give one a better idea of the cryptologic methods of the North and the South, each government's efforts are addressed below.

Union Cryptology

• The most commonly used cryptographic system used by the Union government and senior military officers was the route system as developed by Mr. Stager (see Example 1). The message was written in a number of predetermined columns, which were then read up or down and in a random order thereby scrambling the meaning of the message. The key was given by a prearranged first word that informed the receiver how many columns of how many words and in what sequence to restore the original message.

• At the beginning of the war all cipher information could be carried by the Union signals officer on the back of a card. By the end of the war there were 12 pages of route indicators and 36 pages for the 1,600 codewords used.

• In order to further confuse the enemy, frequently used words such as *President Lincoln, General Grant, Washington* and *division* were replaced with codewords, i.e., *WORM* could mean *Lincoln,* etc. The codewords came into being at the suggestion of Samuel H. Beckwith, General Grant's cipher operator.

• As the war went on, the routes became more and more complicated, i.e., not only up or down columns but also diagonally across and in interrupted columns. The keyword dictated the size of the rectangle and the route.

• In Washington there were three very young men named David Bates, Charles Tinker and Albert Chandler who not only enciphered and deciphered the Union messages received, but also broke the Confederate messages obtained via wiretappings and intercepted couriers. They successfully diagnosed and read the Confederate government Vicksburg Square system. Examples of their success include:

—Decipherment of a message concerning a shipment of rifles for the Confederacy. The shipment was subsequently intercepted by the Union army.

—Deciphering of a Confederate text making possible the arrest of the printer in New York producing Confederate money and consequent destruction of the plates.

As a reward for their excellent work all three received a $25 a month raise. They were known as the Sacred Three and President Lincoln often looked over their shoulders as they worked on a decipherment.

• For lower level encipherment the Union used what is known as a dictionary code. Both the sender and the recipient held copies of the same dictionary with all the words numbered consecutively. Messages were sent merely by substituting the corresponding number for the desired word. This system is easy to read once you have the proper dictionary.

Confederate Cryptology

The Confederate government used the Virgenere Tableau or as they called it the Vicksburg Square throughout the entire course of the war. This system is easy to use and requires the cipher clerk to have very little material. As can be seen in Example 2, this system is based on a codeword that can vary from message to message. The weakness of the Confederate use of the system is that they use only three codewords during the entire course of the war: *Manchester Bluff*, *Complete Victory*, and *Come Retribution*. It is ironic that the last message sent by the Confederate government that fell into Union hands used the codeword "Come Retribution"—and it was coming! the message when deciphered read:

The hostile government rejects the proposed settlement, and orders active operations to be resumed in forty-eight hours from noon today.

• The Confederate operators often missed a letter or in other ways garbled the messages which made them very hard to read. In one instance a Major Cunningham, on the staff of General Kirby Smith, tried for 12 hours to read a cipher message from a subordinate unit. Finally, in frustration, he jumped on his horse, galloped around Union lines to the sender unit and asked them what they were trying to say.

• The multiple systems used within the Confederacy led to confusion among the communicating people, and confusion always aids the other side. Some examples of the systems used are:

—J. David to General Johnston: Identical dictionaries

—Beauregard to General Anderson: Monoalphabetic substitution

—Secretary of Navy to vessels: Identical dictionaries

• The Confederacy used the want ads section of Northern newspapers to exchange information. An advertisement offering so many acres of farm land for sale could provide an opportunity to inform Richmond (via the *New York Herald*) how many pounds sterling were being transferred from secret service funds in Canada and England.

Just prior to the war a Union officer (surgeon by profession) by the name of Albert J. Myers developed a flag system for communicating when line-of-sight could be maintained. Assisting him in his endeavors was another officer by the name of E. Porter Alexander. The system later known as the wigwag employed large flags during the day; at night burning torches were used. When the war commenced Lieutenant Alexander joined the Confederacy and initiated the wigwag system in the Confederate army. The result was that both sides could read the other's wigwag system during the war and even though the code values were frequently changed it did not take long for the opposition to understand them. The information passed on the wigwag system was almost without exception of a tactical, perishable nature, and the ability to transmit tactical information rapidly did play a part in some of the major battles, for example the Battle of Gettysburg. In addition the ability to read the enemy's wigwag signals had great tactical value.

If a spy could obtain the code groups used with their meanings he had given his side a definite advantage. One can easily see why cipher clerks and communications officers were prime targets for espionage operatives. Spies made great efforts to get inside a general's headquarters to find a copy of the dictionary he used in his private codes, to obtain listings of the codewords, the cipher discs used, and to become a friend of the cipher clerk. Just as in today's society the enemy cipher clerk is a prime target for another country's espionage efforts.

Cryptology was obviously in a transitional state during the Civil War due to the introduction of the telegraph. It did contribute to the intelligence systems of both combatants. In the case of the Union, the Confederate governmental messages that took 12 hours to decrypt were obviously of strategic intelligence value, as the examples show. For both combatants the reading of the ciphers of the local armies, accomplished at a much faster pace, could and probably did impact on current operations.

It is interesting to note that the three young men in Washington, the Sacred Three, were the forerunners of much larger governmental operations in most nations today. And today the Sacred Three would have the advantage of being able to employ the computer instead of the pencil, paper and brain.

Example 1
Route Ciphers

This apparently simple cipher was not so simple to decipher as it may seem. Here, for instance, is a message sent by President Lincoln to Colonel Ludlow on June 1, 1863. In plain the message read:

> For Colonel Ludlow. Richardson and Brown, correspondents of the Tribune, captured at Vicksburg, are detained at Richmond. Please ascertain why they are detained and get them off if you can. The President.

When enciphered, Code 9 was used and provided the following codeword substitutions: VENUS for colonel, WAYLAND for captured, ODOR for Vicksburg, NEPTUNE for Richmond, ADAM for President of U.S. and NELLY for 4:30 PM. The encipherer chose to write out the message in seven lines of five words each with three nulls to complete the rectangle. Nulls were inserted at the end of each column. The message as prepared for transmission looked like:

1	2	3	4	5
(kissing)		(Commissioner)		(times)
For	VENUS	Ludlow	Richardson	and
Brown	correspondents	of	the	Tribune
WAYLAND	at	ODOR	are	detained
at	NEPTUNE	please	ascertain	why
they	are	detained	and	get
them	off	if	you	can
ADAM	NELLY	THIS	FILLS	UP
	(turning)		(belly)	

The route for transmitting the message was up the first column, down the second, up the fifth, down the fourth, and up the third. With the key word GUARD heading the message to indicate the size of the rectangle and its route, this cipher text resulted:

GUARD **ADAM** THEM THEY AT **WAYLAND** BROWN FOR KISSING **VENUS** CORRESPONDENTS AT **NEPTUNE** ARE OFF **NELLY** TURNING UP CAN GET WHY DETAINED TRIBUNE AND TIMES RICHARDSON THE ARE YOU FILLS BELLY THIS IF DETAINED PLEASE **ODOR** OF LUDLOW COMMISSIONER.

Words in **BOLD** type are codewords
Words underlined are nulls

Example 2
Virgenere Tableau

	A	B	C	D	E	F	G	H	I	J	K	L	M	N	O	P	Q	R	S	T	U	V	W	X	Y	Z
A	a	b	c	d	e	f	g	h	i	j	k	l	m	n	o	p	q	r	s	t	u	v	w	x	y	z
B	b	c	d	e	f	g	h	i	j	k	l	m	n	o	p	q	r	s	t	u	v	w	x	y	z	a
C	c	d	e	f	g	h	i	j	k	l	m	n	o	p	q	r	s	t	u	v	w	x	y	z	a	b
D	d	e	f	g	h	i	j	k	l	m	n	o	p	q	r	s	t	u	v	w	x	y	z	a	b	c
E	e	f	g	h	i	j	k	l	m	n	o	p	q	r	s	t	u	v	w	x	y	z	a	b	c	d
F	f	g	h	i	j	k	l	m	n	o	p	q	r	s	t	u	v	w	x	y	z	a	b	c	d	e
G	g	h	i	j	k	l	m	n	o	p	q	r	s	t	u	v	w	x	y	z	a	b	c	d	e	f
H	h	i	j	k	l	m	n	o	p	q	r	s	t	u	v	w	x	y	z	a	b	c	d	e	f	g
I	i	j	k	l	m	n	o	p	q	r	s	t	u	v	w	x	y	z	a	b	c	d	e	f	g	h
J	j	k	l	m	n	o	p	q	r	s	t	u	v	w	x	y	z	a	b	c	d	e	f	g	h	i
K	k	l	m	n	o	p	q	r	s	t	u	v	w	x	y	z	a	b	c	d	e	f	g	h	i	j
L	l	m	n	o	p	q	r	s	t	u	v	w	x	y	z	a	b	c	d	e	f	g	h	i	j	k
M	m	n	o	p	q	r	s	t	u	v	w	x	y	z	a	b	c	d	e	f	g	h	i	j	k	l
N	n	o	p	q	r	s	t	u	v	w	x	y	z	a	b	c	d	e	f	g	h	i	j	k	l	m
O	o	p	q	r	s	t	u	v	w	x	y	z	a	b	c	d	e	f	g	h	i	j	k	l	m	n
P	p	q	r	s	t	u	v	w	x	y	z	a	b	c	d	e	f	g	h	i	j	k	l	m	n	o
Q	q	r	s	t	u	v	w	x	y	z	a	b	c	d	e	f	g	h	i	j	k	l	m	n	o	p
R	r	s	t	u	v	w	x	y	z	a	b	c	d	e	f	g	h	i	j	k	l	m	n	o	p	q
S	s	t	u	v	w	x	y	z	a	b	c	d	e	f	g	h	i	j	k	l	m	n	o	p	q	r
T	t	u	v	w	x	y	z	a	b	c	d	e	f	g	h	i	j	k	l	m	n	o	p	q	r	s
U	u	v	w	x	y	z	a	b	c	d	e	f	g	h	i	j	k	l	m	n	o	p	q	r	s	t
V	v	w	x	y	z	a	b	c	d	e	f	g	h	i	j	k	l	m	n	o	p	q	r	s	t	u
W	w	x	y	z	a	b	c	d	e	f	g	h	i	j	k	l	m	n	o	p	q	r	s	t	u	v
X	x	y	z	a	b	c	d	e	f	g	h	i	j	k	l	m	n	o	p	q	r	s	t	u	v	w
Y	y	z	a	b	c	d	e	f	g	h	i	j	k	l	m	n	o	p	q	r	s	t	u	v	w	x
Z	z	a	b	c	d	e	f	g	h	i	j	k	l	m	n	o	p	q	r	s	t	u	v	w	x	y

TO ENCIPHER: Key word: COMPLETE VICTORY

Plain: THE ARMY WILL MOVE TONIGHT
Key: Com plet evic tory complet
Cipher: vvq-pcqr-adtn-fcmc-vczxrlm

To cipher take the plain letter T at the side of table look to key letter C across the top of table and take the letter at the intersection—
cipher letter v.

46

To decipher:

```
cipher:   v v q - p c q r - a d t n - f c m c - v c z x r l m
Key:      c o m  p l e t  e v i c  t o r y  c o m p l e t
Plain:    t h e  a r m y  w i l l  m o v e  t o n i g h t
```

Find the letter C at the top of the table, trace down the column until you come to the letter V, look to left column and take letter T.

Chapter 6

Unique Spy Groups

*I*n addition to the individual spies there were several rather unique spy groups active during the Civil War. Treating these groups as entities in themselves, rather than the individual parts, provides a much clearer picture of the groups, their characteristics, contributions and uniqueness.

Most of the groups represent a "first" for American spying, and each made a unique contribution to the outcome of the Civil War. The groups are:

• The Confederate espionage effort in Toronto, Canada. Unlike the majority of Confederate espionage activity in the Union itself this group operated on foreign soil. The Canadian group was instrumental in keeping the Copperhead cause alive, thereby causing considerable trouble for the Union, requiring the use of a very scarce commodity—Union troops.
• The escaping Southern slave, who if found to be educated and brave was frequently recruited to return to the Confederacy as a Union slave. The contributions of the Negro spy group were real. Today we think of the Negro who fought in the Union Army, such as the 54th Massachusetts, and while they too made a contribution, the Negro spy should not be overlooked.

• Young men, serving as newsboys, wandered freely through the encampments of both forces selling newspapers. The troops were anxious for the news and the boys were a welcome sight. In several documented cases the boys were more than newsboys; they were in fact intelligence collectors for their governments. In more than one case they were highly successful in their endeavors.

• Not only Americans served as spies for the Union and the Confederacy. There are several documented cases of Europeans serving as spies during the course of the Civil War. Some were soldiers of fortune, such as Count Solieski, while others appear to have undertaken the role in a spirit of pure adventure. Their role should not be discounted.

• A unique group, for America, was the presence of American spies in Europe. Prior to the Civil War, America did not actively pursue such activities in Europe. However, with the advent of the war, the Union as well as the Confederacy undertook spy efforts in Europe. For both governments, the spies in Europe did have an impact on the outcome of the war, although only a select few are recognized today.

• Technology led to a very unique group of spies. The Civil War represents the first use of the telegraph in a military environment as well as the first spy activities to not only use it to their advantage, but to target the enemies' telegraphic communications. It did not take long to learn that a telegraph line could be tapped or that an undercover telegraph operator, working for the enemy, could be a definite asset.

Details of each group follow, and hopefully the reader will gain an appreciation or the special contributions of these unique spies.

Confederate Operations in Canada

From the earliest days of the Civil War the Confederacy had a secret operation in Canada with two main purposes. First, Canada provided a safe haven for Confederate prisoners of war who escaped from the prison camps in the North, and second, it served as a relay point for communications between England and the Confederacy. During the early days of the war Rose O'Neal Greenhow, of Washington, served as an intermediary between Washington and Toronto.

On 7 April 1864, the mission of the Toronto operation was drastically changed. On that day President Jefferson Davis sent the following telegram to the Honorable Jacob Thompson, in Mississippi: "If your engagements permit you to accept service abroad for the next six months, please come here immediately." Mr. Thompson, a lawyer, statesman, ex-member of Congress, and Secretary of the Interior under President Buchanan, was above all a loyal Confederate. He quickly responded to President Davis' call.

The reason for his summoning by President Davis was that the Confederacy, in a last desperate action, wanted Thompson to go to Canada and from there direct a secret operation to create hostile activities in the Northwest, specifically another secession movement against the Union government—thereby, hopefully, the Union would sue for peace to prevent a further breakup.

Thompson accepted the challenge and was joined in Canada by Clement Clay, an ex-senator from Alabama, who was given the title of Commissioner of the North. The action officers assigned to the effort were James P. Holcombe, a University of Virginia law professor, and Captain Thomas Henry Hines, a veteran Confederate spy (even though he was only in his early twenties).

Why go to Toronto? By 1864, Toronto was much like Lisbon during the Second World War. Everyone had spies there and it was not infrequent that the spies traded information. In addition, C.L. Vallandingham, who was the Grand Commander of the Sons of Liberty and an outspoken sympathizer for the Confederacy, had fled from the U.S. to Canada in 1863. He purposed to detach the states of Illinois, Indiana and Ohio from the Union, if the Confederacy would move sufficient troops into Kentucky and Missouri to ensure their entry into the new Confederacy. Vallandingham wanted to form the five states into a new Northwestern Confederacy and thereby break the Union into three distinct pieces. He felt this action would force the Union to sue for peace. It is for all of these reasons that President Davis sent his powerful delegation north to Canada in the spring of 1864.

Hines and his fellow agents did work closely with all of the Copperhead organizations in the Northwest, mainly the Knights of the Golden Circle, the Order of the American Knights, and the Sons of Liberty, in attempts to create uprisings. All that resulted from this liaison was a great deal of inflammatory talk and no action. It appears that Captain Hines, in his youthful optimism, often misread the rhetoric as a guarantee of action—action that never came to fruition.

The following chronology summarizes the action undertaken by the Toronto operation:

• During May, June and July of 1864 Maine coastal residents noticed artists sketching along the shore. These artists, about 50 in number, were in reality Confederate topographers sent to Maine to map the coastline. They were looking for coves and inlets that could be used by armed steamers in a joint land and sea attack on Maine. The full attack never took place, again stymied by Union actions, and their scaled down attempt met with disaster. On July 14, 1864, the governor of Maine, Samuel Cony, received a telegram from the U.S. Consul in St. John, New Brunswick, Canada. The telegram warned Governor Cony that a Confederate party of 14 men was planning to land on the Maine coast. A later telegram stated the team was headed for Calais, in Maine, to rob a bank. It further stated the team was led by a man named William Collins.

• On July 18, 1864, the man named William Collins and two other men, Phillips and the famous Confederate courier Francis Jones, were captured on the Main Street of Calais walking towards the bank. When arrested and searched, a Confederate flag was found on Collins and he openly stated he was a Confederate, claiming to be a captain in the 15th Mississippi Infantry Regiment. No trace could be found of the other reported 11 men.

• No real connection could be found between the intended robbers and the Confederacy in Richmond or the operation in Toronto, and therefore the men were tried merely for "conspiracy to rob." Each was sentenced to three years in the Maine State Prison.

• Francis Jones, a disenchanted Confederate, confessed not only to his part in the Maine plot but also supplied information regarding

Confederate weapons caches in the North as well as the names of 20 key Confederate agents operating in the Union. The operatives were in Maine, Massachusetts, New York, Pennsylvania, Maryland, Illinois, Mississippi, Kentucky, Tennessee and Ohio. Based on the disclosure mass arrests were made and weapons confiscated.

• In early June of 1864, Captain Hines planned an uprising in the Northwest timed with a raid by General John Morgan's raiders in the Ohio/Kentucky area. General Morgan commenced a raiding mission in Kentucky on the 11th of June and was successful until he met the forces of General Burbridge who drove him out of the area and into Virginia. The raid did not create the desired unrest in the Northwest states.

• An uprising was planned for August 29, 1864, timed with the Democratic Convention in Chicago. While the planning was extensive and assurances were given—no actual uprising occurred in Chicago as planned. President Davis' comment after the failure of the mission was that the Copperheads did not do well as they had no military leaders.

• Political methods were also attempted. The Toronto operation funded the campaign of Democrat James C. Robinson for governor of Illinois. They were led to believe that if elected Robinson would turn over the state's militia and arsenal to the Sons of Liberty. He lost the election.

• In the fall of 1864, operatives from Toronto did go to St. Louis, Missouri, to destroy the Union transports used to ferry Union troops and supplies on the Mississippi. They intended to use an inflammatory known as "Greek fire" (a Molotov cocktail), which was only successful about 50 percent of the time. The group did in fact manage to destroy or damage 5 to 10 of the 75 Union transports in port.

• In need of money, the Toronto operation staged a robbery in St. Albans, Vermont, in mid-October of 1864. The robbery was successful and the agents returned with over $200,000 in gold and U.S. currency. (When pressed by the U.S. for the return of the bank robbers, Canada refused since they were able to prove they were on a military mission—they produced their orders from Richmond).

• Uprisings were next planned in Chicago, New York, Boston, Cincinnati and other locations for Election Day, November 8,

1864. The operation in Canada supplied the money and weapons to make the uprisings happen—but to no avail.

• On November 25, 1864, Confederate operatives from Toronto came to New York City with the intention of "flaming" the city. They selected 19 hotels as targets and hoped to create a riot similar to the New York City draft riots. While some of the hotels did in fact sustain fires, in several cases the Greek fire did not ignite and the total effect was not what was desired. All of the operatives did manage to escape from the city which was a neat trick since a double agent, Godfrey Hyams, had informed the Union of the threat to New York.

• The next target was the USS *Michigan,* the only gun ship on the Great Lakes. The attempt, made on December 19, 1864, was abortive due to a Union counter spy, J. Winslow Ayer, placed in the Confederate prison camp on Lake Michigan as a patent medicine salesman. He heard the Confederate prisoners talking about the fact that when the ship was taken over they were to rise up, take over the camp and then depart on the steamer.

• In December of 1864 Confederate operatives working for Hines decided to kidnap Vice President-elect Andrew Johnson on his way to Washington for the inaugural. They had a specific plan to capture him in his hotel room in Louisville, Kentucky, and take him away in a covered coach. The first night they attempted to execute the plan events made it impossible. On the second attempt, the agents rushed into the vice presidential suite all too easily, then found that the official party had left about an hour earlier. Vice President Johnson had decided to continue on his journey by boat instead of train.

• After the war, at the Lincoln assassination trial, a witness testified that the Toronto operation actually attempted "pestilence warfare" late in the war. The effort was reported to involve the delivery of "Yellow fever infected" blankets and clothing to Washington, D.C., in hopes of infecting the President and his cabinet with the disease.

The Union was well aware of the threat represented by the actions of both C.L. Vallandingham and the Toronto operation and a major effort was made to infiltrate one of the Copperhead organizations to avert surprise. They were very successful in this endeavor in the person of Felix Stidger. Stidger was a Midwesterner by birth and was very familiar with Indiana, Kentucky and Ohio. He was a Union soldier under the command of Brigadier General Henry Carrington, who headed the intelligence operations in Indiana. On orders from Carrington, Stidger successfully infiltrated the Knights of the Golden Circle in Indiana in early 1864 and over time rose to the rank of Secretary General of the Grand Council of Indiana. Until October of 1864 Stidger submitted continual reports on the activities of the Knights of the Golden Circle and their involvement with the Toronto Confederate group to General Carrington. In October of 1864, Stidger along with over 100 of the Knights of the Golden Circle hierarchy were arrested. The Knights did not realize that Stidger was a Union agent until he appeared to testify against them.

All in all, it is estimated that the Confederacy spent over a million dollars funding their efforts to get the Copperheads to rise up, all to no avail due largely to Captain Hines. He was a young idealistic officer who believed that everyone with whom he had contact had the same genuine enthusiasm for the cause that he did. Therefore his reports back to Thompson in Toronto were glowing and full of guarantees that all was well and indeed moving the way the Confederacy wanted it to go. The operation finances could well have been used by the Confederacy for many other purposes, however, in his desperation President Davis felt an uprising had a chance and he refused to let his hopes die.

The overall failure of the Toronto operation was not only the fault of Captain Hines; it was also due to the excellent counter-espionage efforts of the Union. By this late stage of the War the Union had a very sophisticated counter-espionage organization that had great successes—due in no small part to the lack of appreciation of their work by the Confederacy. While the Union began the war well behind the Confederacy in the world of espionage and counter-espionage, by the final stages the situation was completely reversed.

Negro Spying

The greatest single source of military and naval intelligence, particularly on the tactical level, for the Federal government during the war was the Negro.

—Herbert Aptheker

55

From the earliest days of the Civil War the Union had an unexpected source of manpower—not only for regular army duties—but also for spying. That source was the runaway slave, who escaped by the thousands to the North. It is estimated that during the entire course of the war approximately 700,000 slaves escaped from the Confederacy to the safety of the Union.

The value of the Negro was not immediately appreciated by the Union army officers as noted by a newspaper article written after the first Battle of Bull Run. The article contained the statement that "There is little doubt that the rout was owing to General McDowell's ignorance of the Confederate position concerning which any Negro could have informed him."

One of the first to recognize the value of the runaway slave as a potential intelligence source was the chief of General George McClellan's Secret Service, Allan Pinkerton. Pinkerton agents, as early as the fall of 1861, were sent to the front lines to interrogate the slaves as they entered Union lines. The purpose of their interrogations was twofold: first, the escaping slaves had information that would be of use to the Union Army (however one had to be careful of this information since many of the slaves could not read or write, making it hard for them, for example, to estimate troop strengths); and second, the agents were looking for Negroes who were educated and could be convinced to return to the Confederacy as Union spies. As time would prove, this turned out to be an excellent program, probably due to the fact that the Negro was held in such low respect in the South that no one would suspect him as a Union spy!

Today little is known about the specific contribution of the Black spies (as they were called in Civil War times) to the Union effort. Pinkerton mentions only two by name, the first a man named "Jem" whom he met initially in Memphis and later recruited; and the other, a man named John Scobell. Scobell, recruited by Pinkerton in the fall of 1861, represents one of the best examples of the success of Pinkerton's recruiting efforts among the escaping Negroes—who once convinced to go back to the Confederacy as a spy, continued to function as such for the rest of the war. To further illustrate how the South felt about the Negro, Scobell was with Timothy Webster and Hattie Lawton (all Pinkerton agents) when both Webster and Lawton were arrested in Richmond in March of 1862. Webster was eventually hanged, Mrs. Lawton was imprisoned for a year and later exchanged, and John Scobell was left to ply his trade without even being asked to submit to questioning. What an advantage for the Union!

John Scobell had been freed in Virginia, along with his wife. Their master, of Scottish descent, realized that John was an intelligent Negro and had taught him to read and write beyond just the rudimentary skill level. In addition, John Scobell was an excellent musician who had learned all the Scottish songs that his master sang—Scobell even sang them with a Scottish brogue! He therefore had all the necessary skill to become a successful Union spy. Pinkerton said of him, "He had only to assume the role of a light-hearted darky and no one would suspect his real role." Scobell traveled throughout the South as a vender of delicacies in the camps, a laborer on the earthworks, possibly as a cook in the camps or as a deck hand on Confederate steamers. Until her arrest in Richmond, John Scobell frequently traveled as the servant of Hattie Lawton, a Pinkerton agent. Their teamwork was most successful and of proven value to the Union effort.

Scobell's wife had remained in Richmond as a cook when John initially went north. After he was recruited by the Union, Mrs. Scobell obviously became a good source of information for John. It is not known if Mrs. Scobell ever knew that her husband was a Union spy for most of the Civil War. Unfortunately, with the end of the war John Scobell, like many of his compatriots in the Union intelligence service, faded into the woodwork and nothing is known of his later life.

Another escaped slave who is known to have become a spy is mentioned by Colonel Graham, an officer in one of General Joseph Hooker's divisions. The man's name was James Lawson. Lawson escaped, in early 1863, from his master and crossed the lines near Aquia Creek in northern Virginia. He was noticed by the Union officers as being a Negro with more than average intelligence, always truthful and deeply religious, making him an excellent candidate for spying. Initially, the Union sent him behind the Confederate lines just to test his honesty and to see if he would return to their unit. He did. On his next trip behind the lines he succeeded in rescuing his family and bringing them to freedom. He made several more trips at the request of the Union forces, always returning with the required information. On some trips he took other escaped slaves with him and one specific trip, to ascertain the amount of enemy troops in Fredericksburg, a man named "Cornelius" was killed by a Confederate picket. General Hooker sent a report to the War Department in Washington, D.C., about Lawson's spy activities, hoping that he would be compensated for the duties he had performed for the Union. Nothing is known of any subsequent action by the government in Washington. Like his fellow Negro spy, John Scobell, James Lawson fades into oblivion with the cessation of hostilities.

Negro spies were also successful in infiltrating the home of the President of the Confederacy, Jefferson Davis. One such Negro was President Davis' coachman, a man named William A. Jackson. He would listen to the conversations in the home and most importantly in the presidential coach and then steal away, pass through the Union lines north of Richmond, and deliver the information which was then relayed on to the authorities in Washington. His initial trip to the Union lines was on May 3, 1862. Historians credit the coachman as one of the most important of the "intelligent contraband."

Female Black spies also proved useful to the Union, with perhaps Elizabeth Bowser, another Negro who infiltrated the Confederate presidential household, as the best example. Miss Bowser had been a servant of Elizabeth Van Lew in Richmond prior to the war. She had been sent north by Miss Van Lew to obtain an education and to have a better life. However, when Miss Van Lew decided to spy for the Union during the very early days of the Civil War she asked Miss Bowser to return to Richmond and undertake a task for her— and Miss Bowser obligingly returned. She was placed as a servant in the home of the President of the Confederacy as a waitress and nanny to the children. Everything she learned there was dutifully reported to Miss Van Lew who passed the information on to the Union.

In addition, Mary Touvestre, a Negro housekeeper, was working in the home of a Confederate engineer where she overheard him talking about the remodeling of the *Merrimac*. When her master was away, she went into his office, stole a set of plans for the remodeling, and took them personally to Washington, D.C.

The most famous female Negro of the time, Harriet Tubman, known in the South by the codename "Moses," served as a Union spy. It would be logical that on her numerous trips into the Confederacy to assist Negroes in their flights to freedom in the North, she wouled also glean information of use to the Union government and military. She also is reported to have enlisted Negroes in the South to spy for the Union while remaining in place. Many of her trips into enemy territory were made in company with soldier details from Colonel James Montgomery's Negro brigade, the Second South Carolina Volunteers. Colonel Montgomery frequently used Mrs. Tubman as a liaison between the military officers and the slaves in the areas they raided. In appreciation of her work Colonel Montgomery wrote to General Quincy Gilmore on July 6, 1863, stating:

> I wish to commend to your attention Mrs. Harriet Tubman, a most remarkable woman, and invaluable as a scout.

The old Boston newspaper *Commonwealth* carried an article about the exploits of Mrs. Tubman on a Union raiding party:

> Colonel Montgomery and his gallant band of 300 black soldiers under the guidance of a black woman, dashed into the enemy's country, struck a bold and effective blow, destroying millions of dollars worth of commissary stores, cotton, and brought off nearly 800 slaves and thousands of dollars worth of property without losing a man or receiving a scratch.

Upon her death, in 1913, Mrs. Tubman was given a military funeral.

The lesser known Black spies include the following for which only limited information is available:

• A runaway from Winchester, Virginia, joined the 13th Massachusetts, and was quickly discovered to be a very clever man. He was sent on many occasions behind enemy lines armed with needles, thread and medicine to sell. On his first trip he was able to ascertain the location of Stonewall Jackson which was the main objective of the mission.
• When Louisville, Kentucky, was threatened in the fall of 1862, Henry Blake, a Negro living in the area, spent his nights spying on Confederate positions and reporting his findings to local white Un-

ionists who in turn passed the information to the Union forces. When his activities became known to the Confederates, a $1,000 reward was offered for his capture.

• Furney Bryant, an ex-slave escaped from his master's plantation early in the war. He not only crossed the lines frequently himself but also controlled a whole corps of Negro spies. It is through Bryant's spies that the Union Army learned the whereabouts of a Confederate cache of $800,000 in silver coins. In late 1863, Bryant enlisted in a Union Negro regiment where he served for the remainder of the war.

• At New Bern, North Carolina, Vincent Colyer reported that over 50 Negro spies were employed as scouts and spies (probably under the control of Furney Bryant). They went behind rebel lines in North Carolina at Kinston, Goldboro, and points along the Roanoke River. Frequently they went as far as 300 miles behind the lines gathering information.

• A young Negro man, named "Charley," deployed to Kinston, North Carolina, reported the retreating of a large portion of the Confederate forces from Kinston. His report proved valid and consisted of information previously unknown to the Union.

• Sam Williams became a scout for the 3rd New York Cavalry, and his commander said of him, "There's no braver man alive."

• Alfred Wood (Ol' Alf) of the 3rd United States Cavalry was very successful in the Mississippi area. Once when captured, he passed himself off as a runaway slave and was permitted to serve with the Confederate Army. Due to his light skin he later joined a Texas Ranger unit and after collecting information deserted to the Union lines.

While Negro husband and wife spy teams were rare there is one account of such a team that is worth noting, if for no other reasons than the ingenuity involved. The account was written by a Union officer in 1863 when the Union Army was encamped on the banks of the Rappahannock River in Virginia. It states:

> There came into the Union lines a Negro from a farm on the other side of the river, known by the name of Dabney, who was found to possess a remarkably clear knowledge of the topography of the whole region; and he was employed as cook and body servant at headquar-

ters. When he first saw our system of army telegraphs, the idea interested him intensely, and he begged the operators to explain the signs to him. They did so, and found that he could (readily) understand and remember the meaning of the various movements. . . .

Not long after, his wife, who had come with him, expressed a great anxiety to be allowed to go over to the other side as a servant to a "secesh woman," whom General Hooker was about sending over to her friends. The request was granted. Dabney's wife went across the Rappahannock, and in a few days was duly installed as laundress at the headquarters of a prominent General. Dabney, her husband, on the north bank, was soon found to be wonderfully well informed as to all the rebel plans. Within an hour of the time that a movement of any kind was projected, or even discussed, among the rebel generals, Hooker (the Union general) knew all about it. He knew which corps was moving, or about to move, in what direction, how long they had been on the march, and in what force; and all this knowledge came through Dabney, and his reports always turned out to be true.

Yet Dabney was never absent, and never talked with the scouts, and seemed to be always taken up with his duties as cook and groom about Headquarters.

How he got his information remained for some time a puzzle to the Union Officers. At length, upon much solicitation, he unfolded his marvelous secret to one of our officers.

Taking him to a point where a clear view could be obtained of Fredericksburg, he pointed out a little cabin in the suburbs near the river bank; and asked him if he saw that clothes-line with clothes hanging on it to dry. "Well" said he "that clothes line tells me in half an hour just what goes on at Lee's headquarters. You see my wife over there; she washes for the officers, and cooks, and waits around, and as soon as she hears about any movement or anything going on she comes down and moves the clothes on that line so I can understand it in a minute. That there gray shirt is Longstreet; and when she takes it off, it means he's gone down about Richmond. That white shirt means Hill; and when she moves it up to the west end of the line, Hill's corps has moved upstream. That red one is Stonewall. He's down on the right now, and if he moves, she will move that red shirt."

One morning Dabney came in and reported a movement over there. "But" says he, "it don't amount to anything. They're just making believe."

An Officer went out to look at the clothes-line telegraph through his field-glass. There had been quite a shifting over there among the army flannels. "But how do you know but there is something in it?"

61

"Do you see those two blankets pinned together at the bottom?" said Dabney. "Yes, but what of it?" said the officer. "Why, that her way of making a fish-trap; and when she pins the clothes together that way, it means that Lee is only trying to draw us into his fish trap."

As long as the two armies lay watching each other on opposite banks of the stream, Dabney, with his clothes-line telegraph, continued to be one of the most prompt and reliable of General Hooker's scouts.

When Scobell or other Negro spies would go into the Confederacy they were aided by a Negro organization known as the "Legal League." This organization served as spies in place gathering data from other League members and local sources. The most legendary member of this league was a Negro by the name of "Uncle Gallus." Entry to the Legal League meeting was obtained with the following sequence, subsequent to rapping on the door:

Doorkeeper: "Who comes?"
Stranger   : "Friends of Uncle Abe."
Doorkeeper: "What do you desire?"
Stranger   : "Light and loyalty!"

The League would either pass the information gathered by League members to a known Union man, such as John Scobell, or would on occasion use one of their members as a courier to take the information to the Union line. The League also provided safe havens for the Negro Union spies that passed through their areas as well as for escaped Union prisoners of war. While we hear much of the Underground Railroad for the slaves, we hear little of the underground railroad, operated by slaves, that aided Yankee escapees making their way back to the Union lines. There are many surviving stories provided by the men they helped escape—the line did exist!

The acquisition and movement of intelligence by the Negroes behind Confederate lines came to be known as the "Black Dispatch." The term was coined by General Rush Hawkins, the Union commander at Cape Hatteras, North Carolina, in 1861, who said of the Negro:

If I want to find out anything hereabouts I hunt up a Negro; and if he knows or can find out, I'm sure to get all I want.

The Black Dispatch was used effectively not only by General Hawkins, but also General George Sharpe on the Virginia front, and General Grenville Dodge on the Western front.

Those Negroes who could not escape were often of use to the Union efforts. With the encouragement of such people as John Scobell and the Legal League, these Negroes often aided the Union with their sabotage efforts and continued unruliness. It was very easy for them to wreck farm equipment, thereby making the harvesting of crops very difficult if not impossible. In addition, their attitude often led to the wife of the farm pleading with her husband to come home so that he could handle the unruly slaves. While some of the behavior was spontaneous, much of it was generated by such agents as Scobell working with the Legal League.

General Dodge continued and expanded upon Pinkerton's initiative regarding the use of Blacks as Union spies, as did General Sharpe, particularly with the Pamunkey Indians, many of whom had bred with the Negro. General Dodge went so far as to organize the escaping Negro men into military units—the 1st Colored Alabama Infantry and the 1st Colored Alabama Cavalry. Like Pinkerton he looked for the brighter Negroes and convinced many of them to return to the South as spies. He would have his Negro spies use their family members, who had remained in the South, as a local spy network and even as necessary to courier information back to General Dodge.

It is interesting to look at the Black spy efforts through the eyes of a prominent Negro of the time, Frederick Douglass, who wrote, in 1862:

> The true history of this war will show that the loyal army found no friends at the South so faithful, active and daring in their efforts to sustain the Government as the Negroes. It will be shown that they have been the safest guides to our army and the best pilots to our navy, and the most dutiful laborers on our fortifications, where they have been permitted to serve. It is already known that the tremendous slaughter of loyal soldiers at Pittsburgh Landing, where our army was surprised and cut to pieces, would have been prevented had the alarm given by a Negro, who had risked his life to give it, been taken. The same is true of the destruction of the Maryland Regiment the other day at Port Royal. Gen. Burnside, in the difficult task committed to him of feeling his way into the intricate rivers and creeks of

Virginia and North Carolina, has found no assistance among the so-called loyal whites comparable in value to that obtained from intelligent Black men. The folly and expense of marching an army to Manassas, after it had been evacuated more than a week, would have been prevented but for the contemptuous disregard of information conveyed by the despised men of color. Negroes have repeatedly threaded their way through the lines of the rebels exposing themselves to bullets to convey important information to the loyal army of the Potomac.

Douglass' assertion to the lack of belief in the Negro was in fact one of the major problems facing the Black spy, both Union controlled and independent.

The use of the Negro by the Union for spying purposes was very successful as long as stringent recruiting policies were upheld and men like John Scobell prove the point. By their own blindness to the innate abilities of some Negroes, the Confederacy provided the Union with a unique spy system that continued to operate in the South until the final surrender.

In contrast to the Negro spy efforts for the Union there is no available evidence that the Negro served as a spy for the Confederacy at any point in the war. Just as there are no records of a Southern Black ever turning in an escaped Union military prisoner.

Much like the Negro that served in the Union fighting forces, the Negro's contribution to the spying efforts of the Union Army has not received the recognition that it is due. One of the major contributing reasons for this may be the fact that there are very few written records of the Black spy that have survived to this day—or at least have come to light to the researcher.

Newsboys

Newspapers were very important to the Civil War soldier in the field and newsboys selling local papers were a very common sight among the troops. Both the Confederacy and the Union made use of these newsboys to collect information as they sold their papers.

One of the more interesting reports regarding the Confederate use of newsboys was written on November 1, 1864, by Union General George Sharpe, General Grant's intelligence chief on the Virginia front. The report written at City Point, Virginia, states:

> Scouts returned this morning, bringing communications from Richmond agent which is to the following effect:—
>
> General Lee has two little boys trained as spies, who give him all manner of information. They are very young and travel along our lines in the character of newsboys. They have given General Lee much valuable information, and traveling under this guise are little apt to be suspected as spies. Their names are Smith.

An interesting follow-up letter regarding the young spies was written to the Union Provost Marshal's office on November 4, 1864; it states:

> It is reported by Richmond agent that the father of the two small boys (spies mentioned in previous communications) holds a position on General Lee's staff as an acknowledgment of the services of his sons.

It is quite possible that these same two Confederate newsboy spies are the two mentioned by General Philip Sheridan in his memoirs of the Civil War. The pasage regarding newsboys is as follows:

> The rest of the day we remained on the battlefield undisturbed . . . and reading the Richmond journals, two small newsboys with the commendable enterprise having come within our lines from the Confederate capital to sell their papers. They were sharp youngsters, and having come well supplied, they did a thrifty business. When their stock in trade was all disposed of they wished to return, but they were so intelligent and observant that I thought their mission involved other purposes than the mere sale of newspapers, so they were held till we crossed the Chickahominy and then turned loose.

The Union also utilized young men, disguised as newsboys, as collectors of tactical information for use of their local armies. The best known example was Charles Phillips, the son of John Phillips, who was only 14 years old when he joined his father in espionage work.

Initially Charles served as a courier to relay the information gathered by his father but later became an information gatherer himself. His "cover" was to serve as a paperboy and sell newspapers all over town and in the local encampments. He continued to be very successful in his endeavors until he was arrested in January 1865. He spent the last few months of the war in prison in Richmond. However, he was content, as on at least one occasion he had delivered the intelligence he had gathered directly to General U.S. Grant.

Spies from Europe

Although the Civil War was entirely an American war there are authenticated cases of European citizens in the United States during the war actually serving as spies—some for the Union and some for the Confederacy. In a few cases their motivation was strongly anti-slavery, but in most it appears to be a sense of adverture. In at least one instance, that of the Pole John Sobieski, the Union was able to use his foreign birth to their advantage—the Confederacy thought he was a Polish aristocrat sympathetic to the cause of the Confederacy. He was in fact an aristocrat but his feelings were very pro-Union!

In addition to pointing out that Allan Pinkerton was born and raised in Scotland before coming to America where he later became General George McClellan's "spymaster," there are four known specific cases in which European born men served as spies for the Union: "Dr. Lugo," Northern Italian; John Sobieski, Polish; Mr. Pole, English; and Messers John Scully and Pryce Lewis, English. The specifics for these four cases are:

"DOCTOR LUGO" (Orazio Lugo de Antonzini)—On New Year's Eve 1863, a handsome and well-mannered foreign young man registered at the Ballard House Hotel in Richmond. He soon introduced himself to Bishop John M. McGill, Catholic bishop of Richmond, as the nephew of the personal secretary to Pope Pius IX—a pure fabrication but very effective since within a short period of time he was introduced to not only the socially prominent of

Richmond but also the major figures of the Confederate government, specifically Secretary of the Navy Stephen R. Mallory.

Secretary Mallory upon learning that Dr. Lugo was an expert in explosives, especially those used for torpedoes, quickly made Dr. Lugo his protege and gave him a pass to travel throughout the Confederacy to check on the deployment of torpedoes in the various harbors and other locations. He was so impressed with this young man that he also employed him at the Confederate arsenal for research on torpedoes. Little did Secretary Mallory know that simultaneous with his employment of Dr. Lugo, his protege was also working for the Union Secretary of the Navy, Gideon Welles, as a Union spy. He was actively in the employ of both secretaries!

All went well until late in March when the Richmond underground apparently learned that Dr. Lugo was about to be arrested on suspicion of being a Union spy. They alerted him and on 23 March 1864 he vanished from Ballard House, leaving an unpaid bill of over $500, and secreted himself in a Union safe house. Dr. Lugo remained there until the Richmond underground planned an escape route for him. He departed Richmond and proceeded north, with all going well until he reached the banks of the Rappahannock River where he was arrested and found to be in possession of highly sensitive Confederate documents.

Dr. Lugo was tried, found guilty of spying and sentenced to be hanged. Later the sentence was commuted (probably because of his stated association with the Pope—which was a lie!) to expulsion from the Confederacy. He was to be sent to Nassau to be released. Enroute, the Confederate blockade runner carrying him was captured by a Union vessel and Dr. Lugo was ultimately rescued by the Union.

When Washington learned of his capture, Secretary of the Navy Welles ordered his immediate transfer to Washington. Once in Washington Dr. Lugo petitioned the Federal government for repayment of the $6,000 he claimed to have lost in his endeavors in Richmond. The Federal government responded by graciously giving him a check for $50. Nothing more is recorded regarding Dr. Lugo and one can only assume that he returned to his native land—his lust for adventure then over.

Miss Van Lew and her Union spy ring were obviously aware of Dr. Lugo as they warned him of his impending arrest. What is not known is if Dr. Lugo used her ring to relay his collected information back to the Union prior to his arrest. His access and technical expertise could indeed have provided the Union with considerable knowledge about a very serious problem—the Confederate state-of-the-art torpedo making as well as deployment.

Why Orazio Lugo de Antonzini (Dr. Lugo) undertook his mission remains a mystery.

JOHN SOBIESKI—John Sobieski was born into Polish nobility. He was the great-grandson of John III, King of Poland. He and his family had been exiled from Poland after the overthrow of the royal government and John Sobieski became a soldier of fortune.

He came to the United States—a soldier of fortune who believed in the Union cause—and soon was fighting with the Union Army. He was wounded during the Battle of Gettysburg. At this point, some ingenious Union official devised an espionage scheme that proved to be very useful to the strategic efforts of the Union. The Union government gave Sobieski $4,000 and sent him south as Count Kalieski—an exiled Polish count—a role he could easily portray (dueling scars et al.).

Count Kalieski (Sobieski) traveled to the South via Havana, entering the Confederacy at Mobile, Alabama. He traveled north to Richmond and was royally received in the Confederate capital. He had personal interviews with President Jefferson Davis, Vice President Stephens, many of the Cabinet officials and was even escorted to the front, where he had dinner with General Robert E. Lee. One can only imagine the amount of strategic intelligence he derived from these very important interviews.

He returned to the Union via the same route he had taken to enter the Confederacy. Arriving in Washington he presented his handlers with $322 (what remained of the $4,000 given to him prior to his departure) and a great deal of information. While the intelligence was not of great tactical value, it obviously provided a genuine insight into the thinking of the senior officials at a time that such information would be critical to the Union's strategic planning.

MR. POLE—In February 1865 the Union tried to duplicate the Sobieski feat with another foreigner. This time it was an Englishman by the name of Mr. Pole. He went south in the company of a handler, Mr. Babcock—one of General George Sharpe's very best agents. In short order after reaching the Confederacy Mr. Pole developed a case of "nerves" and not only confessed to the Confederacy his true mission but also "fingered" his handler—Mr. Babcock—which was a real loss to General Sharpe.

The only good thing that came out of this mission was that Mr. Pole surrendered so quickly in the Confederacy that he had not as yet met Elizabeth Van Lew—the main Union spy in Richmond. Had he fingered her as well, the Union would have sustained a tremendous loss of information from Richmond.

JOHN SCULLY AND PRYCE LEWIS—Both Scully and Lewis were of British origin. They were working for Pinkerton when he was forming his secret service and they both joined the service. Working initially in Washington, they were used in the counter-intelligence field and were involved in searching the home of Mrs. Jackson Morton, wife of a ex-U.S. Senator from Florida. They were evidently not too gentle in this search effort as they were remembered later!

Sent to Richmond as English subjects to check on the whereabouts of Timothy Webster, Pinkerton's favorite agent, they were immediately suspected and arrested by the Confederacy. Initially they denied any ulterior motives for their trip until they were identified by Mrs. Morton's son. Unfortunately for the pair, the Morton family, after their rude treatment in Washington, had moved to Richmond. The young Morton remembered the two agents from their search of his family home, he identified them and quickly they admitted their true roles—agents for Pinkerton!

While the Confederacy by this time had suspicions about Timothy Webster they could never find the evidence to arrest him—until they had Scully and Lewis in their hands. When convicted as spies and sentenced to hang, both of these men identified Timothy Webster as one of the main spies for Pinkerton along with Hattie Lawton (his traveling companion).

The outcome was that Scully and Lewis were exchanged almost immediately (one wonders about their reception when they returned to Pinkerton's headquarters), Mrs. Lawton was jailed for a period and then released and Timothy Webster, Pinkerton's best operative, was hanged by the Confederate government in Richmond. (One of the witnesses at the hanging was Miss Van Lew.)

In addition to the above specific cases there is the case of Mr. W.F. Gray, a gentleman from Geneva, Switzerland, who apparently had a grand dream of coming to the United States and serving as a spy for the Union. One of his letters to General Halleck survives to this day. It was written on February 5, 1864, and a portion is quoted here:

> Dear sir:, I send you another plan of Richmond that I do not suppost that you have no drawing but I do it to show you I know the place and am desirous of coming to Washington and aid you with my personal knowledge as to all I know about the country in rebellion. . . . I shall wait til the 1st to 10th of March for a reply after that time I shall never write or look for a letter from Seward or anyone in Washington.

There is no record that a response to Mr. Gray's letter was ever sent by any official in Washington. His letter represents what must have been one of many received during the Civil War by the government in Washington.

The Confederacy also had some European spies. None were as dramatic and successful as John Sobieski, but they were equally interesting. We know of two specific cases—Charles Heidsick and Dr. William Passmore. The specifics of each of these men follow:

JOHN HEIDSICK—John Heidsick was the heir to a French champagne winery. When the War began he was in New Orleans on a combined business/pleasure trip. Heidsick got caught up in the spirit of the Confederacy and while he was not interested in fighting with the Confederate Army he did undertake a spy mission—probably on his own initiative.

Heidsick became a bartender on the river boats that plied the Mississippi and other rivers in the area carrying Union troops. Bars are excellent places for soldier talk, especially when they believe that everyone on the boat is from the Union side—how wrong they were! Heidsick was able to relay to the Confederacy a great deal of intelligence, probably the most important of which was information about coming battles planned by the Union.

Heidsick later returned to France and once again assumed his place in the family business of making French champagne—a business that is still thriving today!

DR. WILLIAM PASSMORE—An English doctor, Passmore was a friend of General Robert E. Lee, and undertook in 1862 a spy mission for him.

Dr. Passmore, probably a good ham actor, entered General Ambrose Burnside's camp as a half-wit selling items from his cart. He wandered freely through the camp and since he was very convincing as a half-wit, soldiers spoke freely in front of him. He reported that on one occasion, General Burnside and his officer discussed their plans as Dr. Passmore rearranged the items on his cart—right in front of them!

The information he provided General Lee upon his return is said to have been instrumental in the Confederate victory at Fredericksburg, Virginia. Apparently this was his one and only mission for his general friend as there are no further references to him from any source.

One can see from the above that both the Union and the Confederate side were not hesitant to use any possible ploy in their efforts to derive information. From the little we know about the use of foreigners as spies it would appear that John Sobieski for the Union and Charles Heidsick were the most successful agents—in fact several of the others caused disasters, which can happen in the espionage field with the use of adventurists—it isn't good "tradecraft."

Spies in Europe

The Continental United States was not the only arena for Union and Confederate spying/espionage activities during the Civil War. Both sides had extensive networks on the continent of Europe—and each side was there to work against the other. The Confederate agents in Europe were there to garner support for their independence efforts, i.e., diplomatic recognition, to purchase much needed supplies, and to convince both governments and private individuals to contribute financially to the Confederate cause. The Union agents on the other hand were there to counter each and every one of the Confederacy's goals.

On the Union side the main spymaster in Europe was Harry S. Sanford, the ambassador to Belgium. Mr. Sanford was by profession a lawyer who spoke French, German and Spanish, which made him an excellent choice for his position. He took his role as spymaster in Europe very seriously and among other achievements he is credited with the following:

• Paying European editors to place pro-Union editorials in their newspapers.
• Bribing clerks in the major manufacturing firms to supply tips to him when the Confederacy was about to formalize a contract for supplies and advise him of cost. He would then bid a higher price and deprive the Confederacy of the supplies. (Most of the Confederate supply efforts were made by Matthew F. Maury, a Confederate agent in the U.K.).
• Putting Union men on ships heading for the Confederacy with supplies and have them attempt to convince the crews (sometimes successfully) to seize control of the ship on the high seas and sail into a Union port.
• Hiring Ignatius Pollaky in the United Kingdom to identify and report on the many Confederate spies in that country, particularly a man named Captain James Bulloch. Pollaky did, in fact, identify about 17 Confederate spies in England and he continued to track them during their stays in that country. All results were reported to Sanford on a regular basis.
• Involving himself in the scheme to recruit the Italian General Garibaldi as a Union brigadier general. The scheme was developed by the U.S. envoy to Brussels, a Mr. Quiggle, early in the war (1861) when the Union desperately need a successful general. Garibaldi was approached, appeared interested, but later balked when he discovered that his two demands could not be met. His demands were the rank of General in Chief of the Union Army and the authority to free the slaves. Garibaldi had lived in the United States for three years, liked America and was very popular in the U.S. so the scheme was not as farfetched as it initially sounds.

Sanford took his role as spymaster very seriously and proved to be an able controller of the agents in Europe. Many of his actions regarding the depriving of supplies and support to the Confederacy, while somewhat intangible, obviously aided the Union war effort.

At the same time that Ambassador Sanford was operating in Europe there was a similar operation in Canada. Secretary of State William Seward sent agents to Canada with two major goals in mind. They were to stop the communications channel that existed between the Confederacy and the United Kingdom, using Canada as the relay point (This channel was used for both agent transfer as well as correspondence) and to stop the Canadians from selling shoes to the Confederacy for their army.

The Confederates had no counterpart to Ambassador Sanford, with the possible exception of James M. Mason, who served as the Confederate representative to the government of the United Kingdom. The Confederate government kept Mr. Mason aware of its activities in Europe but did not expect him to interfere in any way. One example of a Confederate action is contained in a letter to Mr. Mason from J.P. Benjamin, the Confederate Secretary of State, written on July 6, 1863, and containing the following paragraph:

No. 29 Department of State, Richmond, July 6, 1863.
Hon. James M. Mason, etc., London.
Sir: I note what you state in relation to the recruiting by the enemy in Ireland. While it is satisfactory to know that you are diligent in the matter, we have decided to send two or three Irishmen, long residents of our country, to act as far as they can in arresting these unlawful acts of the enemy, by communicating directly with the people, and spreading among them such information and intelligence as may be best adapted to persuade them of the folly and wickedness of volunteering their aid in the savage warfare waged against us.
I am, very respectfully, your obedient servant.
J.P. Benjamin, Secretary of State

By far the most successful Confederate agent operating in Europe was a man by the name of James Bulloch (ironically enough the Georgia born Uncle of Theodore Roosevelt) who operated in Liverpool, England, with a very specific mission.

Captain Bulloch had a long naval career and when the war commenced was actually at sea. When his ship arrived in the port of

Boston, Captain Bulloch and most of his crew resigned their commissions and immediately went south to serve the Confederacy. He was soon notified to come to Richmond and there received his orders to proceed to England on his mission. The Confederacy had very few shipyards for the building of major ships and therefore wanted Bulloch to have warships built in England to serve the Confederacy. Such construction, by a neutral foreign power (England), was against the rules of neutrality (the Foreign Enlistment Act— which stated that a neutral country was prohibited from fitting out armed ships for a combatant).

Arriving in Liverpool, Captain Bulloch immediately began his search for suitable shipyards. His plan was to have the ships built, but not armed prior to leaving the shipyards. The armaments would be on a separate ship that would rendezvous with the new ship at another port where the arming of the ship would take place. Bulloch contracted for the first ship to be named the CSS *Florida* at the Miller & Sons Yard, and the second ship the CSS *Alabama* at the Laird Shipyards. Both shipyards were in the Liverpool area.

All proceeded according to plan, however, the Union learning of the construction strongly protested through the U.S. ambassador to England, Charles F. Adams, Sr. The British stated that as far as they knew the ships were to be used for non-combatant purposes and therefore legal. The Union again protested and demanded that the ships were not to be commissioned or to leave port. Captain Bulloch, ignoring the protest arranged for the ships to go out for "sea trials" and not return—which is exactly what happened. The ships met with their companions carrying the armaments, were armed and immediately pressed into active duty. The British could legally say that they had no idea the ships would not return and therefore believed they could not be held in violation of the Foreign Enlistment Act.

During her lifetime, the CSS *Florida* captured or destroyed 37 Union vessels valued at $3.7 million dollars. Finally in October of 1864 she was captured. The CSS *Alabama* captured or destroyed 65 Union vessels worth about $5.0 million dollars. Finally when she was in bad need of repairs, a Union ship challenged her off the coast of France and after a short battle she was sunk. One can see from the contributions of these two ships why the Union was more than a little indignant about the action of the British government as well as the Confederate agent Bulloch who through very clever maneuvering brought the endeavor to fruition.

At the same time that Bulloch was carefully orchestrating the construction of the *Florida* and the *Alabama,* he was also involved in secretly shipping supplies to the Confederacy. In 1861, he contracted with the British ship *Fingal* to transport supplies to the Caribbean where they would be transferred to Confederate blockade runners for delivery to the mainland. The *Fingal* carried the largest cargo ever carried during the course of the Civil War, which consisted of:

200 made-up cartridges, shot and shell per gun
  2 breech loading 2½ inch steel rifled guns for boats
200 rounds of ammunition per gun
400 barrels of cannon-powder

  clothing for sailors

  for Georgia: 3,000 Enfield rifles
  for Louisiana: 1,000 Enfield Rifles

The *Fingal* chose to run the blockade and was successful in arriving at a Confederate port. Once unloaded it was bottled up for such a long period in the Savannah River that the Confederacy decided to transform the ship into a fighting vessel. The sides were covered with thick armor and four large naval guns were placed on board. Renamed the CSS *Atlanta* she made her maiden, and last voyage, as a Confederate ship in late May of 1863. She drew so much water that she ran aground and was forced to surrender to the Union Navy. She was taken as a prize of war and assigned to the Federal fleet. A very ignominious ending for such a historic ship!

Meanwhile in Liverpool, Captain Bulloch, flushed with the success of his supply efforts and the construction of the two ships for the Confederacy, again went into action. He contracted with the British shipyards to build two ironclad ships again under the guise of non-combatants. The Union, at this point, objected strongly— it was one thing to have wooden non-combatant ships, but ironclads were another matter. The U.S. ambassador to England, Adams, went to Lord Russell and stated that if construction continued on the ships it would probably result in a state of war between the United States and England.

This tense situation continued until a man named Clarence Yonge, hired by Bullock to be the paymaster on the *Alabama* but later fired as a drunk, came to Ambassador Adams out of revenge to Bulloch. Yonge told the ambassador the entire scheme was perpetrated by Bulloch, and with that evidence Ambassador Adams was able to stop construction on the ironclads.

Having problems with the British efforts, Bulloch, not to be deterred, secretly approached the French in June of 1863 with a proposal to build four clipper corvettes for the Confederacy. The French clearly understood Bulloch's scheme and they stated there would be no problem delivering the unarmed ships to a neutral point. Based on this assurance Bulloch further contracted with the French for the construction of two ironclads shallow enough to traverse the Mississippi. Pressure immediately was placed on the French by the Union and things did not go well for the Confederate effort. Events that followed were:

Feb. 1864: France declared that the ships could not leave port
Jul. 1864: The ships were declared for sale and all purchasers must be legitimate (not fronts for the Confederacy)
Aug. 1864: Ships were sold to Prussia and Denmark

By the time Denmark received the ship, their war was over and they had no real use for the ship so they sold it to the Confederacy to be commissioned as the CSS *Stonewall*. After purchase, in February 1865, the ship went into a U.K. port for repairs and refitting where it was constantly under surveillance by the Union Navy. The *Stonewall* finally arrived on the U.S. side of the Atlantic in time to learn of the surrender of General Robert E. Lee's army and therefore was of no use to the Confederacy.

Just prior to the conclusion of the war, in fact in early 1865, the final Confederate secret agent missions took place involving the European powers. The first, the mission of Duncan F. Kenner, was sponsored by the Confederacy, while the second, undertaken by C.J. Polignac, was not known to the Confederate government. Kenner's mission was to go to England and meet with Confederate representatives there, Mason and Slidell, conveying a message to them that the Confederacy might be willing to give up slavery in exchange for European recognition. Unknown to the Confederate delegation in the U.K., Mr. Polignac, in March of 1865, independently went to France to discuss with Napoleon III the possibility of establishing a Southwest Confederacy to include Texas, Arkansas and Louisiana along with adjacent land from Mexico. Both plans were too late to save the Confederacy as General Lee surrendered on April 9, 1865.

The final chapter of the Bulloch saga in England was not written until after the war. Later events were:

• After the war the United States sued the British government for damages resulting from the ships they had built for the Confederacy, the CSS *Florida* and the CSS *Alabama*. The Tribunal of Arbitration in Geneva, Switzerland, awarded the United States 3 million United Kingdom pounds to resolve the case.
• The British bank that represented the Confederacy in Liverpool—Fraser, Frenholm & Co—was sued by the United States and driven out of business.
• The Confederate agent responsible for the shipbuilding efforts in the United Kingdom, Captain James Bulloch, remained in Liverpool and was joined there by his family. He died in 1901 after his nephew, Theodore Roosevelt, had become President of the United States.

Captain Bulloch was a very capable agent for the shipbuilding efforts of the Confederacy. While not in the traditional role of a spy, he did accomplish his task in a secret/covert manner. His actions not only impacted on both the Union and Confederate efforts in the Civil War, but also on the British treasury after the war.

Throughout the war, with the exception of the building of ships, the Confederacy made little progress with the European governments through the use of their covert agents. It was not until late in the war that the Confederacy truly understood the strong anti-slavery feelings that permeated Europe. They had no chance of achieving European recognition as long as they insisted on maintaining the institution of slavery, for while the European powers favored the United States splitting into lesser units, they were influenced by their abhorrence of slavery to not recognize the Confederacy.

As a result of the covert spy activities of both the Union and the Confederacy during the Civil War, the United States realized, to a small extent, the value of an intelligence operation in Europe. Post-Civil War covert activities centered on activities of the United States embassies abroad for both military and political intelligence, probably due to the success of Ambassador Sanford for the Union during the Civil War. With the advent of World War I, this activity expanded, and went beyond the diplomatic sphere for the first time. Without the experiences of the Union during the Civil War, the United States probably would have been less prepared for covert activities in Europe during the early 20th century.

Telegraphic Spies

One of the first signals intelligence spies in United States history and the world worked for the Union forces during the Civil War. His participation was not a deliberate move on the part of the Union but an individual effort—he came forth and volunteered to serve as a Union spy, utilizing his telegraphic skills as an entry to service for the Confederacy. The man was J.O. Kerbey—trained prior to the war as a telegrapher for the railroads.

Kerbey went behind enemy lines prior to the first battle of Bull Run in Virginia and in fact was in the Shenandoah Valley when General Joseph Johnston started to move his troops in support of General Pierre Beauregard at Bull Run. Upon observing the beginning of the movement of Johnston's troops, Kerbey found the Union forces and reported what he had seen only not to be believed. Had he in fact been found credible the outcome of Bull Run may well have been very different. The problem of credibility for agents was a serious one throughout the war—on both sides.

Kerbey stayed behind enemy lines and was subsequently captured by Confederate forces. He told them of his telegraphic skills and soon found himself on duty in a railroad depot (proficient telegraphic operators were in very short supply—particularly in the South). From his assigned railroad depot location, Kerbey could and did listen in on all the telegraphic communications in and out of Richmond, the Confederate capital in Virginia, as one of the lines going through his depot was a direct line to Richmond. On one occasion he heard a report that 25 percent of the troops in the Manassas area of Virginia had dysentery—a good opportunity for a Union assault. He tucked the information in his hat band and headed north to the Union lines.

Every time Kerbey tried to get through to the North he kept getting caught by the Confederacy so he decided he needed to find a better way to communicate with the Union forces. At this time he was stationed in Richmond—still operating a telegraphic post—so he located Elizabeth Van Lew, the eminent Union spy in the Confederacy. He soon learned that any information he acquired could be relayed to the Union very efficiently by Miss Van Lew's courier system.

Like Miss Van Lew, Kerbey had his own cipher system for delivering messages. His apparently normal letter to a relative in the North would have seemingly random pen scratches and small blots on the pages. The scratches and blots would in fact be the telegraphic representation numbers and those numbers would tell the reader what words were significant in the letters. For example the number 5 would mean take only every fifth word in the text as sent. An example of this would be the message he sent to the Union:

. . . . Been . . . . all . . . . through . . . . Southern . . . . Army, ...
again . . . . obliged . . . . delay . . . . here . . . . account . . . .
sickness . . . . impossible . . . . Confederate . . . . advance . . . .
are . . . . exhausted . . . . half . . . . army . . . . sick . . . .
balance . . . . demoralized . . . . look . . . . under . . . . front . . . .
portion . . . . Blanks . . . . house . . . . situated . . . . on . . . .
hill . . . . road . . . . Manassas . . . . to . . . . Washington . . . .
black . . . . roll . . . . of . . . . papers . . . . official . . . . proofs . . . .
wish . . . . friend . . . . Covode . . . . secure . . . . them . . . .
officers . . . . are . . . . there . . . . night . . . . night . . . .
students . . . . Georgetown . . . . signal . . . . south . . . . from . . . .
dormitory . . . . will . . . . be . . . . home . . . . soon . . . . as . . . .
I . . . . can.

Periods, e.g., ... , equate to the four random words inserted between the valid text

This particular message not only tells the Union that the Confederate Army is sick, demoralized, and unlikely to move but it alerts the Union to the fact that the dormitory at Georgetown University—high on the hill above the Washington, D.C., side of the Potomac River—was being used as a signal station. The Confederate sympathizers at the University would raise and lower the shades at night, using lamps to signal messages across the Potomac to Confederate spotters on the other side. Based on Kerbey's message this practice soon came to a halt.

While in the Confederacy, the shortage of manpower became critical and Kerbey found himself recruited into the Confederate Army. He was forced to sign a Loyalty Oath to the Confederacy—which later caused him great trouble. As his unit moved north, Kerbey left them and returned to the Union side where he again worked as a legitimate telegraph operator and all was fine until he was asked to sign a Loyalty Oath to the Union. The oath stated that he had never carried arms against the Union nor had he signed a Loyalty Oath to forces against the Union. Kerbey was an honest man and told his superiors he could not sign the oath, thinking that Secretary of War Edwin Stanton would be aware of his spying activity and would solve the problem. Stanton, in fact, ignored Kerbey and his problem and he found himself in the Old Capitol Prison that also housed the famous Confederate female spy Belle Boyd.

The flamboyant Miss Boyd, always a person for intrigue, heard of Kerbey and his Confederate service as well as his arrest on Stanton's orders. In her mind he obviously was of value to the Confederacy and therefore she undertook a plan to help him escape. She not only helped him develop a plan of escape but also told him of all the safe houses along the route to the Confederacy. Kerbey knowing that the information would be of great value to the Union secret service willingly went along with her planning.

On the actual day that the escape was to be executed, Kerbey was taken from the cell and freed. Apparently Secretary of War Stanton had finally realized his mistake. Miss Boyd never knew what happened to him, nor did she realize that all the information she had given to him was then in Union hands.

J.O. Kerbey was then commissioned a lieutenant in the Union Army with a commission signed personally by President Lincoln. While he fades into the masses at this point, it is fair to say that

J.O. Kerbey has a unique place in the history of espionage, not only for the United States but also the world. He is the first documented person to listen in on the enemy's telegraphic communications and to utilize what he heard as intelligence input—in modern terms he was the first signals intelligence operator on record. It is estimated that during the early days of the war his message volume of intelligence back to the Union rivaled that of Rose O'Neal Greenhow.

The Confederacy has an unknown telegraphic spy of its own. General U.S. Grant's own memoirs contain a reference to an unidentified Confederate telegraphic spy on his staff. During the early months of 1862, immediately after the fall of Fort Donelson in Tennessee, General Grant was in Cairo, Illinois, and moved west. Cairo was the end of the telegraph line but a new line had started from Cairo to Paducah and Smithland, in Kentucky, at the mouths of the Tennessee and Cumberland Rivers. Some of General Grant's messages were sent on to him by steamer but some were given to a telegraphic operator at the Cairo end of the advancing wire for transmission on the newly established line extension. These messages never got to General Grant, and many of them were orders from General George Halleck in Washington.

The lack of response from General Grant caused enough concern that General Halleck recommended that he be removed from command and that an investigation be started to uncover the reasons that General Grant was ignoring his (General Halleck's) commands.

It turns out that the telegraphic operator receiving the messages at the end of the advancing Union line was a rebel spy and he was deliberately not forwarding the messages to General Grant. General Grant could not respond to orders he never received. The operator having done his job escaped to the South and took with him all of General Grant's messages from General Halleck! The young Confederate agent's name has never been established but one has to admit he did an effective job of disrupting the Union command in the West.

Both the Union and the Confederacy soon discovered that telegraph lines could be tapped, and information obtained, without the knowledge of the enemy. Wiretapping became a useful technique and some of the more expert wiretappers include:

Union

WILLIAM FORSTER tapped the telegraph line along the Charleston-Savannah railroad for two days. He was later captured and died in a Confederate prison.

F.S. VAN VALKENBERGH and PATRICK MULLASKY tapped the Confederate line along the Chattanooga Railroad near Knoxville, Tennessee. They supplied General William Rosecrans with information about General Braxton Bragg's actions regarding the detachment of troops to reinforce Vicksburg.

OPERATOR LONEGRAN tapped General Wheeler's lines and provided a warning to General Sherman about General Wheeler's upcoming raid.

Confederacy

Operator GEORGE "LIGHTNING" ELLSWORTH, General Morgan's telegraph operator, served not only as a wire tapper but was also expert at inserting bogus messages on the Union telegraphic lines. He successfully confused the Union for several hours with bogus messages during General Morgan's raid into Union-held Kentucky.

GENERAL LEE'S OPERATORS tapped the Union lines between the Union War Department and General Ambrose Burnside's headquarters at Aquia Creek in Virginia.

C. A. GASTON successfully tapped the Union line between General Grant's headquarters in Virginia and President Lincoln in Washington from a location disguised as a logging camp. While the tap lasted about two months, the Confederacy was never able to read the enciphered messages that passed between the two men. However they did make use of the unenciphered messages. One of the messages taken on the tap reported that 2,586 beeves were to be landed at Coggins' Point on a certain day. This information enabled the Confederate Wade Hampton to make a timely raid and capture the entire shipment.

The telegraph was a new weapon in modern warfare and its usefulness to intelligence was not clearly understood until much later. The selected individuals discussed were in the vanguard in the use of what was to become a very valuable intelligence tool. One has only to think of the value of the ENIGMA messages transmitted by the Germans and intercepted by the Allies in World War II.

Chapter 7

Imprisonment, Exchange and Execution of Spies

Civil War spies caught by either the Confederacy or the Union were initially imprisoned for a length of time that could vary from one to twelve months. During that time they may or may not have been under sentence for their activities. In most cases the spies were exchanged after such a duration as to make the captured spy of little use to the enemy. Spies were usually exchanged in an even swap, however if the spy was a particularly important one the exchange was often uneven. The two men responsible for arranging the parole or swap of prisoners including spies were Colonel W.H. Ludlow for the Union and R.O. Ould for the Confederacy. A great deal of correspondence between the two men can be found in *The War of the Rebellion* published by the U.S. Government in 1899.

Civilian operatives arrested were always classified as "spies." However, when a military man was captured, it became very important to him to be classified as a "scout" and not a "spy." While both operated behind enemy lines to gather information, scouts were normally sentenced to time as a prisoner of war while spies could be sentenced to the gallows. The wearing of the uniform did not necessarily prevent a man from being classified as a spy since according to the "Rules of Land Warfare" (a 19th century War Department document):

> The fact of being in the enemy's lines dressed as a civilian or wearing the enemy's uniform is presumed to constitute a spy, but it is possible to rebut this presumption by proof of no intention to obtain military information.

The determination of scout versus spy apparently depended on the mood of the local general, the embarrassment the detainee had caused him, and the value of the information found on the man. Sam Davis, the Confederate courier, is a good example of a man being classified a spy while in fact he was no more than a courier. The information he carried was the damning factor.

In the greater Washington area, arrested Confederate spies were placed in the Old Capitol Prison. The prison had been the meeting place of Congress during a renovation of the Capitol after the War of 1812 (the site is now the location of the Supreme Court Building). Its famous residents include many Confederate generals, the Confederate spies Rose O'Neal Greenhow and Belle Boyd as well as Captain Wirz, the keeper of Andersonville Prison. Executions were done on the grounds.

Civilians held in Old Capitol Prison, or any other Union prison, could be released only if they signed an Oath of Allegiance to the United States (see Example 1 on page 88). Antonia Ford, the Confederate spy, is someone who did sign such an oath. Both Belle Boyd and Rose O'Neal Greenhow refused to sign either an Oath of Allegiance or a Pardon with Honor. In cases such as these, where exchange was the outcome, the persons exchanged were required to sign a statement such as the one below for Mrs. Greenhow:

Headquarters, Fort Monroe, Va. June 2, 1863
We the undersigned, late prisoners in the Old Capitol at Washington, do pledge our word of honor that in consideration of our being

set at liberty beyond the lines of the U.S. Army we will not return north of the Potomac River during the present hostilities without the permission of the Secretary of War of the United States.

ROSE O'N GREENHOW

NOTE: Mrs. C.V. Baxley and Mrs. Augusta Morris also signed this parole and were sent South with Mrs. Greenhow.

Military personnel in order to be released from a Union prisoner of war camp were compelled to agree to the terms of a Pardon of Honor (Example 2 on page 89). As with the Oath of Allegiance, military persons loyal to the Confederacy refused to agree to the terms of the Pardon and chose to remain in a prison camp.

Union sentiment regarding the execution of Confederate spies changed in late 1861 when three Union spies were sentenced to death in Richmond. One of the Union spies was a man named Timothy Webster, Pinkerton's best agent. In an effort to avoid the execution, Pinkerton went to President Lincoln and in his own words describes events:

Mr. Lincoln was readily seen, and he, too, filled with sympathy for the unfortunate man, promised to call a special session of the Cabinet to consider the case that evening. . . . In the evening the Cabinet convened, and after a full discussion of the matter it was decided that the only thing that could be done was to authorize the Secretary of War to communicate with the rebel authorities on the subject. He was directed to authorize General Wool to send by flag-of-truce boat, or by telegraph, a message to Jefferson Davis, representing that the course pursued by the Federal government toward rebel spies had heretofore been lenient and forbearing; that in many cases such persons had been released after a short confinement, and that in no instance had any one so charged been tried for his life or sentenced to death. THE MESSAGE CONCLUDED WITH THE DECIDED INTIMATION THAT IF THE CONFEDERATE GOVERNMENT PROCEEDED TO CARRY OUT THEIR SENTENCE OF DEATH INTO EXECUTION, THE FEDERAL GOVERNMENT WOULD INITIATE A SYSTEM OF RETALIATION WHICH WOULD AMPLY AVENGE THE DEATH OF THE MEN NOW HELD. (Capitalization not original).

OATH OF ALLEGIANCE.

I, Charles H. Andrus of Blue Earth County, do hereby solemnly swear That I will bear true allegiance to the United States, and support and sustain the Constitution and laws thereof: that I will maintain the National Sovereignty paramount to that of all State, County or Confederate powers; that I will discourage, discountenance, and forever oppose secession, rebellion and the disintegration of the Federal Union: that I disclaim and denounce all faith and fellowship with the so-called Confederate Armies, and pledge my honor, my property, and my life, to the sacred performance of this my solemn Oath of Allegiance to the Government of the United States of America.

C. H. Andrus

Subscribed and sworn to before me this
2 5 day of February 1865
at Beg Lincoln Co Mo

Ja M Meaden Capt apt Pro Mar
4 Sub Dist North Mo

WITNESSES:

.... of

Savannah Mo

DESCRIPTION.

Age, Thirty
Height, Five feet Eight inches
Color of Eyes, Brown
Color of Hair, Brown
Characteristics:

88

Head-Quarters, Middle Department, 8th Army Corps,

OFFICE PROVOST MARSHAL,

Baltimore, *Oct 25* 1864

PAROLE OF HONOR.

I, _E. J. Smith_ _____

hereby give my Parole of Honor, that I will demean myself in every respect as a
true and loyal citizen of the United States, neither doing myself, nor aiding, abetting
or countenancing in others any act or speech injurious or prejudicial to the good of
these United States, or to the Government thereof, or to the preservation of the Union,
nor speaking or acting contemptuously of, or respecting the same. I furthermore
solemnly promise not to attempt to go into any of the States now in Rebellion, or
to correspond either by word, letter or sign, with any person in such States, or have
any other correspond for me with any such person, unless under the proper Military
supervision and approval. _✓ Not to leave the City of Baltimore_

All this I promise without any mental reservation or evasion whatever, and
of my own free will and accord.

WITNESS:

E. J. Smith _____

and Provost Marshal.

89

The Confederacy did in fact execute Timothy Webster and the Union in response did initiate a system of retaliation, as did the Confederacy.

Immediately after the war the Union released the Confederate military men still held in Union prisons as spies. An example of this action is the following General Order extract:

GENERAL COURT MARTIAL ORDERS, NO. 283
WAR DEPARTMENT,
Adjutant General's Office
Washington, June 12, 1865.

In compliance with General Orders, No. 98, War Department, Adjutant General's Office, May 27, 1865, the sentences of the following named prisoners, now in confinement for "during the war," are remitted, and the prisoners will be immediately discharged upon taking the oath of allegiance:

Albany Pententiary.

1. John, R. H. Embert, now or late of the so-called Confederate Army.

Charge I.—"Acting as a spy."

Charge II.—"Violation of the laws of war, as laid down in paragraph 86, General Orders, No 100, from the War Department, April 24, 1863."

Finding.—"Guilty."

Sentence

"Confinement at hard labor in the Albany Pententiary, during the War."

BY ORDER OF THE PRESIDENT OF THE UNITED STATES:

E. D. Townsend
Assistant Adjutant General

Similar General Orders exist for Samuel B. Hearn, and Braxton Lyon, convicted Spies from the "so-called Confederate Army."

There is no record of either a female or a Black captured spy being executed by either the Union or the Confederacy (although at least two Union female spies were sentenced to death—Jane Ferguson and Pauline Cushman). They were always exchanged, or in the case of Pauline Cushman, rescued. The execution of Mary Surratt as an accomplice in the Lincoln assassination plot was the first female executed not only in the Civil War but in the history of the United States.

Military records for the Union Army show a total of 270 executions of military personnel. Only three of these are Union soldiers executed for spy activities. The major categories are murder and desertion. Records identifying the captured spies actually executed are very sparse for several reasons, to include:

• To preserve anonymity, spies carried no documentation of their true identity. Therefore when a spy was executed the record would merely document the event and not the person.
• The spy could not wear his uniform and thereby claim protection of the uniform. He was for all intents and purposes a civilian and for a civilian spy the penalty was death, particularly if captured in the field.
• The spy sentenced to death was not allowed to write to any loved one, and many would not have done so even if allowed—they wanted to maintain the anonymous standing.

What is known about the execution of spies during the Civil War is listed here.

Spies Executed During Civil War Period

Union Spies Executed by the Confederacy

J. J. ANDREWS*	7 June	1862
SPENCER KELLOGG BROWN	25 Sept.	1863

WILLIAM CAMPBELL**	18 June	1862
JOHN M. FLINN†	20 May	1863
SAM GIBBONS		1864
PVT SAMUEL ROBERTSON**	18 June	1862
SGT MARIAN ROSS**	18 June	1862
HENRY W. SAWYER†	20 May	1863
SGT JOHN SCOTT**	18 June	1862
PVT PERRY SHADRACH**	18 June	1862
PVT SAMEUL SLAVENS**	18 June	1862
LEVI STRAUSS		
A. C. WEBSTER, CAPT.	10 April	1864
TIMOTHY WEBSTER	29 April	1862
GEORGE D. WILSON**	12 June	1862

*Civilian leader of the Union raid on Confederate railroad to capture the locomotive *The General*, previously had acted as spy for Union.
**Union soldiers who volunteered to go with Andrew on his railroad hijacking mission. Picked at random to be hanged from the 12 captured Union troops. Hanged as spies as they were all in civilian clothes. Only William Campbell was in fact a civilian. In March of 1863 the remaining captured raiders were exchanged. All survivors were presented the Congressional Medal of Honor.
†Hanged in retaliation for Union hanging of Corbin and McGraw as spies.

During October 1862, 45 members of a pro-Union society in Gainsville, Texas, were executed after conviction by a people's court as follows:

26 hung by people's court to include:

BARNABAS BIRCH
EPHRAIM CHILDS
DR. HENRY CHILDS
M. D. HARPER
I. W.P. LOCK
RICHARD MARTIN
A. D. SCOTT

In addition, 15 were hanged by the mob and four men—two of the order and two loyalists—were shot. Three others were turned over to the provost marshal and were hanged by the military.

In 1863, in retaliation for the Union hanging of the Confederate spy/courier Sam Davis, the Confederacy hanged two young Union boys, one 14 and one 16 years of age, in Richmond.

Confederate Spies Executed by the Union

GEORGE ATZERODT	7 July	1865
JOHN Y. BEALL, LT.	23 Feb.	1865
JOHN E. BOYD	12 Jan.	1865
WILLIAM BURGESS	20 Apr.	1863
CORBIN, CAPTAIN	15 May	1863
SAM DAVIS	27 Nov.	1863
RICHARD DILLARD		
DAVID DODD	8 Jan.	1864
E. S. DODD	8 Jan.	1864
A. C. GRIMES, PVT	Jan.	1865
DAVID HERAD	7 July	1865
DEWITT JOBE	Sept.	1864
ROBERT KENNEDY, CAPT	25 Mar.	1865
CHARLES E. LANGLEY	6 Apr.	1865
MC GRAW, CAPTAIN	15 May	1863
WALTER G. PETERS, LT	9 June	1863
T. PETTICORD, LT	Dec.	1863
LEWIS POWELL	7 July	1865
WILLIAM RICHARDSON	6 July	1863
MARY SURRATT	7 July	1865
URZ		1864
JAMES WILLIAMS	25 Jan.	1863
WILLIAM O. WILLIAMS, COL	9 June	1863

NOTE: References found to four unknown Confederate spies being caught and hanged in Kentucky in the spring of 1865 by Union forces.

Union Troops Executed by Union for Acting as Spy

PVT. ALEXANDER J. JOHNSON 139th Infantry, New York	7 March	1864
PVT. THOMAS ABRAHAM	3 July	1863
PVT. CHARLES KING 3rd Cavalry, New Jersey	6 Jan.	1863
PVT. HENRY REGLEY 3rd Cavalry, New Jersey	6 Jan.	1863

Chapter 8

The Individual Spies

Why look at the lives of the individual spies? First and foremost, for many of the spies it gives the reader an opportunity to learn about individual contributions to the war efforts of both the Union and Confederate. In addition, by looking at the lives of some of the active spies of the Civil War one can better understand the feelings and atmosphere that permeated both societies during this turbulent time of American history.

The Civil War represents a time when feelings were running high, patriotism for both the Union and the Confederacy was rampant and patriots wanted to contribute as best they could. It was also a time of chivalry regarding women, complete disregard for the intelligence of the Negro and utter naivete as to the world of intelligence gathering. It was a time when anyone could and many did become spies, making it very difficult for the counter-espionage efforts of either side, and hampering the credibility of the professional agents in the field. How did one differentiate between a legitimate agent, an amateur or a "plant" from the opposing side?

The men involved in spying, for both the Union and Confederacy, had a high coincidence of similar characteristics in their personalities, careers and political feelings:

95

• Many of the men involved in spying during the Civil War were lawyers by profession, and they returned to the practice of law after the war. These men made excellent spymasters as they were organizers and could give concise orders to their spies.

• Another profession that appears among the male spies is acting. Two of the more important espionage figures, the Confederate spy Harrison at Gettysburg and John Wilkes Booth, the assassin of President Lincoln, were well known actors. This profession is a natural since actors can easily assume the role of another person.

• All were virtually untrained when they entered the covert world of spying. While not all were educated, they consistently had innovative and creative minds and a great deal of native intelligence.

• They believed strongly in the "cause" of the government for which they spied, both the Confederate and Union.

• Not all of them came from the ranks of the military, but virtually all of them freely volunteered for the intelligence service of their government.

• They all appear to have enjoyed the challenge of spying and were not afraid to take chances in order to complete their mission.

The other major group of spies during the Civil War were the women of both the Confederacy and the Union. The female spies did make major contributions to the war efforts of the government and often at great risk to their own lives. Some of the characteristics that depict the Civil War female spy are:

• They had a very strong belief in the "cause" of their government. In many cases that belief was stronger than that of their male counterparts.

• The female spy was not as well educated as their male counterparts, a characteristic of the times in which they lived.

• Many of the female spies joined the covert world since, except for nursing, it represented the only way they could actively contribute to the war efforts of their government.

• All of the female spies, both Union and Confederate, plied their skills with the clear understanding that the male world of that day gave the female little credit for intelligence and absolutely none for understanding anything "technical." This was a major advantage for the female and they all used it to their advantage.

- It was not unusual for females, of either side, to assume the role of a male for their spying purposes. This enabled them to join troops actually on the front lines in order to derive intelligence of immediate value.
- Many of the female spies were married, and not always to a male from the same side for which they were spying. The husbands, in most cases, had no idea that their wives were actively engaged in a covert activity.

It must be noted that for both the male and the female spy characteristics given above, only the white spies are in either group. The Black spies, of whom only a limited number are known by name, represent a grouping of their own. Their characteristics were:

- Without exception all references to Negroe spies refer to Negroes who have escaped from the South and run North. There are no references to any Negro spying for the Confederacy.
- The ex-slaves chosen for spying were the educated ones who generally knew how to read and write and more importantly had a basic knowledge of arithmetic (for estimating troop strengths).
Negro spies were successful and part of their succcess comes from the basic inbred bias of the South at that time: No Negro had any intelligence nor could he function on his own without a master telling him what to do. The Negro spies used this fact to their great advantage.
- With the exception of John Scobell, Uncle Gallus and a few others, the majority of Negro spies of the Civil War remain unknown. This is probably due to the fact that after the war they just wanted to settle down in the North and continue with their own lives.
- The Southern bias toward the lack of intelligence of the Negro was present in the Union as well. This made it difficult for a Negro spy to convince his Union spymaster of the validity of the information he was reporting.

As one reads the following individual Civil War spy cameo biographies, keep in mind not only their individual actions and contributions but also how their performances were driven by the times in which they lived. Their lives present an interesting reflection on the moods of both the Union and the Confederacy during the Civil War. Some of their stories, when read today, read like cheap dime-store novels—but they are basically true, probably embellished over time—and they present an interesting insight into the Civil War period.

Chapter 9

The Confederate Male Spies

Thomas N. Conrad, Lafayette Baker's Nemesis

*T*homas Conrad was one of the more elusive Confederate spies that operated in and around the Union capital city of Washington, D.C., during the Civil War. He was very familiar with the city since when the war began he was the headmaster of Georgetown College, a boy's school in the city of Washington, D.C. His action at the school led to his initial arrest on June of 1861.

Headmaster Conrad had the students sending messages to the Confederate side of the Potomac by raising and lowering the shades on their windows. In addition, on graduation day in June of 1861, the speeches were inflammatory to the Union and the processional march was "Dixie"—all too much for the Union and Conrad was arrested that night. But not for long. He was merely chastised and sent South.

Arriving in Virginia, he enlisted in the 3rd Virginia Cavalry of J.E.B. (Jeb) Stuart where he became a chaplain for the troops. Conrad soon discovered that a chaplain could easily enter the Union lines and minister to the troops, gathering information as he went—which he did for several months until he was called to Richmond to undertake a special mission. His mission consisted of going to Washington, finding certain French and English diplomats, and escorting them safely through the Union lines to Richmond. Reportedly the diplomats represented their governments in a $3 million loan proposal. Conrad succeeded in his mission but nothing is known of the outcome of the loan proposal.

At this point, Conrad returned to Washington to take up residence and to conduct covert activities. In order to avoid recognition he changed his hair style and type of beard, homemade Southern style boots to machine-made Northern boots, and altered his chewing tobacco to Northern style—all good spy tradecraft. He took up residence in Washington and almost immediately went into business.

His first idea was the assassination of General of the Army Winfield Scott. After purchasing a musket he queried Richmond on the idea and was soundly turned down by the government. Not to worry. By this time Conrad had made contact with several Confederate-sympathizing clerks in the War Department, whom he visited on a regular basis. He evidently had free access to the building as the clerks would leave papers on their desks at lunch and Conrad would pass their desks, read the papers and depart with the desired information. The system was so successful that prior to General George McClellan's Peninsula Campaign, Conrad sent the entire Order of Battle for the Union Army, along with the operational plan, to the Confederate Army.

In November of 1862 he advised Richmond 24 hours in advance of the change of command from General George McClellan to General Ambrose Burnside and of General Burnside's intention to attack Fredericksburg, Virginia. He personally delivered this information to General Robert E. Lee, who later soundly defeated General Burnside at Fredericksburg.

Residing in Washington and actively spying was a risky business for anyone, especially one who was already known in the city. To avoid compromise, Conrad placed a double agent on the staff of

Lafayette Baker's Secret Service. The man by the name of Edward Norton passed himself off as a Confederate deserter, and he proved to be of great value to Conrad. By mid-1863 Baker's men were highly suspicious of the activities of Mr. Conrad and prepared to arrest him. Norton got to him first, advised him of the pending arrest and assisted Conrad in getting out of town. As an indication of the excellent tradecraft of Conrad, he advised Norton to make a full and complete report of his (Conrad's) activities to Baker, thereby taking any suspicion off himself and ensuring his continuance on Baker's staff.

At this juncture, Conrad appears to be under the operational control of the Confederate Secret Service headed by Major William Norris. He was sent to a spot on the Potomac River about 35 miles south of Washington (Boyd's Landing, Virginig) to set up a courier relay station. He built a hut there and named it "Eagle's Nest." From this location he received communiques from agents in the North and with the assistance of two mounted couriers was able to have the information in Richmond within 24 hours.

Bored with the inactivity, Conrad again went to Washington and developed a plan to kidnap President Lincoln as he rode from the White House to his summer residence at the Soldiers' Home in suburban Washington. Again, as with the General Scott assassination plan, the Confederate government turned down his proposal. During this same period he traveled to Annapolis as a minister and preached to General Burnside's troops and discovered that the troops would be joining General U.S. Grant's efforts in Virginia. He sent the following message to General Lee:

Burnside will reinforce Grant and that at an early date.

About this time Conrad decided that he had had enough of being a spy and went to Richmond to work in counter-espionage, at which he was totally unsuccessful. Seeing the war coming to an end he decided to go north and seek other employment, again changing his hair and beard style (unfortunately to look just like John Wilkes Booth). He was arrested on April 16, 1865, as John Wilkes Booth! When the mis-identification was known as well as his true identity, he was introduced to his nemesis, Lafayette Baker, who shook his hand and released him on the spot.

After the war, Conrad married a woman by the name of Minnie Ball (ironic that one of the bullets used in the Civil War was nicknamed the minnie ball for the Frenchman Minie' who invented it). He also went back into the education field and subsequently served as the president of two different colleges. He did write about his experiences as a Confederate spy, but never exploited his past for his own monetary gain.

Thomas Conrad stands as one of the most successful of the Confederate spies that we know of today. He made excellent use of his talent for disguise, was not easily discouraged, and had a self-developed spy tradecraft well beyond most of his contemporaries. He is one Confederate spy who made a real contribution to the Confederate war efforts through his espionage efforts. His philosophy for spying can be well summed up in his own statement:

> Was it not possible that as a spy I might discover that which would soon give the Southern cause the upper-hand in its struggle for Secession?

That hope of ultimate success is one of the best attributes for any spy—not only in the Civil War but today as well.

Major W.P. Gorman, Confederate Emissary to the Copperheads

In 1890, the marshal of the Birmingham Confederate Memorial Day parade was a man by the name of Major W.P. Gorman. He spoke freely to bystanders at the parade about his very special role during the Civil War. Hearing this, an enterprising reporter interviewed him and published the account in May of 1890. All that we know of the man comes from this inverview. Although nothing can be authenticated it does present a consistent picture of Confederate spy operations during the Civil War.

Gorman was born in Michigan and spent the early years of his life there before moving to Memphis, Tennessee. He entered the U.S. Army and when the war broke out went south to the Confederate Army serving initially with General Nathan B. Forrest, and seeing combat at the Battle of Stone's River in Tennessee. He was next called to Richmond for a special assignment, that of organizing a Copperhead military unit to support simultaneous raids by Generals Nathan Forrest and John Marmaduke into Missouri.

According to Gorman he went to Missouri and as required had a 7,000 man Copperhead military unit ready to march in support of the raids. He then heard of General Forrest's defeat at Jackson, Tennessee, and General Marmaduke's at Springfield, Missouri. His troops were dispersed back into their normal lives to wait for another occasion.

Later in St. Louis on personal business for General Forrest he met two ladies, the daughters of Lt. Colonel Kibble of General Sterling's regiment. They took him to their home where that night 1,662 "Confederates" met—within 4 miles of downtown St. Louis. Arriving back in Richmond he was again sent north to organize the Copperhead men into Confederate units. According to Confederates in Richmond there were 30,000 in Illinois, 12,000 in Missouri, 16,000 in Indiana, 4,000 in Ohio, and 5,000 in Pennsylvania, all loyal to the Confederacy and ready to rise up against the Union.

An interesting sidelight of his next trip is Gorman's statement that on his way north he stopped in Washington, D.C., and presented a serving United States senator a lieutenant general's commission in the Confederate Army. The senator is not named. On this trip he traveled throughout the states of Ohio, Pennsylvania and Indiana reviewing the Copperhead "Confederate" troops. Since the Copperhead organization was infiltrated by Union spies, he soon became identified as a person most wanted by the Union. Even with his frequent changes of name, he was a marked man.

Upon his return, General John H. Winder insisted that he make one more trip north even though Gorman contended that he was too well known by this time to return. But he did go. His stops included Indiana, Illinois and Kentucky—where he was arrested by Union forces who soon discovered they had a true prize. As they moved his coat that he had taken off, they noticed a rustling and when they ripped open the coat they found documents, maps and messages for President Jefferson Davis. The messages were in code and that is what saved him.

When interrogated, found guilty and sentenced to be executed, he was asked if he could read the encoded messages. He could not but convinced the Union panel that he could indeed read them.

Stalling for time he asked to see a Catholic priest and explained his predicament, to which the priest responded. Next came a woman by the name of Curd who brought him clean clothes, including a shirt with a file in it! Using the file he was able to work an escape.

At this point he returned to regular Confederate Army duty and once again became a prisoner in October of 1863. He spent the remainder of the war in a Union prisoner of war camp, refusing parole as it required signing a Union loyalty oath.

After the war, W.P. Gorman returned to the North. He settled in Detroit and became a member of the Michigan state legislature. He served one term, was defeated and then moved to Birmingham, Alabama, where the enterprising reporter caught up with him.

His actions, as personally reported, appear to be quite independent of the Montreal operation for a Northwest Conspiracy. It is interesting to note the figures of Copperhead troop strengths in the Northwest states. Even if exaggerated the true total could have been a sizable force, one that could definitely have caused trouble for the Union. It is also interesting to note his reporting on the United States senator who held a lieutenant general's commission in the Confederate Army—just waiting for the Copperhead uprising.

None of the Gorman story can be verified but it does have a ring of truth about it from other sources that the Confederacy, in their desperation, looked to the Copperheads of the North to ease the pressure on the Confederate armies. If Gorman's numbers are even near correct, they could have done just that.

Harrison, the Mystery Man at Gettysburg

The name "Harrison" became famous after the Battle of Gettysburg, but to this day there is an air of mystery about the person. Harrison's actions prior to the Battle of Gettysburg are an established fact; what remains a mystery is exactly who the man was.

Harrison arrived in the camp of General Longstreet in the spring of 1863. He delivered to Longstreet a letter of introduction from the Confederate Secretary of War, James A. Seddon, stating that he thought Harrison's skills would be of use to General Longstreet. Longstreet who apparently knew of Harrison's spy activities quickly decided to employ his new asset. Harrison was known for excellent and accurate reporting, and since the Confederacy was paying him $150 in U.S. currency a month for his spying activities, he must be good. Longstreet sent Harrison out to ascertain the activities of the Union forces concurrent with the movement of the Confederate forces to Pennsylvania.

Harrison undertook the mission and went among the Union troops on their route north, ending up in Washington, D.C., in mid-June. When he had derived the needed information he set out to find General Longstreet, with no real idea of his location. He arrived in Gettysburg in late June, quickly located Longstreet and made his report stating that General Joseph Hooker's army was on the move north and the pace of the movement was much faster than General Lee had thought possible. Based on Harrison's reputation for reporting reliable intelligence, General Longstreet believed him and immediately took him to see General Lee where once again he gave his report. General Lee initially did not believe Harrison since he had no corroborating data of his own (Jeb Stuart's cavalry had not reported). Finally, General Lee was convinced of the validity of the report and acted accordingly. Harrison's report represents the first valid information that General Lee received regarding the movement of the Union forces.

After returning to Longstreet's camp, Harrison was deployed to the town of Gettysburg to ascertain what and how many Union troops were in the town. And it is here, in Gettysburg, that Harrison disappeared and the mystery of the true identity of Harrison arises.

For many years, Harrison was thought to be James Harrison, an actor by profession who had enlisted in the Confederate Army. In Gettysburg, he apparently told one of Longstreet's officers that he would be appearing on the stage in Richmond in September of 1863. Longstreet was in Richmond that September and his aide went to the theater to see a Shakespearean play and is said to have recognized Harrison on the stage.

But James Harrison, it seems, had a tendency to imbibe and also to gamble, habits that soon became known to the Confederate authorities, and he was never again used as a Confederate spy. He was paid off by the authorities as a poor security risk. He did continue to appear on the stage for the rest of his life. He died in poverty on

22 February 1913. At no time in his later life did he ever speak of his spy activities for the Confederacy.

The second version of the identity of Harrison is that he was Henry Thomas Harrison. This version is based on work done in the mid-1980s by James Hall using the National Archives records. In many ways the lives of James Harrison and Henry Thomas Harrison agree in that:

- Both Harrisons were initially scouts for the Confederates.
- They both were special agents for War Secretary Seddon.
- They both had an association with General Longstreet and they were regarded as excellent collectors and reporters of intelligence.
- Their release from Confederate service was due to heavy drinking and potential security risk.

What differs about the two men is their occupations and actions after the Battle of Gettysburg. Henry Thomas Harrison, after being paid off in 1863, attempted to find General Longstreet for further employment. By this time Longstreet was in eastern Tennessee and Harrison did not locate him. He is next mentioned in Mexico where he supposedly went to aid Maximilian. Henry Harrison finally appeared in the Montana Territory around 1900, and then vanished forever.

While the debate over the true identity of the spy Harrison may never be completely solved, it is an established fact that his work as a Confederate spy just prior to the Battle of Gettysburg did have a major impact on the actions of the Confederate Army at Gettysburg. His reporting represents the first valid intelligence provided to General Lee regarding the movement of the opposing Union forces.

Harrison remains a mystery man. Was he James or Henry Harrison or a totally unknown person just using the name of "Harrison" as an alias? We may never know, however there is no doubt that his place in Civil War history is secure.

Thomas H. Hines, "The Fox"

One of the less familiar Confederate spies of the Civil War was also one of the most active; Captain Thomas H. Hines of the Confederate Army was the key player in the Confederate efforts for the Northwest Conspiracy. While he was instrumental in devising and attempting to execute the Northwest Conspiracy, he was also the man who probably had the biggest role in the failure of the conspiracy.

Prior to the war, Captain Hines was on the faculty of the Masonic University at La Grange, Kentucky. When the war broke out Hines, a young and idealistic adventurer, lost no time in enlisting in the Army of the Confederacy. He initially served as a "Buckner" guide for General Simon B. Buckner but soon found his way to Morgan's Raiders—their adventures were more to his liking.

While with General John H. Morgan, head of Morgan's Raiders, fellow raiders reported that Hines would disappear for periods of time and then reappear to again take up his military duties. In his time away he was working as a Confederate spy and as a liaison with the Copperhead organizations organizing in Kentucky and the other northwest states. His activity fit with that of the Morgan's raiders since they frequently took money that was then given to the Copperhead organizations to purchase weapons.

In July of 1863, General Morgan along with Captain Hines and several other of his officers were captured and sent to the Ohio State Penitentiary. They were not there long. Hines very quickly decided to dig out of the prison via a tunnel. By November of 1863 it was complete and on 20 November, they successfully escaped via their hand-dug tunnel.

Captain Hines went about his military duties along with his spying activities until he was called to Richmond in early 1864. A Captain Longuemare had recently presented a plan to President Jefferson Davis aimed at assisting the Northwest Union states in secession from the Union. His plan consisted of:

- The overthrow of state and local governments and the murder of the political leaders.
- The freeing of all Confederate prisoners of war.
- The burning of Chicago and New York City.
- The military push of Morgan's raiders into the Northwest states.

Captain Hines was selected as the military leader of the Northwest effort and was given the following letter of instructions:

Confederate States of America
War Department
Richmond, Va., March 16, 1864

Captain T. Henry Hines:

Sir—You are detailed for special service to proceed to Canada, passing through the United States under such character and in such mode as you may deem most safe, for the purpose of collecting there the men of General Morgan's command who may have escaped, and others of the citizens of the Confederate States willing to return and enter the military service of the Confederacy, and arranging for their return either through the United States or by sea. You will place yourself, on arrival, in communication with Hon. J.P. Holcomb, who has been sent as special commissioner to the British Provinces, and in his instructions directed to facilitate the passage of such men to the Confederacy. In passing through the United States you will confer with the leading persons friendly or attracted to the cause of the Confederacy, or who may be advocates of peace, and do all in your power to induce our friends to organize and prepare themselves to render such aid as circumstances may allow; and to encourage and animate those favorable to a peaceful adjustment to the employment of all agencies calculated to effect such consummation on terms consistent always with the independence of the Confederate States. You will likewise have in view the possibility, by such means as you can command, of effecting any fair and appropriate enterprises of war against our enemies, and will be at liberty to employ such of our soldiers as you may collect, in any hostile operation offering, that may be consistent with the strict observance of neutral obligations in the British provinces.

Reliance is felt in your discretion and sagacity to understand and carry out, as contingencies may dictate, the details of the general design thus communicated. More specific instructions in anticipation of events that may occur under your observation cannot well be given. You will receive a letter to General Polk in which I request his aid in the transmission of cotton, so as to provide funds for the enterprise, and an order has been given to Colonel Bayne, with whom you will confer, to have two hundred bales of cotton purchased in North Mississippi and placed under your direction for this purpose.

Should the agencies you may employ for transmitting that be unsuccessful, the same means will be adopted of giving you larger credit, and you are advised to report to Colonel Bayne, before leaving the lines of the Confederacy, what success has attended your effort for such transmission.

Respectfully,

(Signed)   James A. Seddon

Secretary of War

Hines who was an adventurist, an idealist and a "doer" took this letter and used its authority in the broadest terms. He actively worked with the Copperhead organizations in Illinois, Indiana, Ohio and Kentucky and planned uprisings in Chicago, New York and other smaller cities. None ever came to pass. Hines in his idealism believed that the enthusiasm shown by the Copperhead leaders in meetings with him was directly translatable to actions without precise planning or proof of intent. He consistently passed glowing reports back to Toronto as well as Richmond—glowing reports that without exception proved to be wrong!

As an indication of the zeal of Captain Hines, the following quote is extracted from a report that Commissioner Thompson sent to President Jefferson Davis, dated December 3, 1864, regarding the freeing of Confederate prisoners of war in the North:

> All projects of that sort were abandoned, except that Captain Hines still believed he could effect their release. We yielded to his firmness, zeal and persistence but treachery defeated him before his well laid schemes were developed.

The above reference "treachery defeated him" is a good indication that while Hines was very successful as a spy he tended to forget the enemy could also achieve success. His efforts were constantly thwarted by double agents and Union infiltrators. He never seemed to realize that caution should be taken with fellow conspirators.

The only actions that had any success at all were those carried out by Captain Hines' own men. Those included the burning of the Union vessels in St. Louis, Missouri, the burning of the Union warehouses in Matoon, Illinois, the limited success of the hotel fires in New York City and the bank robbery in St. Albans, Vermont. All of the proposed uprisings and other disturbances planned with the Copperheads without exception came to no fruition. The failures were most likely due to slipshod planning on the part of the

Copperheads and a Confederate agent who was all too quick to accept their word that all was in order. It is however true that the activities of Captain Hines and his group did cause concern in the Union and did require the detailing of valuable Union troops to counter his moves. In that sense he was successful.

Captain Thomas H. Hines known as "the Fox" was no doubt an elusive man. He was frequently in tight spots and was always able to elude his captors. He was fearless and seemed to enjoy the challenge of escaping capture. One of the great advantages he had was that he was most attractive to women and frequently they were responsible for his evading capture.

After the war Hines and his wife fled to Canada to avoid any possibility of arrest. They remained there for several years and while there Hines wrote his memoirs. He later returned to the United States, passed the bar examination and became a lawyer in his native state of Kentucky.

Hines' endeavors cost the Confederacy dearly in financial resources with little to show for his efforts. Idealism as well as his own personal trust in accepting the word of others seemed to have clouded his thinking as it has for many agents.

"Renfrew," Who Was He?

In the fall of 1864, Secretary of War Edwin Stanton sent a confidential adviser named Lomas to be assigned as a member of General Philip Sheridan's staff. General Sheridan was not pleased with the assignment, but as it had come from Secretary of War Stanton he complied. Not fully trusting the man he ordered that he be kept under constant surveillance. No derogatory reports resulted from the surveillance but General Sheridan remained wary.

After a short period of time, Lomas came to General Sheridan with a tall, dark and handsome man he said was a deserter from the Confederacy. The man claimed to have had a falling out with Colonel John Mosby and now wanted to work for the Union. According to Lomas, the man whose name was Renfrew, was an excellent make-up artist and master of disguise—which could be put to use in the Union secret service.

General Sheridan allowed the man to stay in camp but as with

Lomas, he had Renfrew followed at all times. In short order, General Sheridan's suspicions proved to be valid as both Lomas and Renfrew were found to be sending more information out of camp than they were bringing in. They were in fact both Confederate spies.

The pair were arrested and ordered imprisoned at Fort Warren in Pennsylvania; unfortunately both escaped while going through Baltimore on the way to the fort. A few weeks later Secretary Stanton came to believe that his friend Lomas was closely allied to the President Lincoln assassination plot. At this point, General Sheridan realized that Renfrew, the accomplished make-up man, master of disguise and a handsome actor, was probably none other than John Wilkes Booth, the man who killed President Lincoln. Had he not escaped during the trip to Fort Warren, would there have been the assassination attempt?

Benjamin Franklin Stringfellow, A Much "Wanted" Spy

Benjamin Franklin Stringfellow, commonly known as "Frank," was a Virginian to the core—born, raised, educated and fighting for his state in the Confederate army. With the war on the horizon Stringfellow quickly enlisted in Company E, 4th Virginia Cavalry commanded by another famous Virginian, Jeb Stuart.

His talents for scouting and spying soon came to the fore and Private Stringfellow found himself serving first as a scout and then a spy for General Stuart. His fearless nature, coupled with his intelligence and quick reactions, made him a natural.

Shortly after the secession of Virginia from the Union, Stringfellow was sent to the Washington, D.C., area in conjunction with E. Pliny Bryan, to organize a spy ring that would supply intelligence of value to the Confederate military. For this mission he assumed the role of dental assistant and took the name of Edward Delcher (an actual person who lived in Boston). He settled in Alexandria, Virginia (on the outskirts of Washington), a city he knew well as he was engaged to a local girl in the city. There he worked for a Confederate sympathizing dentist by the name of Dr. Richard M. Sykes. (The city of Alexandria, while in Virginia, had been occupied by the Union almost immediately after the secession of the state of Virginia.)

From the dentist's office, Stringfellow recruited and organized a spy ring that remained in place throughout most of the Civil War. His agents visited the dental office as patients, bringing information or newspapers of value to the Confederate cause. Stringefellow condensed the newspaper articles, combined them with the other information delivered to him and then, at close of the business day, placed it all outside at a corner of the dentist's office. A Confederate courier would pick it up during the night and proceed south to waiting Confederate authorities who were always anxious to receive Stringfellow's information.

Stringfellow remained in place until advised by the dentist's wife that Dr. Sykes was about to turn him in to the Federal authorities. Stringfellow at this point returned to Jeb Stuart's command but his agents and couriers remained in place and the information flow continued throughout the war.

One of his scouting successes under Jeb Stuart came just prior to the Second Battle of Bull Run in Virginia (29–30 August 1862). He went to Warrenton, Virginia, to find the extreme right flank of General John Pope's army. He not only found the flank but also found General Pope's field headquarters at Catlett's Station. When Jeb Stuart was advised of this he conducted a raid on the headquarters capturing many horses, over 300 prisoners and most significantly many important papers of General Pope. Stringfellow himself said of the importance of the raid that:

> Gaining the knowledge of the enemy's location, his force, the position of his reinforcements, and his "notions" of where "we" were and what we were trying to do, was of great value to us (in fighting Second Bull Run—a rebel victory)

After the Battle of Antietam in Maryland (September 17, 1862), Frank Stringfellow again went into the city of Alexandria, which served as his base on all of his missions to the north. This time he went to work in a shop run by James Sturrett who was totally unaware of his covert activities. This mission was specifically ordered by General Robert E. Lee, who, although he distrusted spies in general, had great faith in the work done by Stringfellow. His mission from General Lee was in preparation for the invasion of the North by General Lee's army and while Stringfellow did acquire a great deal of strategic information, General Lee never received it. Stringfellow was recognized by some local residents and arrested, taken to Old Capitol Prison and later on 12 August 1863 returned to the Confederacy in a prisoner's exchange.

Upon returning to the Confederacy, Stringfellow, as always, returned to his army unit under Jeb Stuart and continued his army scouting. On one occasion he got so close to General U.S. Grant that he could have killed him—but he could not do it. While President Grant was in office, Stringfellow sent him a letter describing the incident and how he had spared the General's life. President Grant in return thanked him warmly and said that any request made by Stringfellow of him or any future President would be honored. (This came into play during the Spanish American War).

Finally in March of 1865, Stringfellow was sent to Washington with a Confederate surrender proposal from President Jefferson Davis. He was to present it to a foreign party who in turn had promised to present the proposal to President Lincoln. The proposal was delivered and Stringfellow remained in Washington, as instructed, to collect more intelligence. He remained too long as he was once again arrested, but this time he managed to escape back to the Confederacy.

During the final days of the war, the Union had a reward offer of $10,000 for the capture of Benjamin Franklin Stringfellow, but he was never captured again. Fearing for his safety after the war, Stringfellow and his fiance fled to Canada where they married and remained for several years.

When he returned to the United States from his self-imposed exile he became an Episcopal priest. Later when the Spanish American War broke out, Stringfellow desperately wanted to enter the military but was told he was too old. He then remembered the promise made to him by President Grant. Determined to serve, he wrote to President McKinley, who did in fact honor President Grant's promise and Stringfellow entered the United States Army at the grand old age of 57 years.

Benjamin Franklin Stringfellow was a very dangerous, elusive Confederate intelligence operative. He was most effective in recruiting and establishing a Confederate spy ring in the Washington area along with its communications line back to the Confederacy. The only Confederate spy ring older than his was the one handled by Rose O'Neal Greenhow. Stringfellow was a very daring man, who knew the value of "time-sensitive" intelligence and was smart enough to be able to distinguish it from the "strategic" intelligence. He must have been exceptional to be specifically recognized by General Lee who had a very strong dislike for spies.

And he must have been effective against the Union or they would not have put a price of $10,000 on his head!

He lived until the year 1913.

Lesser Known Confederate Male Spies

COLONEL TURNER ASHBY—Served as a member of General Stonewall Jackson's cavalry. He frequently put on a Union uniform and went behind Union lines as a veterinarian. After treating the animals and gathering information he would return to General Jackson with the Union intelligence he had gathered.

Colonel Ashby is also credited as the person responsible for the early training of Belle Boyd in intelligence gathering.

WALTER BOWIE—A thirty-year-old lawyer at the beginning of the war, Bowie became one of the more important spies for the Confederacy in southern Maryland (particularly in the Prince George's County area). He used the nickname "Wat."

In November of 1862, Bowie was captured by Union troops, sentenced to hang and actually escaped on the way to the gallows. He then joined Colonel John Mosby's raiders as a lieutenant and scout but continued his spying operations.

During his active spying days, Bowie is credited with informing General Robert E. Lee of General U.S. Grant's strategy for the Wilderness Campaign in Virginia. The date of Bowie's report is 27 April 1864 and the actual campaign opened on 4 May 1864. He is also famous for disguising himself as a black mammy in order to escape Union troops who had trailed him to a home in southern Maryland.

Bowie devised a plan to kidnap the governor of Maryland who had blocked the secession of the state of Maryland in the early days of the Confederacy. Bowie felt that if the governor was held for ransom the state would then secede—and an important border state would join the Confederacy and Washington, D.C., would then be within the boundaries of the Confederacy. The operation was not a success and on the return trip from Annapolis, Maryland, to Virginia, Union troops spotted Bowie and his troops. The Union troops attacked the Bowie party in Sandy Springs, Maryland, (known as the Battle of Rickett's Run). Bowie was killed in the ensuing battle.

E. PLINY BRYAN—Early in the war, E. Porter Alexander, chief signal officer for the Confederacy, noted that the Confederate lines were only about five miles south of the Potomac in the area of Washington, D.C.—an area known as Mason Hill. He suggested opening a secret line of communications from Washington to Mason Hill, on the Virginia side of the Potomac and from there on to Richmond. E. Pliny Bryan was selected for the job.

Bryan was ordered to Washington, where he was to secure a room on the upper floor of a house, visible from Mason Hill. He was ordered to denote the room by placing a coffee pot in the window. Major Alexander, with his telescope on Mason Hill, would then read the messages that Bryan would wigwag from his room. It was planned that he would report the news carried in the Northern newspapers as well as any information brought to him by agents. Before the system could be put into effect the Confederacy pulled back and thereby lost the advantage of Mason Hill.

Bryan then moved to a location about 15 miles south of Washington in Southern Maryland. This station did become operational and here Bryan received information from Southern sympathizers. They brought him the newspapers, he condensed the news, and then flagged it across the river.

The system worked until the spring of 1862 when the Union learned of the transmitting station and Union troops arrested Bryan and all operations ceased.

JOHN BURKE—A highly respected Confederate spy. Burke was blind in one eye and used this to his advantage. He would remove his glass eye and appear as a one-eyed man, or wear a patch over the empty space. He very effectively spied for the Confederacy in the Washington, Philadelphia, and New York areas throughout the war years. At one point he was captured—he escaped and remained in Union territory where he continued his spying activities.

C.E. COLEMAN—His real name was Henry Shaw and prior to the war he had been a clerk on the river run from Tennessee to New Orleans, Louisiana, which made him very familiar with Tennessee.

During the war he was a captain in the Confederate Army, and frequently deployed on spying missions behind enemy lines. When on his secret missions, he used the name of C.E. Coleman and represented himself as an itinerant doctor. He was a very successful spy and considered, by the Union, as one of the most dangerous spies in the West. Eventually, he and his courier were among a group of Confederates captured by Union forces. His courier, Sam Davis, chose to hang rather than reveal that Coleman was in the captured group. Coleman was later unwittingly exchanged by the Union as a regular prisoner of war. His true identity was never compromised.

During the time he was in captivity, his organization continued to sign messages with the signature C.E. Coleman, in order to not alert the Union to the fact that Coleman was in their possession.

GODFREY HYAMS—Functioned as a double agent for the Union. He infiltrated the Confederate Toronto operation and passed advance word of the plans for the burning of the New York City hotels to the New York City police.

A.D. LYTLE—A member of the Confederate secret service he served as a photographer in the southwest area of the conflict. He photographed the First Indiana Heavy Artillery in the New Orleans area, providing information on troop strengths and armaments.

CAPTAIN JOHN MAXWELL—Confederate spy who on August 9, 1864, led the raid on City Point, Virginia, then held by the Union. He successfully blew up the train depot and associated buildings. The raid killed 58 Union soldiers, injured 128 more and did significant damage to the transportation system in that area of Virginia. General U.S. Grant was in the area at the time and several of his aides and people around him were wounded by the shrapnel. General Grant could easily have been killed in the raid.

CHANNING SMITH—A career military man. Favorite spy/scout for General Robert E. Lee and other Confederate generals. Frequently worked with Benjamin F. Stringfellow in the Washington, D.C. area. Was highly successful during the entire course of the war.

WILLIAM SMITHSON—Prominent member of Rose O'Neal Greenhow's espionage ring in Washington, D.C. Used the alias of "Charles Cables" when communicating with the Confederates. When Mrs. Greenhow was arrested, Smithson served as the point of contact for members of the ring desiring to transmit information to the South. After Mrs. Greenhow's exchange to Richmond, Smithson served not only as her personal banker in Washington, where he attended to her stocks and other monies, but also assisted the Confederacy in selling Southern securities and handling currency exchanges. He was arrested in 1862 and sent to Fort Lafayette in New York, then released later in the war.

After the war, General Philip Sheridan testified that a Sister of Charity nun reported to him that in 1861 Smithson had tried to send a plan of the Washington fortifications through the lines enclosed in a small plug of tobacco. Smithson's plan evidently failed when the Sister of Charity returned the papers to Smithson because a paroled Confederate prisoner of war refused to carry them South as it would violate the terms of his parole.

There is no doubt that Smithson was a key player in the Washington spy ring controlled by Rose O'Neal Greenhow.

DR. AARON VAN CAMP—Washington dentist and a member of the Greenhow spy ring. He made frequent trips through the Union lines to the Confederate forces to relay military information. One of his prime sources of information was a clerk for the U.S. Senate Military Committee named John Callan. Dr. Van Camp was arrested in 1862 and spent the remainder of the war in prison. Nothing is known about his later life.

Chapter 10

Union Male Spies

Spencer Kellogg Brown, A "Brown" Hanged by the Confederacy

> Did you ever pass through a tunnel under a mountain? My passage, my death is dark, but beyond all is light and bright.
>
> Spencer Kellogg Brown

Spencer Kellogg Brown was born in Kansas in 1842. There in his early life he saw the burning of the family home in the sack of Osawatomie, continual violence between the abolitionists and the anti-abolitionists and was eventually sent to live in a pro-slavery house to "correct" his thinking. No wonder he was an avid abolitionist. It is ironic that he left Kansas because he was told the name "Brown" was not a good one to have in Kansas, and he ended up just like John Brown—on the end of a rope—but hanged by the other side.

Spencer Kellogg (he did not use the name Brown) arrived in St. Louis, Missouri, where he initially enlisted in the U.S. Army to serve in Missouri against the violence happening in that state. He received an honorable discharge when his enlistment ended and at this time he entered the U.S. Navy (1861) where he served on the Union vessel *Essex*.

Prior to the attacks on Forts Henry and Donelson, in Tennessee, both the army and the navy were in need of intelligence about the shore batteries and troop strengths of the opposing force and Brown volunteered to go ashore and collect as much information as he could. He was given 10 days to complete his mission and was accompanied by his friend Trussel.

Brown and Trussel left the *Essex* in a small boat and later found the Confederate ship *Charm* which they boarded. Brown had handcuffed his hands and they passed themselves off as Union deserters. Initially suspected they were so convincing that later the Confederate navy wanted them to join their force. Brown said "no" because if the ship was captured by the Union, they would surely be recognized and shot.

As the ship plied the Mississippi, Brown and his friend kept their eyes open to collect as much information as they could. For example, Brown noted that the Confederate Parrott canons were mounted on carriages and slides, developed by the Confederates, that were far superior to those of the Union—fact duly noted.

The pair was then put ashore to assist the Engineers with construction work. All went well until two Confederates noted Brown spending a great deal of time near the river observing. He was arrested and eventually sent to Fort Pillow, Tennessee, where he talked the commanding officer into releasing him in order that he could go south to Corinth in Mississippi and enlist in the Confederate army. On the way south he met an enlisted man of the 1st Louisiana Cavalry Volunteers and he did join the unit—temporarily! As the unit neared Pittsburg Landing, Tennessee (the Battle of Shiloh was underway at this point), Brown successfully escaped and found his way to the Union lines. He was taken to General U.S. Grant to whom he reported all the intelligence he had gathered on his mission.

At this juncture, Spencer Kellogg Brown rejoined the crew of the *Essex* with no further thought of espionage work—until the Navy discovered that Fort Hudson in Georgia was being resupplied by a ferry boat traversing the river. The Union wanted the ferry removed prior to any attack on the fort and Brown quickly agreed to undertake the task.

With the assistance of about 40 men Brown successfully attacked the ferry and destroyed it by sinking it in the river. As he went ashore after the sinking he was met by a group of strangers who after a short conversation arrested him on the spot—they were Confederate soldiers! On August 15, 1862, Spencer Kellogg Brown's luck finally ran out. He was taken to Richmond, Virginia, tried as a Union spy, found guilty and sentenced to be hanged.

When Commodore W.D. Porter of the Union Navy learned of Brown's arrest by the Confederacy he initiated an extensive effort to secure his release. At least 11 separate pieces of correspondence regarding Brown's release, covering the period from March 19, 1863, to September 28, 1863, are in various volumes of *The War of the Rebellion,* published by the U.S. Government in 1899.

The hanging took place in Richmond on September 25, 1863, over a year after his arrest. One of the spectators present at the hanging was the Union spy Elizabeth Van Lew who recorded the final statement of Spencer Kellogg Brown:

Did you ever pass through a tunnel under a mountain? My passage, my death is dark, but beyond all is light and bright.

It is not hard to understand why Spencer Kellogg Brown became a Union spy so readily. His early years in Kansas during the turmoil of the slave/anti-slave period made him a staunch abolitionist and he would do whatever was required to further the cause. The information he gathered on his initial mission behind Confederate lines was probably of little value since he had no timely means of getting the information back to the Union forces. By the time he was able to report in person to General Grant, much of what he had learned had been overtaken by events.

Spencer Kellogg Brown does represent many of his Union and Confederate spy counterparts. He was a man totally untrained in the tradecraft of the profession, but very willing to undertake the missions requested of him. His hanging was not so much due to the value of the information he delivered to the Union on the Confederate military establishment as it was a Confederate reaction to Union spying in general. All Union spies were equally dangerous in the eyes of the government in Richmond.

The Union hanged John Brown and the Confederacy hanged Spencer Kellogg Brown—a true irony of the Civil War.

George Curtis, the "Subterranean" Insider

George Curtis was about 25 years old when the Civil War began. He was living in New York at the time and quickly enlisted in a New York Infantry Regiment. Curtis was cool headed, brave in nature, very determined and had a superb mind. These traits made him an excellent candidate to become a Pinkerton man. Which is exactly what he did. He was, however, not from the same mold as the Pinkerton men who had been detectives with Allan Pinkerton prior to the war; he was not a detective but a war-time Pinkerton spy, and a very good one.

In early 1862, the Union decided that more intelligence was needed from the Confederate capital and George Curtis was selected to accomplish the mission. He was sent south as a contraband merchant willing and able to sell gun caps, ammunition and most importantly quinine to the Confederacy. He took the same river boat south that carried General George McClellan and openly entered the South on the Virginia side of the Potomac River.

The next day he was taken in by Confederate pickets and he found himself in the presence of General A.P. Hill. Upon learning his mission of contracting for contraband goods for the Confederacy, all goods that were desperately needed, General Hill gave him a pass to proceed to Richmond. He also asked Curtis to carry some dispatches to Richmond for him (a very naive general as he had just met the man) and Curtis most willingly agreed to do so.

That night at his hotel he met a fellow contraband merchant by the name of Leroy from Baltimore, and having much in common they became friends and traveled onto Richmond together. The next day the two merchants met with Secretary of War Judah Benjamin and successfully negotiated contracts for the delivery of contraband goods. Secretary Benjamin also gave Curtis a pass to freely travel in and out of Richmond.

That same day Mr. Leroy introduced George Curtis to the Subterranean Club, a quasi-governmental intelligence operation. The club, which met in one of the local hotels, was composed of both government personnel and local businessmen. The main interest of the club was the gathering of intelligence that would be helpful in the acquisition and movement of contraband goods to the Confederacy. Mr. Curtis, the contraband merchant from Washington, was a welcome addition to the group and he remained a member throughout the war.

The Subterranean Club had about 50 agents scattered throughout the Union with the majority being in Baltimore and Washington. At the club's request, Mr. Curtis became a member of the Washington Subterranean group.

When Curtis left Richmond after his first visit, a precedent was set that continued throughout the remainder of the war. He was asked to carry dispatches to Confederate General John B. Magruder—which he gladly did. But first the dispatches were delivered to Mr. Bangs, Pinkerton's field supervisor, where they were copied prior to delivery. This practice continued uninterrupted for the next three years.

The Curtis adventure also has a side for the romantics. During his visits to the South, Curtis had made the acquaintance of a Unionist farm family by the name of Harcourt. They had a charming daughter, Mary, with whom Curtis soon fell in love. Curtis assisted the family in escaping to the North, where after the war he married Miss Mary Harcourt and lived happily ever after as a salesman in Chicago.

The main point of the Curtis saga is that the Union in using Curtis as a contraband salesman was willing to trade contraband goods for accurate and reliable intelligence. All of the contracts that Curtis initiated with the Confederacy were in fact honored by the Union. They knew that by doing so they were increasing the credibility of their agent Curtis. His value was not only in the intelligence he gathered on his trips to the Confederacy but also in the dispatches he was asked to carry to and from the Confederacy. Curtis was the only Union spy to successfully infiltrate the Subterranean Club where he was able not only to glean intelligence but to pass it on to the Confederacy, that is the "intelligence" the Union wanted the Confederacy to receive.

George Curtis had to be an exceptional agent to be able to function as a Union spy for the entire period of the Civil War and never come under suspicion. His superior mind coupled with his non-flamboyant manner were great assets to him not only in protecting his life but in completing his missions for the Union.

James A. Garfield, Intelligence User Extraordinaire

James A. Garfield, who later gained fame as the twentieth President of the United States, was not actively a spy. He is included herein as he is probably the best example of a Union officer who understood what to do with the raw intelligence he received from the various Union spies and scouts reporting to him. He represents a conscious one-man effort to function in the role of a Union army intelligence collection point—a role he performed for the Union Army of the Cumberland.

Garfield entered the Union army in 1861 when he was commissioned a lieutenant colonel in the 42nd Ohio Volunteers. Prior to entering the army Garfield had been a preacher and educator in Ohio. He soon rose to the rank of colonel and was promoted at the age of 31 to the rank of brigadier general after the Battle of Fredericksburg in Virginia. As the result of his promotion he was assigned to General William S. Rosecrans, head of the Army of the Cumberland, as Chief of Staff and it was here that he began his role at the center of intelligence.

In most Union army units, the spies reported back to the officer for whom they worked and that information was often used in isolation from other intelligence that may have been gleaned on the same subject. In the case of the Army of the Cumberland, information was received from the spies of General Grenville Dodge, General Stephen Hurlbut, General Gordon Granger and General George Thomas and until General Garfield became the Chief of Staff the information was used on a piecemeal basis. Putting all of the information together and analyzing it, Garfield soon became a master of tracking troop movements and gauging Confederate troop strengths. While this may sound simple, it was not generally done in either army.

Some examples of General Garfield's successes are:

• In his June 12, 1863, report to General Rosecrans he estimated that the Army of Tennessee was comprised of 41,680 active soldiers. He based this number on incoming reports and his own independent analysis of the data. General Braxton Bragg, head of the Army of Tennessee, on June 10, 1862, reported a strength of 46,260, proving Garfield's number to be very realistic.

• In another report in June, Garfield reported that General Bragg was sending a total of 12,000 men to General Joseph Johnson, when in fact the actual number was 11,300—again not a bad estimate.

• He urged both Generals Granger and Thomas, corps commanders, to form "bureaus of information" in order to keep themselves advised of troop movements and other important military intelligence.

The information reported by the spies, and more importantly collected at one point and analyzed by General Garfield, gave General Rosecrans a real advantage in the Battle of Tullahoma in Tennessee. Based on Garfield's input, Rosencrans was able to maneuver General Bragg out of mid-Tennessee back to Chattanooga on the Georgia border.

From the viewpoint of Civil War intelligence efforts, the most important aspect of General Garfield's endeavors is that he is one of the very few officers, either for the Confederacy or the Union, to establish a central point for the collection of intelligence reports from military spies. More importantly he represents one of the first military officers to serve as a command intelligence officer, who took incoming reports, consolidated them, analyzed them and produced a comprehensive report for his general. His reports were the result not only of the incoming reports but also his interpretation of the meaning of the intelligence reported. He was way ahead of his time in this endeavor.

General Rosecrans himself, when Garfield was running for President, was quoted as saying, "His views were large and he was possessed of a comprehensive mind," and that is what it took then and what it takes now to function as a military intelligence collection and analysis officer.

Garfield was elected to the House of Representatives in 1862 and left the army in 1863 to serve in his congressional role. Had he remained in the military and continued his active intelligence collection and analysis efforts, the Union army, in general, may well have adopted his techniques—much to their advantage.

James A. Garfield was later elected to the United States Senate, his life long goal, but he never served as a Senator. Before his term began he was nominated and elected to be the twentieth President of the United States in 1881.

"Colonel" Philip Henson, the Spy of Many Generals

Philip Henson was born and raised in Alabama but when the war came he was outcast from his family, then living in Mississippi—he was a loyal Unionist, but a quiet one. To avoid entering the Confederate military he convinced a plantation owner to make him the manager of his plantation and thereby avoided military service.

When General U.S. Grant and the Union forces entered Mississippi in late 1862, Henson left his family on the plantation and embarked on a dangerous mission—that of Union spy. His first assignment was to go to Corinth in Mississippi and buy all the cotton he could find for the Union. He was so successful in this endeavor that he soon found himself working for General William Rosecrans, but that did not last long. Returning from a mission to the Confederacy, he was stopped at the Union lines where the soldiers were very wary of any "Southern drawl" speaker. He was taken to General Grenville Dodge, the spymaster in the West, and interrogated. General Dodge was not only impressed with the information the man had uncovered in his trip south but also the man himself. Henson soon found himself working not for General Rosecrans but for General Dodge.

At this time Vicksburg, Mississippi, was the central interest of the Union army and intelligence regarding the Confederate military forces in the city was needed greatly. Henson was given the task of acquiring that information. To ease his entry into the city, he persuaded an old friend, Jessie Johnsey, who had a son in the Confederate army, to visit Vicksburg and check on his son and take Henson with him. They succeeded in entering the city and obtained an interview with General John C. Pemberton, commander in the city.

Henson proceeded to inform General Pemberton about the sub-

126

human treatment that the Confederate prisoners of war were receiving from the Union captors. He so impressed the general that he was asked to talk to all the troops in Vicksburg about the subject (General Pemberton thought it would make them better fighters when the battle came). To accomplish this task Henson was given complete freedom to enter all areas of Vicksburg—a dream come true for a spy!

When he had collected all the intelligence he could, he left Vicksburg, after being congratulated by General Pemberton for a job well done, and returned to General Dodge's headquarters. One can only imagine the amount and value of the intelligence he was able to supply to General Grant prior to the attack on Vicksburg.

Just prior to his next mission to the Confederacy, General Dodge advised Henson to go into his tent and take whatever he thought would be useful from his desk. It was General Dodge's philosophy that his agents should have valid information about the Union forces to use as either "bargaining power" in case they were arrested, or as a method of impressing the Confederate generals (as pseudo double agent). In this case, when Henson went south he so impressed the Confederate Generals Lucius Polk and Sterling Price that he was able to become a member of their staff and stay with their forces—that is until he had acquired all the information he needed at which time he once again headed north. On these trips to the South, Henson frequently stayed in the John W. Thompson house near Corinth, which was a safe house for traveling Union spies.

On subsequent missions the same scenario was repeated as Henson became a Confederate spy for Generals Daniel Ruggles, Samuel Gholson, Samuel Ferguson and one very well known general by the name of James Longstreet. His association with General Longstreet began right after the fall of Vicksburg when he went to Atlanta, Georgia. As in the past, he impressed General Longstreet with the information he had on the Union and was asked to be a member of his immediate staff. General Longstreet at the time was on his way to reinforce General Braxton Bragg. Henson was able to supply General Rosecrans with the size of the Longstreet force, the route of movement and other valuable information well in advance of any battle. General Rosecrans was able to use the intelligence to his advantage.

Once again returning to the Union lines he was next assigned to spy on the activities of General Nathan Forrest, the highly respected Confederate cavalry leader. At this point, Henson's luck seemed to have run out as he was arrested in Tupelo, Mississippi, by some of Forrest's men. Knowing he was in trouble he informed Forrest that he knew the names and locations of many of the Union spies that had been sent into Georgia by General Dodge. What General Forrest did not know, and Henson did, was that all of the Union agents named had already returned to the Union lines. Impressed with this knowledge, General Forrest sent Henson on to Georgia to assist General Polk in locating the Union spies. He was once again so convincing that General Polk gave him $500 to find the Union spies. Henson took the money and returned to Union lines.

Henson was finally arrested on a trip behind enemy lines in late 1864 by the troops of General Philip Roddey who wanted to turn him over to General Forrest. But General Forrest would have nothing more to do with the man and he was held in prison until February 1865. At this point the Confederacy, desperate for manpower to fight the war, released Henson at his request to serve in the 26th Mississippi. On route to join his unit, he jumped from the train and somehow managed to make his way back to the Union lines in time for the Confederate surrender.

At this same time, Mrs. Henson had also been arrested, and was held in prison. Like her husband she remained stalwart and was finally released.

Later when General Forrest learned of Henson's escape he regretted the fact that he had not hanged him when he was his prisoner. But he paid him the utmost compliment that could be paid a Union spy. General Forrest called him "the most dangerous Federal spy operating in the Confederacy," which was probably true.

The appreciation that General Dodge had for Henson can clearly be seen in the following excerpts from letters written by General Dodge regarding his favorite spy. The first written on March 31, 1865, was addressed to General H. Thomas, commanding the Department of the Cumberland. It contained the following passage:

> I can vouch for Mr. Henson; he was probably one of the best—if not the very best—men we ever had in our employ, and the information

given us by him, in all campaigns, was of incalculable benefit to us; he never failed us, and in all our campaigns in the Southwest, up to the Atlantic campaign, he performed service that no other man would; he has suffered almost death for us, and deserves our assistance.

General Dodge's opinion of Henson did not change over the years, as in 1887 he wrote the following to Henson prior to a G.A.R. encampment in St. Louis:

> No. 1 Broadway, New York City
> August 31, 1887

Philip Henson, Esq, Corinth, Miss:

Dear Sir: It will be impossible for me to be present at the G.A.R. encampment in St. Louis. Your efficient services as a scout (probably the best who ever went through our lines), are a matter of official record in Washington, and have time and again received my commendation and elicited my efforts to your behalf. Not only that, but I received letters from General Grant, at the time you were sending information from the South, stating that my reports as to the movements of the rebel troops were so accurate and found afterwards to be so correct, that he was anxious to know who acted for me, and I named to him you among others, who were inside of the enemy's lines so long for me. You are at liberty to show this to any of my friends of the Grand Army; but I do not think you will need it to give you a standing among them.

> Yours truly
> G.M. Dodge

After the war Henson petitioned the federal government requesting payment for his years as a Federal spy. Even with glowing letters of recommendation, similar to those quoted above, his petition, like those of others, was turned down. As a protest for this action "Colonel" Henson took to the lecture circuit and decided not to shave his beard until the issue was settled. His beard grew to a length of 6 feet 4 inches!

There is no doubt that Philip Henson was a very effective Union spy in the Western campaign. He had all the attributes required for the job—a Southerner by birth, a Southern drawl, knowledge of the area and the local populace and most important a good intelligence and a sense of when and how to employ it. The tactical intelligence developed by Henson was a major assist to the Union commanders in the West. His first hand reporting on Vicksburg alone makes him a very unique Union Civil War spy—beard and all.

William A. Lloyd, Lincoln's Own

One of the most secret of the Civil War secret agents was in fact generally unknown until his case for non-payment of salary arrived at the United States Supreme Court. The defendant in the case was none other than the United States Government, in the person of Abraham Lincoln. It seems that even presidents in the time of the Civil War had their own secret service—and William Alvin Lloyd served that purpose for President Lincoln from July 1861 until the end of the war. His services in the Union cause were apparently unknown even to President Lincoln's closest advisers!

In the early summer of 1861 William A. Lloyd, a publisher of railroad and steamer guides for the Southern states, came personally to President Lincoln with a request for a passport. He wanted to enter the Southern states in order to conduct research for his guide book publications. Without current information regarding trains and steamers in the South Mr. Lloyd could not remain in business—a fact that did not go unnoticed by the President. Lincoln saw the potential of this man, a known personality in the South able to move freely throughout the Confederacy. His response was that he would issue the passport only if Mr. Lloyd would serve as his personal secret agent while in the Confederacy. Mr. Lloyd, who was accompanied in his visits to the President by a fellow employee, Thomas Boyd, and a friend F.J. Bonfanti, initially did not like the idea—he knew nothing of spying. However, being a shrewd businessman, and realizing that the $200 a month offered as his salary (plus expenses) was an excellent arrangement, he agreed to the terms. A passport was issued in July 1861, personally signed by President Lincoln. Passports were also issued for Mr. Boyd, Mr. Bonfanti, and Mrs. Lloyd, as well as her maid.

At the time Mr. Lloyd received his passport he signed a contract with the President stating that he would in fact serve as Mr. Lincoln's personal spy in the Confederacy for the duration of the war. The terms of his contract were:

- He would report on the number of troops at specific points.
- He would procure the plans of the Confederacy forts and other battle structures.
- He would receive no codes or ciphers to use for his messages back to Washington—he should find Union couriers to report back.
- Most importantly he was to report only to President Lincoln, and no one else.
- He would be paid for his expenses and in addition would receive a monthly stipend of $200.

With the signed contract in hand, Mr. Lloyd departed for the Confederacy on 13 July 1861. He remained in the Confederacy for four years, both on his own business and that of the President. During this entire time he was assisted in his spying endeavors by his employee, Mr. Boyd. The efforts of the two men to collect intelligence are impressive but their problem was getting the data to President Lincoln in a timely manner. By their contract the information had to go directly to President Lincoln and no one else. They even resorted to sending letters to Boyd's family and then his brother would take them personally to the White House for delivery to President Lincoln.

The information that Lloyd and his associate sent to Lincoln was not shared by the President with his military commanders.

It appears he used it in a quality check on his commanders. Some examples of the information forwarded by Lloyd are:

Oct. 1861—Information on the forts and strengths of General Benjamin Huger's troops

Oct. 1861—A map of the harbor of Norfolk and Portsmouth in Tidewater Virginia

Jul. 1862—Information on the artillery and forts of Richmond

Dec. 1863—Maps of forts and encampments throughout the Confederacy

Mar. 1865—General Robert E. Lee's force strength and map of the port at Wilmington, North Carolina

After one of the deliveries made personally to the President by Boyd, Lincoln was so impressed with the information and his efforts to deliver it that he provided him with $100 a month salary.

Lloyd's time in the Confederacy included four separate prison incarcerations. Once when taken in for questioning by the Confederacy, Mr. Lloyd destroyed the signed contract that he had with Lincoln. He had been carrying it in his hat and felt, rightly so, that it would be incriminating evidence. He saved his life but the destroying of the contract lead to a Supreme Court decision denying his case years after his death in 1868.

After the assassinaion of President Lincoln and the cessation of hostilities, Mr. Lloyd returned to Washington and presented his bill to the United States government. Secretary of War Edwin Stanton did in fact pay his expenses—a total of $2,380 (which could indicate that he was aware of Lloyd's activities)—but he refused to pay any salary (a total of $9,753.32) as he had no evidence of the contract between President Lincoln and Mr. Lloyd. The assassination had taken away the only other person who knew of the contract. Hence a major dilemma existed for Mr. Lloyd. He had conscientiously performed his duties in good faith and felt that President Lincoln's side of the contract should also be executed in good faith. The problem was the lack of evidence to prove his point.

After his death, the administrator of his estate, Enoch Totten, sued the United States government for non-payment of salary of $200 per month ($9,753.32) as promised by Mr. Lincoln in the signed contract that had been destroyed. The case was accepted for review by the Supreme Court, and the final decision was handed down in 1876. The court's decision was:

• Claim denied since the six-year statute of limitation had run out on 14 May 1871 (six years after the return of Lloyd from the Confederacy). There was no reason to prevent his being paid by President Lincoln at any time during the war if his accounts had been presented.
• "The Court, being equally divided in opinion as to the authority

of the President to bind the United States by the contract in question, decided, for the purposes of an appeal, against the claim, and dismissed the petition."

• "Both employer and agent must have understood that the lips of the other were to be forever sealed respecting the relation of either to the matter." The case was denied.

• The court said "The President is undoubtedly authorized during the war, as commander-in-chief of the armies of the United States, to employ secret agents to enter the rebel lines and obtain information respecting the strength, resources, and movements of the enemy; and contracts to compensate such agents are so far binding upon the government as to render it lawful for the President to direct payment of the amount stipulated out of the contingent fund under his control. If he does not have sufficient 'contingency funds' Congress must come up with the money—not the President."

This case established the precedent that an intelligence agent cannot recover by court action against the government for SECRET service. Said the court, "Agents . . . must look for their compensation to the contingent fund of the department employing them, and to such allowance from it as those who dispense the fund may award. The secrecy which such contracts impose precludes any action for this enforcement."

The case also set the precedent that secret agencies do not have to reveal all they know if it impinges on security.

No one to this day has any real idea of the value of Mr. Lloyd's secret agent work in the Confederacy. His reports went directly to President Lincoln and it is apparent that he shared them with no one. Lloyd's reports served as an independent source of intelligence by which President Lincoln could evaluate what he was hearing from other sources. That is a very logical procedure and it is still used today and known as "independent sources."

Mr. Totten's actions in behalf of the Lloyd estate and the subsequent Supreme Court actions set precedents that still guide the United States Intelligence Community today. Therefore one has to say that Mr. Lincoln's association with Mr. Lloyd has had a very long lasting impact on the secret service of the United States, even though most Americans do not even know of the existence of William A. Lloyd, secret agent for the President Abraham Lincoln.

"Corporal Pike," A Sherman Spy

The following is extracted from the memoirs of General William T. Sherman. While it is a specific description of "Corporal Pike," it also represents many of the Civil War spies.

The bearer of this message was Corporal Pike. . . This Pike proved to be a singular character, his manner attracted my notice at once and I got him a horse, and had him travel with us eastward about Elkton, whence I sent him back to General Crook at Huntsville; but told him, if I could ever do him a personal service, he might apply to me. The next spring then I was in Chattanooga, preparing for the Atlanta campaign, Corporal Pike made his appearance and asked a fulfillment of my promise. I inquired what he wanted, and he said he wanted to do something "bold," something that would make him a hero. I explained to him that we were getting ready to go for Joe Johnston at Dalton, that I expected to be in the neighborhood of Atlanta about the 4th of July, and wanted the bridge across the Savannah River at Augusta, Georgia to be burnt about that time, to produce alarm and confusion behind the rebel army, I explained to Pike that the chances were three to one that he would be caught and hanged; but the greater the danger the greater seemed to be his desire to attempt it. I told him to select a companion, to disguise himself as an East Tennessee refugee, work his way over the mountains into North Carolina, and at the time appointed to float down the Savannah River and burn that bridge. In a few days he had made his preparations and took his departure. The bridge was not burnt, and I supposed that Pike had been caught and hanged.

When we reached Columbia, South Carolina, in February 1865, just as we were leaving the town, in passing the asylum, I heard my name called and saw a very dirty fellow followed by a file of men running toward me, and as they got near I recognized Pike. He called to me to identify him as one of my men; he was then a prisoner under guard, and I instructed the guard to bring him that night to my camp some fifteen miles up the road, which was done. Pike gave me a graphic narrative of his adventures, which would have filled a volume; told me how he had made two attempts to burn the bridge, and failed; and said that at the time of our entering Columbia he was a prisoner in the hands of the rebels, under trial for his life, but in the confusion of their retreat he made his escape and got into our lines, where he was again made a prisoner by our troops because of his looks. Pike got some clothes, cleaned up, and I used him afterward to communicate with Wilmington, North Carolina. Some time after the war, he was appointed a lieutenant of the Regular Cavalry, and was killed in Oregon, by the accidental discharge of a pistol. Just before his death he wrote me, saying that he was tired of the monotony of garrison-life, and wanted to turn Indian, join the Cheyennes on the Plains, who were then giving us great trouble, and, after he had gained their confidence, he would betray them into our hands.

It is interesting to note how easily Pike was made a spy by General Sherman. Here was a man who wanted a dangerous mission, so it was given to him with hope for the best. General Sherman had just met the man, had no idea about his background or his real loyalties but he was willing to give him an espionage mission, with the attitude that if it works great and if it doesn't nothing is lost but the life of one man. This attitude permeated the minds of many of the senior army officers, Union and Confederate, when it came to assigning spy/espionage missions. No wonder so many missions failed.

The attitude of Corporal Pike is one that is prevalent among the soldiers of the Civil War. The thought of undertaking a spy/espionage mission was appealing to many for the adventure rather than out of loyalty. Not all soldiers went to their senior officers to find a mission to undertake; many just struck out on their own with results that to this day remain unknown.

Both the attitudes and actions represented by General Sherman and Corporal Pike were very common throughout the Civil War.

Archibald Rowand, Jr., A Spy Who Won the Congressional Medal of Honor

Archibald Rowand, Jr., was a young man with a devotion to his country and a love of adventure. A good combination for a future spy. He volunteered for service in the Union army early in the war

135

and served almost his entire military career in the Shenandoah Valley of Virginia with General Philip Sheridan, initially as an infantry man and later as a scout and spy.

At the age of 19, he answered a call from his commander for volunteers to undertake a very dangerous mission. The cadre selected for the mission were to don Confederate uniforms, infiltrate the Confederate lines to uncover the intentions of the enemy army and then report back to the Union side. Rowand relished the thought and willingly went off in his Confederate uniform. He successfully returned and was then recruited to be a member of "Jessie's Scouts" in the Valley.

Jessie's Scouts originated not in the Valley but in Missouri where they were started by General John C. Fremont. The group was called "Jessie's Scouts" in honor of Mrs. Fremont, whose first name was Jessie. When General Fremont was transferred to the Valley, Jessie's Scouts came with him, and they stayed there for the duration of the war. The group was, in fact, about half scout and half spy in composition and many of them wore Confederate uniforms more than they wore their own Union uniforms.

In order to avoid any identification confusion upon meeting another Confederate, Jessie's Scouts in the Valley established methods of ascertaining if the "Confederate" they met was a real one or one of Jessie's Scouts:

- All of Jessie's Scouts wore white scarves, always knotted in a very specific way.
- Upon meeting a "Confederate" they would initiate a prearranged conversation to prove the true identity of the other party. The conversation went:

Party A: Good morning (or evening)!
Party B: These are perilous times.
Party A: Yes, but we are looking for better.
Party B: To what shall we look?
Party A: To the red and white cord.

While the first four lines could conceivably occur at random, there is no way that the last line could be spoken by chance. The famous Confederate raider, Major Harry Gilmor, and his troops did discover the white scarf identifying feature and used it successfully against the Union, but they never uncovered the conversation identification technique.

Archibald Rowand, born and raised in South Carolina, was a natural to be a Union spy in the South—he spoke the language—which is always a real plus for any agent. In addition, he was young, good looking and completely fearless. Rowand almost always wore a Confederate uniform and in his early days worked as a team with another young man by the name of Ike Harris. Ike was killed on one of their trips south and that only made Rowand that much more daring. He did however have one major security fault that could have caused serious problems. He always wrote long letters home detailing his adventures in espionage—and not always past adventures—also those planned for the future. This lack of security never got him captured as his family did not reveal the letters until long after the war—and Rowand lived to a very old age.

In January of 1865, the notorious Major Gilmor returned to the Valley to continue his raiding for the Confederate Army. He was a real problem and a very difficult man to pinpoint for potential capture. Rowand was sent into the field in his Confederate uniform to ascertain the location of Major Gilmor and his troops. Within two days Rowand reported his whereabouts, troops were dispatched and the infamous Gilmor was captured and sent to Boston to sit out the remainder of the war.

On the way back to the Union camp with Gilmor in tow an interesting turn of events, reportedly, occurred that not only gives an insight into Rowand's personality, but also the human side of a very cruel war. Rowand, in Confederate uniform, spotted a Confederate soldier standing in a doorway and immediately went to arrest him. When he got closer he recognized the man as a Confederate he had arrested the year before. When he called the rebel by name, the startled man responded, "How did you know my name?" He had just gotten out of a Union prison and here was his original arrester to send him back!

When they returned to the Union camp, Private Rowand asked if the Confederate he had arrested could be released and not imprisoned again. Major Harry Young, the commander of Jessie's Scouts, knowing perfectly well that no Union enlisted man had the authority to release a prisoner, told Rowand to take the Confederate aside and do as he pleased. The Confederate was released and probably felt forever indebted to a man whose name he did not even know.

For his intelligence work in Jessie's Scouts during the Shenandoah Valley Campaign, Private Rowand was recommended by General Sheridan for the Congressional Medal of Honor. The recommendation read:

TO THE ADJUTANT GENERAL OF THE ARMY, Washington, D. C.:

SIR,—I respectfully recommend that a Medal of Honor be given to Private Archibald H. Rowand, Jr., First W. Va Cavalry, for gallant and meritorious services during the war.

During the James River Raid, in the winter of '64–65, private Rowand was one of the two men who went from Columbia, VA. to General Grant, who was encamped at City Point.

He also gave information as to the whereabouts of the Confederate Scout Harry Gilmor(e) and assisted in his capture, besides making several other daring scouts through the enemy's lines. His address is L.B. 244, Pittsburg, Pena.

I am, sir, very respectfully, your obedient servant,
(signed) P.H.Sheridan
Lieut.—Gen. USA

The actual citation read:

Private, Company K, 1st West Virginia Calvary. MOIH citation issued 3 Mar 1873 Citation: "Was one of two men who succeeded in getting through the enemy's lines with dispatches to General Grant."

It is interesting to note that his Medal of Honor was not given to him specifically for his work in the capture of Major Gilmor, but more for his accomplishments in the field of support of General Grant. Many years after the war, Rowand dictated a book based on his recollections. It is obviously not as accurate as it would have been at an earlier time. However, many of his letters did survive the war and are still available for some very interesting reading.

Rowand is one of many Union military spies that contributed to the Union victory, but he is one of the very few to receive official recognition for his accomplishments. His commander Major Young of Jessie's Scouts was instrumental in recommending Rowand for the medal. He worked with him on a very close personal basis and was well aware of his unique talents as a scout/spy and the contributions he had made to the Union effort.

Samuel Ruth, a Union Railroad Man in Richmond

Samuel Ruth, a Northerner by birth, had come to Richmond prior to the war to be the supervisor for the Richmond Fredericksburg and Potomac (RF&P) Railroad. The railroad became important during the war as it was the only line carrying rail traffic north from Richmond. Because of the Union presence in Northern Virginia the RF&P railroad had shrunk to only 55 miles—but a very important 55 miles to the Confederacy as well as the Union. It is about the rail activity of these 55 miles of track (from Richmond to Hamilton Landing in Virginia) that Samuel Ruth kept the Union informed throughout the war.

Ruth worked both as a collector of intelligence and an espionage agent for the Union. He had a railroad to run and he made sure that the efficiency of the railroad was to the Union advantage. For example, a mail train could make the 55-mile run in about three hours, while a troop train took seven hours to make the same journey. His tampering with the delivery of supplies to the front so infuriated General Robert E. Lee that in late 1862, just prior to General Ambrose Burnside's attack on Fredericksburg in Virginia, General Lee wrote to President Jefferson Davis complaining about the efficiency of Ruth's handling of the railroad. General Lee said:

> Unless the Richmond and Fredericksburg Railroad is more energetically operated, it will be impossible to supply this army with provisions and oblige its retirement to Hanover Square.

General Lee continued to complain to President Davis throughout the war, but to no avail.

As to example of his astute work, when the railroad bridge to the north was rebuilt after being destroyed by the Union, Ruth dutifully placed an advertisement in the Richmond paper giving the new schedules for the trains traveling north. He was not only obliging the local citizens but he also knew that the Union forces would obtain copies of the paper and have the full schedule for their own use.

During the entire length of the war Mr. Ruth continually supplied the Union forces with information of the following nature:

- Damages to the rolling stock of his railroad and others operating out of Richmond to the south
- Strength of the railroad guards
- Disposition of troops in Southwest Virginia just prior to the cavalry raid in December of 1864
- The number of troops dispatched by railroad to meet the Union expedition to Wilmington, North Carolina.

An example of Ruth's reporting is contained in a letter from General George Sharpe, General Grant's intelligence chief, to the provost marshal, written on December 15, 1864, which states:

> Scouts returned this A.M. with the following information from Richmond agents. . . .
>
> The Superintendent of the Richmond & Fredericksburg reports that provisions are becoming very scarce in Richmond and that the Danville Road is being run to its utmost capacity—but can scarcely supply the demands of the army. This informant reports that the cutting of the central RR at Hanover Junction would be a matter of great annoyance to the enemy, as most of the supplies used by the citizens are brought over the Central and Richmond Roads.
>
> This person is well informed with regard to the usefulness and capacity of all Rail Roads above Richmond.

Finally on January 23, 1865, Mr. Ruth was arrested and thrown in jail. The hue and cry from the citizens of Richmond about the arrest of an "outstanding citizen" was so massive that he was released nine days later and was immediately back in action.

His biggest coup occurred in February 1865 when he advised the Union that the Confederacy was shipping 400,000 pounds of Southern tobacco to Hamilton Landing in Virginia to be illegally exchanged with a Northern merchant for 95 tons of bacon valued at over $300,000. The Union forces intercepted the shipment and confiscated 28 railroad cars, took over 400 prisoners and destroyed four railroad bridges. They effectively put Ruth and his railroad out of business. (Although Ruth had alerted the Union to the shipment, he was never compensated for the loss of his rolling stock.)

Finally in March of 1865, Ruth advised the Union of General Lee's last ditch attempt to break General U.S. Grant's hold on Richmond which resulted in heavy losses for General Lee. He also advised the Union of the location of his rolling stock which was captured or destroyed by Union raiders—despite the fact that the rolling stock was his railroad.

Samuel Ruth was assisted in his spy/espionage endeavors by his assistant Frederick W.E. Lohman as well as by Charles Carter, who served as his courier. In addition, the Ruth operation had a connection with the spy ring operated by Miss Van Lew, probably for the transmission of information.

After the war, both General Grant and General George Sharpe supported his claim for reimbursement for his rolling stock. Congress failed to act during his lifetime and when the final compensation was made it amounted to a total of $500 for his widow. When General Grant became President he did however obtain a position for Mr. Ruth in the Internal Revenue Service, as the collectorship of internal revenue for the 2nd District of Virginia.

There can be little doubt that the information supplied to the Union forces by Ruth was of value to the planning and actions of the Union Army. The fact that Ruth was not suspected, only thought of as inefficient by some people, says a great deal about his ability as a spy and espionage agent. His actions clearly show that he placed the Union cause above his own personal gain—his railroad was destroyed by his own actions.

Felix Stidger, the Union's Copperhead

Felix Stidger, an uneducated farm boy, was one of the most successful of the Union spies employed in infiltrating the enemy during the Civil War. By infiltrating one of the Copperhead organizations, the Knights of the Golden Circle in Indiana, and attaining a statewide position, he was able to keep the Union informed of the subversive activities of the organization and their associations with the Confederates of the Toronto operation.

Stidger initially entered the army in an infantry regiment and was later sent to the Provost Marshall's office in Tennessee as a clerk. In the Provost Marshall's office he worked for a man named Captain Jones. In early 1864 when General Henry Carrington, the man charged with the intelligence operations in the state of Ohio, Illinois, Indiana, Tennessee and Kentucky, asked Jones for candidates to infiltrate the Knights, Jones recommended the 34-year-old Stidger. General Carrington had known Stidger and agreed that he had the potential to do the job—even though he was totally untrained in the world of espionage. When approached, Stidger agreed to undertake the mission.

In the spring of that same year Stidger started out on his mission representing himself as a "Peace Democrat & Copperhead." He soon met other Copperheads and before long found himself in the company of the leaders of the organization. He must have been very convincing because he was soon elected to serve as the secretary for the Knights of the Golden Circle in Indiana—a great position to have as an infiltrator.

Throughout the entire time Stidger was reporting to General Carrington on the events of the Knights. In his reports he used the name "J.J. Eustis" to avoid identification. Among the reports he forwarded were:

• May 11, 1864: Described his meeting with the Copperheads, his introduction to the leader Dr. Bowles, the "Greek fire" demonstration, and the details of the proposed revolution which included:
    —Indiana, Ohio and Illinois would fall to revolution.
    —The guns would be supplied by Captain Hines of the Toronto operation.
    —State heads would be murdered.
    —Confederate prisoners in northern camps would revolt.

• June 3, 1864: Sent list of co-conspirators, and the fact that a fellow Union agent by the name of "Coffin" was to be murdered.
• June 25, 1864: Talked of his meeting with Confederate Agent Hines in the company of Bowles and that the date of the revolt had been set for July 4, 1864.

• July 1864: Informed General Carrington that Justice Bullitt, a Knights leader, would be returning from Canada with a large sum of money collected from the Confederates to buy arms. Stidger was to meet him at the Louisville Ferry. In addition to the cash, Bullitt would have checks and currency, indisputable evidence of his treason. The information provided the evidence needed to arrest him and all the other leaders in one large raid. The arrests, in the early fall of 1864, netted over 100 of the Copperhead leaders.

In order not to alert the arrested leaders to Stidger's true mission, Stidger was himself arrested and spent several weeks in jail where he continued to gather intelligence. His fellow Copperheads did not realize his true role until he appeared in court to testify against them. Based on his work, all of the leaders were found guilty of treason and sentenced to die. The sentences were however commuted by President Andrew Johnson.

Stidger was truly an excellent agent. He infiltrated the organization, gained their confidence and successfully reported on their activities without ever coming under suspicion. When one realizes that Stidger was an uneducated country boy, his accomplishments become all the more remarkable. He was, as stated by General Carrington, "a natural spy."

After the war, Stidger married, raised a family, and chose like many of his Civil War spy contemporaries never to speak or write of his experiences within the Knights of the Golden Circle until after the turn of the century (his book was published in 1903). Part of his reasoning had to be his own personal security, as when his identity came to light at the Knight's trial he received many assassination threats. He did, none the less, live a long and healthy life, and while he got no official recognition he had to know that he deserved a "well-done" for his work.

Timothy Webster, Pinkerton's Premier Agent

Timothy Webster is recognized to this day as the most famous and effective of Allan Pinkerton's agents active in the Civil War. His loss, early in the war, was a severe blow, personally and professionally to Pinkerton and more importantly to the early intelligence gathering efforts of the Union.

Webster was born in 1821 in the United Kingdom and immigrated to the United States in 1833 with his parents. After finishing school he became a New York City policeman, and a very effective one. He was soon noticed by a friend of Pinkerton's in New York, who recommended him to Pinkerton for detective work. His pre-Civil War work for Pinkerton was excellent and he quickly became the top agent.

When Pinkerton entered federal service at the request of General George McClellan, many of his agents—including Timothy Webster—made the transition from detective to Union spy. While many of the agents never completely understood the difference, Webster successfully made the transition and did in fact become a very effective Union spy—for the short remainder of his life.

Pinkerton always felt that "any man meeting Webster would . . . immediately be impressed with the conviction that he was a man who could be trusted; that any duty devolving upon him would be sacredly kept" and Webster's performance during his career proved this assessment to be correct.

Prior to the inauguration of President-Elect Lincoln, Pinkerton sent Webster to Baltimore to infiltrate the Sons of Liberty organization, which was suspected of hatching a plot to assassinate Mr. Lincoln on his way through Baltimore. Webster did become a member of the Sons of Liberty and warned Pinkerton of their intended plot. When the Federal troops moved in and arrested the plotters, Webster, who was present, "escaped" and maintained his value as an agent and infiltrator.

With the commencement of war he was sent south to Tennessee and Kentucky to gather intelligence on secession sentiments of these border states. Again he achieved his goal and was even offered a colonelship in an Arkansas regiment of the Confederate army.

Upon returning to Washington he went to Baltimore and the Sons of Liberty. At this time there was intense pressure from many residents of Maryland to hold a session of the legislature to vote for secession—Maryland was in many ways a Southern state. Webster, working within the Sons of Liberty, was able to identify many of the instigators of the movement and thereby prevent the secession movement from becoming a fact. During his stay in Baltimore, his cover was so effective that a new, aggressive Pinkerton agent arrested him as a Confederate spy. In order to maintain his true identity, Pinkerton arranged for him to again "escape" when they moved him from one prison to another—his cover was never blown.

Pinkerton next sent Webster south to Richmond where his skills as an intelligence agent came into their own. His accomplishments include:

• Being hired by the Confederate Secretary of War Judah Benjamin to be a secret agent for the Confederacy. His main mission was to carry mail and important dispatches to Confederate agents in the Union. On three return trips to the Union he did "carry the mail" and it was delivered—after first being read by Union officials!
• Secretary of War Benjamin supplied Webster with the necessary travel papers that allowed him to move freely throughout the Confederacy.
• On one trip south he actually accompanied a Confederate contractor who was looking for leather for saddles. They visited Knoxville, Chattanooga and Nashville in Tennessee, all important points of interest to the Union. Webster was allowed to tour the cities as he wished throughout the entire trip.

On his third trip back to Richmond, he was accompanied on the Potomac River crossing by two young ladies and their children. When they reached the Virginia coast the weather was bad and the boat could not land, so the ever chivalrous Webster carried the children and the ladies to the shore. Upon landing they spent the first night in a cabin where Webster slept on the floor with no bed covers. This led to his developing rheumatism which plagued him the remainder of his life. That cabin visit was not without its blessings, however. As Webster was lying on the floor he noticed a small oilskin packet that had evidently fallen out of the dress of one of the ladies. Webber took the packet and discovered it was full of maps of Union forces. He sent the packet back to Washington and it led to the arrest of a Confederate spy who was working as a clerk in the Provost Marshal's office.

On Webster's fourth and last trip south, he was stricken with a bout of rheumatism upon arriving in Richmond and was confined to a hotel room. At the time Hattie Lawton and her Negro servant,

John Scobell—both Pinkerton operatives—were also in Richmond and Mrs. Lawton took on the responsibility of nursing Webster back to life. No word was sent to Pinkerton about Webster's condition and over time he became greatly concerned about the safety of his prime agent. His reaction caused a human disaster and again indicates his lack of appreciation of covert operations.

Pinkerton decided to send two agents, Scully and Lewis, to Richmond to ascertain the status of Webster. Upon arrival in Richmond they were immediately followed by Confederate counter-intelligence personnel. Once they had learned the whereabouts of Webster, they paid him a visit—along with their Confederate "tails." Scully and Lewis were arrested as Union spies and Webster was placed under considerable suspicion.

As events would have it, the counter-espionage "pasts" of Scully and Lewis came into play. Early in their careers both Scully and Lewis were involved in Washington in a house search of a suspected Confederate sympathizer, a woman named Mrs. Morton, whose husband had been a U.S. senator from Florida. The search had been conducted in a heavy handed way by Scully and Lewis, much to the consternation of the family. As fate would have it, the Morton family had moved to Richmond and when Chase Morton, the son of the Mortons, heard the news of the capture of the Union agents, he came forward and positively identified the two men as Pinkerton agents!

Scully and Lewis were sentenced to death and put under heavy pressure to tell what they knew of the man Webster—the Confederate agent. Both finally broke and in return for a commutation of their death sentences they implicated Webster.

Webster was arrested, tried and sentenced to death. He was a major embarrassment to the Confederate government. He was a man they had trusted with valuable documents to deliver to their agents in the North—a man who was in fact a Union spy. His death sentence was just retribution.

When Webster was arrested, Mrs. Lawton, who was still nursing him, was also arrested as a Union spy, but John Scobell, the Negro and also a Union spy, was not even suspected. This is a good indication of why Negro spies for the Union were so effective—the Confederate did not give them any credit for intelligence.

Pinkerton, upon hearing the news of the sentence, went immediately to the President who called an emergency session of the Cabinet to discuss the subject. The Union sent a message to the Confederacy stating that if the hanging did take place that the Union had no choice but to hang a Confederate spy in retribution. Up until this time it had been the Union policy to incarcerate the spies for a period and then exchange them for Union prisoners.

The Confederacy ignored the Union warning and on 29 April 1862 Webster was hanged in Richmond. He became the first American to be hanged as a spy since Nathan Hale. At his hanging the rope broke and he had to be hanged the second time. Just prior to the second hanging he said, "I die a second death." One of the observers of the hanging was Elizabeth Van Lew, the Union spy in Richmond.

Scully, Lewis and Mrs. Lawton were imprisoned for a period and then exchanged for Confederate prisoners. All three of these agents' careers ended at this point, Scully and Lewis because of their actions in Richmond and Mrs. Lawton since her true identity had been compromised and she was now known throughout the South.

Timothy Webster is considered to be one of the most effective Union spies in infiltrating the Confederate government. The true importance of the documents he couriered north to be reviewed by the Union officials will never be completely known. We do know, however, that many Confederate agents were compromised by correspondence addressed to them. The value of his overall intelligence gathering was of the strategic nature since he had no courier system to relay time-sensitive information back to Washington. Neither Webster or Pinkerton understood the value of early receipt of time-sensitive intelligence.

It is ironic that while Timothy Webster was Pinkerton's favorite agent, it is Pinkerton who must be ultimately held responsible for his death. His actions in sending Scully and Lewis to Richmond, not realizing that their actions as counter-espionage agents in Washington made their true identities suspect, was a tragic mistake. A mistake that an accomplished spymaster would not make!

Captain Harry H. Young, Sheridan's Valley Man

Captain Harry H. Young, assigned to General Philip Sheridan in the Shenandoah Valley, was at the same time a spy, a local spymaster and a Regular Army officer. He was one of the most valuable officers that General Sheridan had with him in the Valley campaign. Sheridan thought so much of this officer that in April of 1865 he sent the following letter to the Secretary of War:

> Cavalry Headquarters
> Petersburg, Virginia, April 19, 1865
> TO HONORABLE E. M. STANTON,
> Secretary of War, Washington, D. C.
>
> Sir—. . . ; I desire to make special mention of the valuable services of Major H.H. Young, Second Rhode Island Infantry, Chief of my scouts during the cavalry expedition from Winchester, Virginia, to the James River. His personal gallantry and numerous conflicts with the enemy won the admiration of the whole command. In the late campaign from Petersburg to Appomattox Court House he kept me constantly informed of the movements of the enemy and brought in prisoners, from Brigadier-Generals down. The information obtained through him was invaluable. I earnestly request that he be made a lieutenant-colonel by brevet.
> Very respectfully,
> Your obedient servant,
> (signed) P.H. Sheridan
> Major General, Commanding

Young, a member of the Second Rhode Island Infantry, had been assigned to General Sheridan prior to the Shenandoah Valley expedition. At the time of his assignment he was strictly an infantry officer, but over time he became more and more interested in spying and scouting. For the remainder of the Civil War he took great delight in donning a Confederate uniform and infiltrating the enemy lines to gather information. On one occasion he actually joined a Confederate unit and marched with them through the valley. He soon was noticed by General Sheridan and made the head of Jessie's

Scouts, the spy/scout element of Sheridan's army (called Jessie's Scouts in honor of General John Fremont's wife Jessie; Fremont had started the unit).

At its peak Jessie's Scouts consisted of about 40 agents that scoured the Shenandoah Valley for information of value to General Sheridan. One of Young's most famous spies was a young man by the name of Archibald Rowand, who later was awarded the Congressional Medal of Honor for his work as a Jessie's Scout. His spies, like their spymaster, worked in Confederate uniforms, infiltrated the enemy lines, remained there until they had the required information and then returned to the Union lines.

The entire time that Captain Young commanded the Jessie's Scouts unit he remained a regular infantry officer and frequently saw combat. He had the unique ability to be able to keep his two assignments separate and nonconflicting—a special ability, even in today's army.

One of the big coups for Jessie's Scouts and Captain Young's Infantry unit came very near the end of the war. His spies uncovered the information that a Confederate supply train was approaching Appomattox and would probably be the last available for General Lee's troops. Having the intelligence in hand, Captain Young deployed his unit and captured the supply train prior to its arrival in General Lee's area. His actions may have been instrumental in General Lee's surrender, as he had no choice—he had run out of supplies for his army!

General Sheridan was well aware of the capabilities of Major Harry H. Young and had him on his staff continually until well after the Civil War. In fact, Young (at that time a colonel) was with General Sheridan in California when he died—on active duty.

The contribution of Captain Harry H. Young during the Civil War—particularly his leadership of Jessie's Scouts—can be assessed from the above quoted letter of General Sheridan. His scouts/spies, along with the leader himself, did contribute much of the information General Sheridan used in the development of the Shenandoah Valley Campaign. In addition, his actions against the Confederate supply train cannot but have impacted on the action of General Lee just prior to his surrender.

Harry Young was very aware that the intelligence his men collected was of a time-sensitive tactical nature and he made every effort to make sure it was available to General Sheridan prior to any troop deployment or action. He is an excellent example of an early military intelligence man.

Other Male Spies Operating for the Union

JAMES J. ANDREWS—Gained the confidence of the Confederacy by smuggling quinine to them for their medical use in the field. He later was involved in a daring attempt to capture a Confederate train locomotive *The General*. Pursued by the Confederates in a high speed train chase, Andrews and his gang were caught and he was later hanged in Richmond as a spy, despite the fact that he was a Union military man. He was in civilian clothes and therefore considered to be a spy. All members of the group, who survived, were awarded the Congressional Medal of Honor.

"TINKER" DAVE BEATTY—The leader of a band of guerrillas working for the Union in middle Tennessee. He often worked with Dr. Jonathan P. Hale, the chief scout for the Army of the Cumberland under Generals William Rosencrans and George Thomas. Beatty kept watch on the movements and activities of Generals John Morgan, Nathan Forrest and Joseph Wheeler when they were in his area and constantly reported their strength and location to the Army of the Cumberland.

HARRY DAVIES—A Pinkerton man. Prior to the war he had lived in New Orleans and other Southern cities, was familiar with, and capable of imitating or exploiting the customs, chief characteristics and prejudices of the local gentry. He was personally acquainted with many of the leaders of the secession. He had a polished manner, was a handsome man of French descent and had been educated by the Jesuits for the priesthood. However, he found the discipline of a vocation to be distasteful so he turned to the Secret Service for his career. Davies spoke three foreign languages and was widely traveled so it was easy for him to assume the role of an international merchant. Allan Pinkerton thought that Davies' Jesuit education had not been a total failure—he had the power of persuasion of the Jesuits.

Davies was very active for Pinkerton in Baltimore prior to the arrival of President-elect Abraham Lincoln in Washington for his first inaugural. His work was key to the foiling of the attempt to assassinate Lincoln on his way through Baltimore in 1861.

Davies later joined a Union cavalry regiment and served as a cavalry officer throughout the remainder of the war.

"CHARLIE DAVIS"—In reality, Robert W. Boone, the great grandson of Daniel Boone. He was a captain in the Confederate Army when he joined the Union Secret Service. Headquartered in Knoxville, Tennessee, he operated his organization in East Tennessee, western North Carolina, northern Georgia and South Carolina. During his term of service he belonged to eight different Confederate regiments, serving a part of the time as a private, and part as an officer. In both capacities he gained military intelligence of value to the Union. He was known during his time in the Union Secret Service by the name of "Charlie Davis" and is credited with rescuing hundreds of Union prisoners of war and helping them get back to the Union lines.

ALEXANDER GARDNER—When the war began Gardner was the manager of the Matthew Brady Photograph Studio in Washington. He left the studio in 1861 and joined Pinkerton's group as a covert photographer. He worked mainly in conjunction with the U.S. topographical engineers. He created photographs of the terrain that were subsequently turned into maps. He photographed potential battlefields for General George McClellan.

In addition, Gardner took unit photographs of the Union troops. These photographs proved an excellent way to spot a Confederate infiltrator to a unit. The commander would check the photo to isolate any unknown soldiers. The system was so effective that the Confederacy told their potential infiltrators not to ever pose for a unit photograph.

When Pinkerton left the federal service, Alexander Gardner returned to his position at the Brady Studio in Washington. He is credited with taking the last portrait of President Abraham Lincoln, just prior to his assassination.

JOSEPH E. McCABE—Member of Jessie's Scouts in the Shenandoah Valley of Virginia under the command of Major Harry Young. Frequently went behind enemy lines dressed as a Confederate soldier.

On the night before the Battle of Five Forks (near Petersburg, Virginia), March 31, 1865, McCabe went behind enemy lines and succeeded in cutting the telegraph lines between General George Pickett and General Robert E. Lee. The loss of communications was one of the factors that resulted in the evacuation of Petersburg and Richmond.

During the Confederate retreat to Appomattox, in April of 1865, McCabe was involved in the capture of the trains filled with rations intended for the Army of Northern Virginia at Appomattox Station just prior to the surrender. As fate would have it these rations were used to feed the Confederate troops—after the surrender.

THOMAS MCCAMMON—An amateur spy from Hagerstown, Maryland. He carefully watched the movements of the Confederate troops on their way north in June of 1863. Once troops had passed he found the Union forces and reported to General Joseph Hooker and his staff on the movements of General Robert E. Lee's army. The date of his briefing the Union army was 25 June 1863.

JOHN AND CHARLES PHILLIPS—John Phillips arrived in Richmond in 1863 to set up and operate the presses for *The Richmond Dispatch* newspaper. He later sent for his family to join him in Richmond and the family remained there throughout the war. Not only John, but his son Charles, actively worked as spies for the Union during the entire course of the war.

Charles, the son, was only 14 when he joined his father in espionage work. Initially he served as a courier to relay the information gathered and later became an information gatherer himself. His "cover" was to serve as a paperboy and sell newspapers all over town and in the local encampments. He continued to be very successful in his endeavors until he was arrested in January 1865. He spent the last few months of the war in prison in Richmond. However, he was content, as on at least one occasion he had delivered the intelligence he had gathered directly to General U.S. Grant.

B.W. SAUNDERS—Successfully infiltrated the Confederate government and continually passed information back to the Union capital. On one occasion he discovered that the Confederacy had about 2 million dollars worth of supplies on the docks in England ready to ship to the Confederacy. He proposed to the Union that they buy a ship, lend it to him, and he in turn would lend the ship to the Confederacy for the shipment. Once at sea the shipment would be diverted to the Union instead of the Confederacy.

Unfortunately, the Union did not act fast enough and the supplies were shipped on a Confederate ship. Saunders, not to be deterred, did remain inside the Confederate government throughout the war.

WILLIAM T. WOOD—Mr. Wood was the superintendent of the Old Capitol Prison in Washington, D.C., and was also a Pinkerton man. He would interrogate the prisoners upon their arrival at the prison and frequently during their incarceration. Any information derived would immediately be sent to his boss.

In July of 1865, Wood became the chief of the detectives under the direction of the solicitor general of the Department of the Treasury. This represents the beginning of the United States Secret Service. Initially the force was targeted against counterfeiters, smugglers and other criminals of importance to the Treasury Department, and did not include protection of senior government officials until 1901, after the assassination of President McKinley.

Chapter 11

The Confederate Female Spies

Belle Boyd, the Self Appointed "Cleopatra of the Secession"

*B*elle Boyd may well be the most famous female spy of the Civil War. However, her notoriety is not due to her spy success (which appears to be dramatic and marginal at best), but to her love of publicity and fame—areas that professional spies do their best to avoid!

The Boyd family, during the Civil War, appears to have had a family love of spying as not only Belle but at least three of her relatives served as Confederate spies—Captain William B. Compton (cousin), Colonel John Boyd (uncle) and Captain James W. Glenn (uncle). However, Belle can claim the title of the youngest of the Boyd spies as she was only 18 years old when she began her spying career and only 19 when imprisoned in the Old Capitol Prison in Washington, D.C.!

When the Civil War began Belle was living in Martinsburg,

155

West Virginia, where her parents ran a hotel. She gained instant notoriety on the Fourth of July 1861, when she shot a soldier who came to the house to replace the Confederate flag hanging over the front of the house with a United States flag. The soldier later died of his wounds and Belle was tried for her actions, chastised and released. This began her career and exemplified her actions throughout the remainder of the Civil War.

Belle Boyd was not blessed with a pretty face, but a good body. She was particularly noted for having the best looking ankles known—and she used them to her advantage. She evidently had a "winning way" with the Union troops and was most obliging in taking care of their needs. The "beguiling woman" became her modus operanti during her entire espionage career.

Her first success came when the Union forces in the Shenandoah Valley of Virginia were about to face General Stonewall Jackson. From the local Union troops Belle learned of their plan to surround his forces and hopefully take Stonewall prisoner. Having gathered the intelligence she rode about 15 miles to the camp of Stonewall Jackson and personally delivered the information to his staff. Returning to her home she acquired more information and even though the Battle of Front Royal (May 23, 1862) was underway she was determined to deliver her latest intelligence. She arrived at the Union lines, dressed in a blue dress and white bonnet and proceeded to run across to the Confederate lines. When she arrived the dress was full of bullet holes but not one shot had hit the courier. She delivered her intelligence and is credited, by some, with being a force that contributed to Jackson's victory at Front Royal.

After the battle she received a "thank you" letter from General Stonewall Jackson himself. The letter said:

Miss Belle Boyd:

I thank you, for myself and for the army, for the immense service that you have rendered your country today.

Hastily, I am your friend,
T.J. Jackson, CSA

What Stonewall was thanking her for was her information that the Union Generals Nathaniel Banks, Julius White and John Fremont were combining forces to go against General Jackson's forces. Jackson was quick enough to be able to change his strategy and thereby defeat the enemy and save his vastly outnumbered forces.

Belle continued to ply her trade both as a spy and a courier in the Valley until the early summer of 1862 when she was arrested and sent to Baltimore, Maryland, for imprisonment. On the train trip north, Belle made her loyalty known as she waved a Confederate flag out of the train window in every town the train went through. When she arrived in Baltimore, she charmed the prison warden into giving her a warning and then releasing her to once again continue her activities in the Valley, and she did just that.

Continuing her flamboyant acts she was arrested four more times, in very short order. Her spy techniques were not the most polished as she rarely used a code or cipher for her messages and was not the least bit subtle about her loyalty to the Confederacy—still she was able to acquire information from the "admiring" troops. Finally on July 29, 1862, she was imprisoned in the Old Capitol prison in Washington, D.C., where she made her feelings clear by such actions as singing "Dixie" at the top of her lungs. In prison she unwittingly assisted the Union spy J.O. Kerbey in a planned escape by revealing to him the Confederate safe houses on the route south and naming people who would help him along the way. She remained in Old Capitol prison until December of 1863 when she was sent south to Richmond in exchange for Union prisoners. But that was not the last of Belle.

When next encountered she was on a ship, the *Greyhound,* bound for England as a courier for the Confederacy. When arrested and put on a Union ship to return to the United States, Belle, totally undaunted, romanced a Union naval officer, Lt. S. Wylde Hardinge, and successfully got him under her spell. Belle was now deported to Canada while her Union naval officer friend was put in prison for "joining" the enemy. Belle went on to England from Canada and became a celebrity as the famous Confederate spy. She wrote a book on her experiences titled *Belle Boyd in Camp and Prison,* and went on the British stage where she gave readings about her career with such interesting titles as "The Dark Days" and "The Perils of a Rebel Spy."

Her lover, Lt. Hardinge, did not fare as well. He was suspected of helping a Confederate spy escape for which he was courtmartialed and thrown out of the U.S. Navy. But true love prevailed; he followed Belle to England where they were married in August of 1864 in the social event of the British season.

Apparently Belle convinced her new husband to return to the United States and work for the Confederacy as a spy. He did return and was soon thrown into prison again, and there he died. Belle, in England at the time, found herself a widow at the age of 21. She remained in England for the remainder of the war, enjoying her popularity on the stage.

When she returned to the United States she continued her stage career, billing herself as the "Cleopatra of the Secession." The press called her "the Rebel Joan of Arc" and the "Siren of the Shenandoah," and Belle relished all of the attention. She continued on the stage, doing readings from her book for many years. She married two more times, and finally died in 1900 in Kilborn, Wisconsin, where she had gone for a personal appearance. She is buried there and her burial was funded by the women's Auxiliary of the Grand Army of the Confederacy.

There is no doubt that Belle Boyd is a dominant personality of the Civil War, however there is some doubt as to her real contributions to the Confederacy as a spy. While her compatriot Rose O'Neal Greenhow acquired both strategic and tactical intelligence, whatever intelligence Belle did acquire was entirely of the tactical nature—acquired from the local Union troops. She apparently loved the thrills associated with working in espionage, was daring but at the same time flamboyant to the point that she lost her true value to the Confederacy (much as Mrs. Greenhow had done).

Belle does reflect the enthusiasm felt for the Confederate cause, while always keeping in mind her own desire for notoriety and fame. She loved being called the "Cleopatra of the Secession" and played it to the hilt—a behavior pattern not normally attributed to the true intelligence professional. For example, the famous Confederate spy Harrison, according to one theory, also an actor, returned to the stage after the Civil War and no one ever knew that he was the same Harrison of the Battle of Gettysburg fame. Quite different from Miss Belle Boyd!

Rose O'Neal Greenhow, "The Victor of Bull Run"

I employed every capacity with which God has endowed me, and the result was far more successful than my hopes could have flattered me to expect.

Rose O'Neal Greenhow

During the first year of the Civil War there was an indisputable premier spy in the Confederate espionage system—a very well established lady of Washington Society by the name of Rose O'Neal Greenhow. She willingly entered the "spy world" prior to the onset of the war and her contributions to the Confederate efforts are legendary.

Mrs. Greenhow was born to wealthy slaveholding parents in southern Maryland. When she was a young girl her father was murdered by one of the slaves and this event made Rose an avid anti-abolitionist for the remainder of her life. She was an avid supporter of the Confederacy from its birth and was quite open about her feelings. It should be remembered that in 1861 Washington, D.C., was considered a very Southern city, so her feelings were not unusual, only her activities.

For many years Mrs. Greenhow had been part of the Washington Establishment, in fact just prior to President Abraham Lincoln's administration she had been a very close confidante of President James Buchanan. She loved to entertain and she frequently had dinner parties at which the guests included members of the diplomatic circle as well as members of Congress. Invitations to her soirees were coveted in the city, not only for the festivities but also the intellectual conversation.

Her position in the city as well as her feelings about the Confederacy did not go unnoticed. Before the actual outbreak of the war, there was a U.S. military officer stationed in Washington by the name of Captain Thomas Jordan, serving overtly as an assistant quartermaster on the War Department staff and covertly as the man responsible for the recruitment of spies for the Confederacy. He knew of Mrs. Greenhow and without too much trouble recruited her to be not only a Confederate spy but also to be in charge of a spy

159

ring located in Washington. Rose gladly undertook the mission and soon lead an established spy ring in the city that included:

Samuel Applegate, Union soldier
Mr. Callan, clerk for Senate Military Comm.
George Donnelon, clerk in Department of Interior
Anson Doolittle, a double agent (probably working for McClellan)
Miss Betty Duvall, courier for Mrs. Greenhow
F.M. Ellis, assigned to Secret Service on Gen. McClellan's staff
Mr. Fox, clerk in Union Navy Department
Mrs. Betty Hassler, courier for Mrs. Greenhow
James Howard, clerk for provost marshall in Washington
Lewis L. McArthur, clerk for Col. Thompson
Miss Lillie Mackall, courier for Mrs. Greenhow
F. Rennehan, government clerk
William Smithson, banker
Col. M. Thompson, Washington socialite
Dr. Aaron Van Camp, dentist
William Walker, government clerk
M.T. Walsworth, clerk for adjutant general

All of her fellow agents collected information and brought it to her for transmission to the Confederacy. Rose in turn would ask them to collect specific kinds of intelligence as requested by the Confederate intelligence personnel.

Her network was well in place when hostilities commenced in April 1861 and her results were almost immediate. Her first real success, and the one for which she is most remembered, occurred immediately before the first Battle of Bull Run. She plied her trade with Colonel E.D. Keyes who was the secretary to General Winfield Scott, General-in-Chief of the Army, as well as with Senator Wilson of Massachusetts. From these two men and her other sources she was able to provide General Pierre Beauregard with the following information prior to the first battle at Bull Run:

• The Union forces would leave Washington on 16 July to advance toward Richmond.
• There would be 50,000 men.

- They would advance via Arlington, Alexandria, to Manassas and on to Centerville.
- The Union would cut the Winchester Railroad Line to prevent General Joseph Johnston from rushing to the aid of General Beauregard.
- A copy of General McDowell's actual order to his troops.

After receiving the information from Mrs. Greenhow, General Beauregard sent her the following note:

> Let them come: we are ready for them. We rely on you for precise information. Be particular to us with descriptions and destinations of forces, quantity of artillery etc.

And immediately after the battle she received the following note from the government in Richmond:

> Our President and our General direct me to thank you. The Confederacy owes you a debt.

Blushed with success Mrs. Greenhow became even more active in her spying activities and also more obvious. She soon fell under the suspicion of Pinkerton, who hesitated to arrest someone who had been a guest of the Lincolns in the White House, but it soon became all too obvious that she was in fact a Confederate spy.

When she was finally arrested on August 23, 1861, Pinkerton's men committed one of the cardinal sins in counter-espionage. They arrested her in front of her own home and took her inside for questioning. One never arrests suspected spies near their own homes or takes them there for questioning—it not only alerts other agents who might be in the area but provides the agent with the potential of destroying incriminating evidence. Both of these potentials were realized by Mrs. Greenhow.

Just prior to her arrest she advised an agent, with whom she had just had a discussion, that she suspected she was about to be arrested. If so, she would raise a handkerchief to her face as a signal of the arrest—she was arrested and she did alert the agent. When taken into her home she feigned a heat stroke attack and asked to go to her room to change her clothing (noticing that there were no female agents present); she was allowed to change and while there destroyed much of the evidence in the house. In addition, her daughter—a true Greenhow—went outside, climbed a tree and shouted, "My Mother's been arrested," a great way of alerting agents to stay away from the house.

Rose was placed under house arrest in her own home, initially with only her daughter but later with other female prisoners taken by the Union. Her jailer during the house arrest was Lt. N.E. Sheldon, who was far too liberal with the cunning Mrs. Greenhow. She continued to correspond with the Confederacy and to transmit information brought to her by her agents (i.e., the map General George McClellan was using in his campaign—given to her by a congressional clerk). The only saving grace during this period was that the Pinkerton operatives were able to break the simple code that Mrs. Greenhow used and thereby knew much of the information that was going to the Confederacy. For example one message read as follows:

In a day or two 1200 cavalry supported by four batteries of artillery will cross the river above to get behind Manassas and cut off the railroad and other communications with our army whilst an attack is made in front. For God's sake heed this. It is positive. They are obliged to give up. . . They find me a hard bargain, and I shall be, I think, released in a few days without condition, but to go South.

Finally in January of 1862 Mrs. Greenhow, her daughter and her maid were transferred to Old Capitol Prison, which has an irony of its own. When Mrs. Greenhow first came to Washington she stayed with an aunt who ran a boarding house frequented by members of Congress. That building was now the Old Capitol Prison and once again housed Mrs. Greenhow!

Even while in prison, Mrs. Greenhow continued to send messages to the South. She used the rubber balls that her daughter played with to start the messages on their way. She would wrap a message around the ball and then toss it out the window, at a predetermined time, to an agent below who would continue the journey south.

Finally in June of 1862, Rose Greenhow and her daughter were exchanged for Union prisoners and sent south to Richmond. When the party arrived in Richmond they were met by President Jefferson Davis who said to Mrs. Greenhow upon greeting her, "But for you there would have been no Battle of Bull Run."

Mrs. Greenhow soon became restless in Richmond and again wanted to contribute to the cause of the Confederacy. She could no longer enter Union territory as she was too well known, so President Davis decided to use her notoriety to its best advantage. He sent her to Europe to elicit support, both financial and political for the Confederate cause. Mrs. Greenhow willingly accepted the assignment.

In Europe, Mrs. Greenhow continued to use her talents as she captivated everyone she met. She was wined and dined by all of the royalty in France and England. While in Europe, Rose wrote a book about her experiences as a Confederate Spy:—*My Imprisonment and the First Year of Abolition Rule at Washington.* The book became a best seller, not only in the Confederacy but also in Europe.

Finally in the summer of 1864 Rose decided that it was time for her to return to her beloved Confederacy. Arriving on the American side of the Atlantic she boarded the blockade runner *Condor,* for the final stage of her trip. The ship ran aground off the coast of North Carolina, well within the striking distance of a pursuing Union vessel. Mrs. Greenhow, fearful of being arrested again, demanded a small boat and some seamen to row her ashore. The captain, who intially refused due to the rough seas, eventually acceded to her demands and the boat was lowered. Almost immediately a swell tipped the boat over and while the crew members were able to hang on to the overturned boat, Mrs. Greenhow was not. She drowned in large part due to her loyalty to the Confederacy.

Before boarding the small boat Mrs. Greenhow had taken all the gold she was bringing back to the Confederacy, to help fund the war, and sewn it inside her dress. When the boat overturned the weight of the gold pulled her down to her death. The next day a young Confederate soldier reportedly found the body along the shore, found the gold, took it, and then pushed the body back in the water. The next day the body was found and identified, and the young soldier returned the gold, out of respect for Mrs. Greenhow.

Her body was placed in the State Capitol at Richmond for public homage and she was given an official state funeral. Her body is buried in Richmond and to this day every year on the anniversary of her death the Daughters of the Confederacy place a wreath on the grave of Rose O'Neal Greenhow—a true Confederate heroine.

There is no doubt that Mrs. Greenhow was a valuable source of intelligence for the Confederacy during the early stages of the war. She not only developed strategic intelligence but also tactical—and she knew the difference. She was well aware of what had to get to the military forces of the Confederacy in a timely manner and she had the courier system to make it happen. Had Mrs. Greenhow been a little more subtle about her activities she could well have extended her usefulness to the Confederacy—but she was going to carry on her spying in her own style—which was eventually her undoing.

Sarah Slater, A True Mystery Woman

Sarah Slater, a reported Confederate spy and courier, was not known to the Union until after the assassination of President Abraham Lincoln and then only through the testimony of other people. She was never found after the Civil War, either by the government, her husband or other members of her family. Mrs. Slater apparently performed her duties for the Confederacy and then disappeared into thin air.

In the interrogation of the suspects arrested for the assassination of President Lincoln, a French speaking woman named Sarah Slater was frequently mentioned, particularly by a man named Weichman. She was known to the conspirators merely as the "French Woman." Reportedly, the French Woman knew about the Lincoln conspiracy and frequently met with John Wilkes Booth whenever she was in Washington. It was also stated that Mrs. Slater often traveled under the names of Kate Thompson or Kate Brown. None of the information derived from the interrogations could ever be proved as Mrs. Slater aka Kate Thompson aka Kate Brown was never found—actively searched for by the government but never found! But she did exist.

Sarah Slater was born in Connecticut to parents of French derivation. The father and three of his children moved to North Carolina in 1858. The family later moved to New Bern, North Carolina, where Sarah was known as "Nettie." In New Bern, Sarah found love and on June 12, 1861, she married Rowan Slater, a local dance instructor, who had just enlisted in Company A, 20th North Carolina Infantry. From the date of his departure for military service, 23 June 1861, Rowan Slater never saw his wife again even though he survived the entire war.

Sarah not only married a Confederate, but she also became an outspoken supporter of the cause of the Confederacy. She was a "rebel."

Little is known about her activities until January 1865 when she went to Richmond to apply for a passport to go north. She wanted to live with her mother in New York City. Mrs. Slater took her request directly to then Secretary of War Seddon who was impressed with the woman and saw her potential for work in the Confederate secret service. He proposed to employ Mrs. Slater as a courier between Richmond and the Confederate agents in Canada. Her refined looks as well as her knowledge of French would make it easy for her to move in the north without suspicion. Mrs. Slater agreed to the proposal and was quickly pressed into service.

The new Confederate courier was given the initial task of delivering important papers and money to the Canadian operation. The papers and money were to be used for the defense of the Confederate agents held by the Canadian authorities for the St. Albans, Maine, bank raid. Along her way north she was assisted by Gus Howell, a Confederate agent in Maryland, who escorted her as far as New York City.

In New York, Mrs. Slater assumed the role of a French woman and spoke only French or very broken English. Obviously never suspected, she proceeded on to Canada where she delivered both the papers and the money. The papers convinced the Canadian judge that the bank robbers were in fact acting on a military mission for the Confederacy and therefore he did not grant the United States request for extradition. Mission accomplished.

Mrs. Slater left Canada with a parcel of dispatches to deliver to Richmond with the understanding that she would meet John Surratt in New York and he would escort her through southern Maryland. They did indeed meet, and Surratt dutifully escorted Mrs. Slater through southern Maryland and ensured that she made the crossing of the Potomac River back into the Confederacy This was about the 22nd of February of 1865.

The first mission of this Confederate agent was so successful that she once again embarked on a mission to Canada during the first week of March in 1865. As always Mrs. Slater traveled with a heavy veil over her face and the firm conviction that if challenged she would appeal to the French consulate for protection.

Her third and last mission was of quite a different nature. By April of 1865 the Confederacy knew that the continuation of the war was a lost effort. Senior Confederate officials were aware that the Canadian operation still had considerable money and they wanted it moved to England for future private use. Such were the instructions that Mrs. Slater carried with her on this last mission.

Mrs. Slater left Richmond on 1 April 1865 for what would be her final mission for the Confederacy. She stopped over in Washington and visited friends to include John Wilkes Booth, and then on the fourth of April headed north to New York. And disappeared into thin air.

Nothing was ever heard of Sarah Slater after her departure from the city of Washington. Not a member of her immediate family, her husband, her Confederate associates, or any friend ever heard from or of her after this date. For all purposes she had vanished!

One can speculate that she did in fact get to Canada and may have been involved in taking the money to Europe—not for the future personal use of the Confederate officials, but for the use of Mrs. Sarah Slater—however this is not known and never will be. One can also speculate that she vanished because she had in fact known about the Lincoln assassination plot and did not want to be implicated in the witch hunt that took place after the actual assassination. Again, no one will ever know.

One thing is certain. Mrs. Sarah Slater was a very effective courier for the Confederacy. Her early action did prevent the extradition of the St. Alban's bank robbers to the United States. Little is known of her second mission to Montreal, and the third leads to a great deal of speculation. No one disappears without a trace without a reason—Mrs. Slater's reason will never be known—only speculated.

A Sampling of the Lesser Known Confederate Female Spies

MRS. BRAXLEY—Arrested in Washington for acting as a Confederate courier between Baltimore and Richmond. Initially held at Greenhow Prison, the home of Rose O'Neal Greenhow, and later in the Old Capitol Prison in Washington, D.C. Exchanged to the Confederacy at the same time as Mrs. Rose O'Neal Greenhow.

BELLE EDMONDSON—Belle lived in Memphis, Tennessee, during the war and was an active Confederate agent. Her given name was Isabella Buchanan Edmondson but she went by the alias of "Brodie West" when involved in agent work. She supplied not only information to the Confederate Army but also provided much needed supplies, such as pharmaceutical drugs to treat the Confederate wounded.

Miss Edmondson kept an extensive diary of her activities during the war, excerpts of which have recently been published.

ANTONIA FORD—Miss Ford lived equidistant from Washington and Manassas, Virginia. She served as a runner for Rose Greenhow and also liked to entertain Union troops and pass what she learned during these "soirees" on to the Confederacy. She was so successful that Allan Pinkerton became suspicious that a Confederate agent was located near Manassas who was passing timely intelligence to the Confederate forces. He sent a female investigator to the area to find the Confederate agent. She became a good friend of Antonia, who made a fatal mistake. Miss Ford showed the Pinkerton agent the following commendation given to her by General J.E.B. Stuart:

> Know ye, that reposing special confidence in the patriotism, fidelity and ability of Miss Antonia Ford, I, James E.B. Stuart, by virtue of the power vested in me, as Brigadier General in the Provisional Army

167

of the CSA, do hereby appoint and commission her my honorary aide de camp to work as such from this date.

She will be obeyed respected and admired by all the lovers of a noble nature.

The commendation had been given to Miss Ford after she had assisted in the kidnaping of the Union General Edwin Stoughton, two of his captains, 30 enlisted men and 80 horses. She had advised Jeb Stuart of the location of the general and his cadre and the best time to catch them literally napping.

When the Pinkerton agent saw the commendation she knew she had her agent. Miss Ford was arrested and taken to the Old Capitol Prison in Washington. Her lover, a Union officer, with the last name of Willard, had himself transferred to duty at the Old Capitol Prison and there succeeded in getting Miss Ford to sign a loyalty oath. They were married and lived happily ever after. Her husband, Lt. Willard was the son of the owner of the Willard Hotel in Washington where Lincoln had stayed prior to his inaugural.

LAURA RATCLIFFE HANNA—Miss Hanna served as an operative for Colonel John Mosby and his raiders in Northern Virginia. Her home was often the place where Col. Mosby held regular meetings with his officers and men. A nearby rock was known as "Mosby Rock" and was a secret hiding place for the money his troops had stolen from the trains. Mosby's Rock was on Miss Hanna's property and was kept under her watchful eye.

Colonel Mosby wrote the following poem to Laura Hanna and gave it to her along with his watch chain, in gratitude for her services during the war:

And when this page shall meet your glance
Forget not him you met by chance.

NANCY HART—A native Virginian from the mountain area. She so successfully supplied General Stonewall Jackson's troops with information and scouted for them that the Union offered a large reward for her capture. When captured, and placed in jail, she overpowered her guard, stole his rifle, shot him, and successfully escaped on the colonel's horse. She continued to spy and scout for

Confederate troops in the mountains of Virginia throughout the war years.

AUGUSTA MORRIS—Daughter of an Alexandria, Virginia, baker and wife of Virginia doctor. Arrived in Washington soon after the war began and offered to sell the Union the Confederate Army signal plan for $10,000. Turned down by the Union government, she began to ply her trade as a Confederate spy. Used aliases of Ada Hewitt and Mrs. Mason. When arrested she was in bed with a man named Walworth, the clerk for the Adjutant General. Mrs. Morris refused to sign a loyalty oath for the Union and was therefore imprisoned in Old Capitol Prison with Mrs. Greenhow. In June of 1862, along with Mrs. Greenhow and Mrs. Braxley, she was sent south to Richmond and her career appears to end there.

There is speculation that rather than a member of the Rose O'Neal Greenhow spy ring in Washington, Mrs. Morris considered herself to be Mrs. Greenhow's competition. The two were not friendly when both were imprisoned in the Old Capitol Prison.

LOTTIE AND GINNIE MOON—The only known sister spy/courier team on either side of the war. The Moon sisters lived in Tennessee and were Confederate sympathizers. They plied their good looks and at one point Ginnie was engaged to 16 Union soldiers and Lottie to 12 Union soldiers simultaneously! All of these men wrote long letters to the Moon sisters telling them of where they were, what was ahead of them and the morale of the troops.

Lottie must have been a real femme fatale, as just prior to the war she was engaged to the future Union General Ambrose Burnside, whom she literally left standing at the altar when she changed her mind. He never forgot this experience. Later in the war Lottie did marry—Judge Clark—who was active in the Copperhead movement in Tennessee and she periodically traveled to Toronto where she coordinated the uprisings planned for Tennessee.

Both girls often carried messages through the Union lines to Confederate military units. They worked most frequently with General Nathan Forrest.

After the War, Lottie and her husband moved to New York where she worked as a reporter. She next went to Europe as a War correspondent and finally ended up in Hollywood where she did some acting.

ANN PATTERSON/KATE PATTERSON—Sisters-in-law who lived in a house overlooking the Nashville, Tennessee, turnpike. They would raise and lower window shades to signal to the Confederate agents and troops in the area when it was safe to be in the area of the turnpike. Their home served as a safe house for Confederate agents and the women served as collectors of information as well as, in rare cases, couriers.

Chapter 12

The Union Female Spies

Mrs. E.H. Baker: Old Friends Can Be Helpful

When the Civil War began, Mrs. E.H. Baker was living in Chicago, Illinois, and working as a Pinkerton agent. She was one of the more adept female agents that Pinkerton employed and could be counted on to keep her composure at all times. In early 1862, her test came when Pinkerton sent her south on a specific mission—to find out about the undersea boats the Confederates were rumored to be constructing.

Mrs. Baker had lived in Richmond prior to her arrival in Chicago and she continued to maintain a correspondence with many of her old friends in Virginia. One of her close family of friends in Richmond were the Atwaters—who conveniently had a son in the Confederate Army in Richmond as a captain. Mrs. Baker wrote and told them that despite the regional differences she intended to come to

Richmond to see the Atwaters and other old friends. The Atwaters were delighted and invited her to stay in their home while she was in Richmond. All was well.

About a week after her arrival, after touring the land earthworks and other fortifications around Richmond, she asked Captain Atwater if she could tour the Tredigar Iron Works (where the secret underwater ships were being built). He agreed immediately and a date was set. As luck would have it, Captain Atwater could not make that date as he had to go to the "sea trials" for the new submarine rams—but would Mrs. Baker like to join him for the day and make a picnic out of the event. Our agent replied that she would enjoy that immensely and so the whole family went to see the new underwater ships.

What Mrs. Baker saw was indeed the underwater ships that the Confederacy was in the process of building. The ships consisted of a submerged craft in which three or four people operated the mechanism. Above the crew at water level was a large raft, painted green, that had air hoses down to the submerged ship so that the crew could breath. The function of the craft was to close in on a ship, probably at night, attach a charge to the side of the ship, back off a distance and then fire the fuse thereby blowing up the ship. And that is what Mrs. Baker saw successfully tested on her picnic day.

The next day, luck again was in her favor as she went to the Tredigar Iron Works in Richmond for a tour and the centerpiece of her tour was an actual inspection of one of the submergible ships under construction. She was told at that time that the Confederacy hoped to have two of the ships in the mouth of the James River within two months. Mrs. Baker had indeed completed the first part of her mission. Now all she had to do was to make copious notes and report all of the information to the authorities in Washington.

Within a few days, Mrs. Baker ended her visit in Richmond, thanked the Atwaters for their hospitality (which was more than they knew) and worked her way back to Union territory. Once there she reported what she had seen to the War Department and the Navy ships in the James River were alerted to watch for the new device.

Just about the time the Confederacy predicted to Mrs. Baker that the boats would be operational, a U.S. Navy boat dragging the entrance to the river did in fact pull up the air hoses from the raft to the ship of the new invention and thereby saved a Union ship. The surprise element hoped for by the Confederacy was lost—due mainly to the expertise of one Mrs. Baker and the gallantry of a Confederate captain—Captain Atwater.

When Pinkerton returned to private business, Mrs. Baker apparently went with him as there are no other records about Mrs. Baker in the Federal Secret Service. She does represent one of Pinkerton's agents whose spying activities in the Civil War can definitely be tied to a successful Union event based on intelligence input.

Mrs. Baker's success was in no small part due to the Southern attitude that women were beautiful objects without a real brain in their heads, and could not possibly understand something as complicated as the new underwater boats under development at the Tredigar Iron Works. How wrong they were!

Pauline Cushman: Sentenced to Be Hanged!

Pauline Cushman has the somewhat dubious honor of almost being hanged by her Confederate captors. Sentenced to death by General Braxton Bragg, her execution was about to take place when a Union raider force attacked the camp and drove the Confederates away. They did not know of the act that was about to take place there (had General Bragg's orders been carried out Miss Cushman would have become the only female spy hanged by either side during the entire Civil War).

Harriet Wood, the true name of Pauline Cushman, was born in New Orleans, but was a truly dedicated Unionist. When the war began there was only one way for her to serve her beloved country and that was as a spy—and she did just that. Early in the war she became a secret agent and was of immediate use to the Union army in the west. Initially she was sent to St. Louis to ferret out the Confederate spies in the area. She did this with aplomb.

Her next assignment was to Nashville, Tennessee, to perform the same task—find the Confederate spies and their methods of communications to Richmond. To assist her in this task Miss Cushman, as she was then known, went on the stage—she was an actress by profession—in Nashville. She connived to have Union officers in the audience dare her to propose a toast to President Jefferson Davis of the Confederacy, which she did much to the glee of the audience. As a result of this action she was "thrown out" of the Union as a Confederate sympathizer. How easy it was for her then to go about her task of identifying Confederate agents!

In May of 1863, as General William Rosecrans was preparing to drive General Bragg across the Tennessee River, Miss Cushman was given a new assignment. She was sent into the Confederate lines to ascertain the strength and location of the Army of Tennessee. She complied and was plying her trade when captured. Papers on her proved without a doubt her true mission and General Bragg, frustrated with all the spies, sentenced her to be hanged on the spot. Fortunately, Shelbyville, Tennessee, where she was under guard, soon had to be evacuated. The harried troops forgot about their hanging mission and retreated, leaving Miss Cushman to be found by the Union troops.

Unfortunately for the Union Army, the news of the rescuing of Miss Cushman spread throughout the land and she became a very famous person overnight. That ended her active career as a spy—her true identity had been compromised. She did however continue to advise the Union army on the geographic terrain of Tennessee, Alabama and Mississippi, all areas that she knew quite well. This information was most useful as good maps were very rare at the time.

After her rescue, the Union bestowed the honorary title of "Major" on Miss Cushman and thereafter she always wanted to be called "Major Cushman." She was a beautiful woman and was very well liked by the Union forces for she was extremely brave and daring in her missions.

After the war "Major" Cushman returned to her stage career and had herself introduced as "Major Cushman" for her performances. She however, unlike Belle Boyd, never talked about her spy activities on the stage. She married in her later life, continuing to act until her career waned. In need of money she later became a dressmaker's assistant and charwoman. At this point of her life she was living in the far West and it is there that she died in 1894. She was buried, with military honors, in the Grand Army plot of a local cemetery. Her simple marker reads:

"Pauline Cushman, Federal Spy and Scout of the Cumberland"

Harriet Wood aka Pauline Cushman was known as the "Belle Boyd" of the Union. There is no doubt there are similarities: they were both actresses, both strongly believed in their causes and both later continued their acting careers, using their Civil War experiences as a drawing card. The difference between the two ladies is that unlike Belle, Pauline was much more subtle and professional in her spying activities. Her work in St. Louis and Nashville is credited with ferreting out many Confederate spies—a task that requires a very quiet manner—and her assistance to the mission of the Union army was quietly undertaken. She was a self-styled professional.

Emma Edmonds, the Woman with a Black Face

Emma Edmonds was one of approximately 400 women who succeeded in enlisting in the army (either Union or Confederate) during the Civil War. Her uniqueness is that she not only succeeded in remaining in the army for several years, but was also eminently successful as a Union spy—all while impersonating a man.

Born in Nova Scotia, Emma had a very difficult early life. Her father greatly resented the fact that she was not born a boy and subsequently he treated her badly in her early life. To counter his temper Emma did all she could to prove that she was in fact a boy underneath her femininity. Finally the father's treatment got so abusive that Emma fled from her home to the United States where she quickly adapted to a new life. The United States became her country and it was a natural thing for her to want to defend "her country" when the war began.

Emma was living in Flint, Michigan, when the first call for Union enlistments went out. She wanted to answer the call. So she cropped her hair, got a man's suit of clothing, took the name of Frank Thompson and tried to enlist. It took her four tries but finally she did in fact get sworn into the Union Army (at that time the physical consisted merely of asking the enlistee questions—no medical examination). On April 25, 1861, Emma Edmonds alias Frank Thompson became a male nurse in the Second Volunteers of the United States Army.

After training in Washington, D.C., Emma's unit was sent south to be part of McClellan's campaign in Virginia. Private Thompson (Emma) was assigned as a male nurse to the hospital unit of the 2nd Michigan Volunteers and had no trouble in maintaining her masculine masquerade. Even before the hostilities erupted on a full scale two events occurred that changed Private Thompson's life forever. The events were:

• A Union agent working in Richmond for McClellan was caught and faced a firing squad. This left a void in the intelligence gathering for McClellan.
• A young officer, named James Vesey, who Emma had known back in Canada, was killed on a patrol. Emma, not knowing this, went to see him and arrived at his unit just as his funeral was about to begin.

As a result of these events, when the word went out that McClellan's staff was looking for a person to act as a spy prior to the campaign—Private Frank Thompson volunteered. She studied all she could find on weapons, tactics, local geography and military personalities and when interviewed for the position, Private Thompson so impressed the staff that the position was his (hers).

Prior to her first mission, Private Thompson had to devise a disguise that would not alert the Confederates to her real mission—and she decided to enter the Confederacy as a black man. Assisted by the wife of the local chaplain, the only person knowing her true identity, she used silver nitrate to darken her skin to the point that the doctor she worked for in the hospital did not recognize her. She donned men's clothing along with a black minstrel wig—chose the assumed name of "Cuff"—and departed on her first mission.

Once on the Confederate front she was soon assigned to work on the ramparts being built by the local Negroes to counter McClellan. Her hands were so blistered after the first day that she convinced a fellow slave to swap jobs with her and the second day she worked in the kitchen and all the time she kept her eyes and ears open. She learned a great deal about the morale of the troops, the size of the army, weapons available, and even discovered the "Quaker guns" (Logs painted black to look like cannons from afar) that were to be used at Yorktown.

After the second day, she was luckily assigned as a Confederate picket, which allowed her to escape and return to the Union side. The information she delivered was well received and she even had a personal interview with McClellan—after which she returned to duty as a male nurse in the hospital unit—but not for long.

About two months later, she once again was ordered to infiltrate the Confederate lines. She did not want to return as "Cuff," so she went as a fat Irish peddler woman with the name of Bridget O'Shea. Once again she successfully gained admittance to the Confederate camps—sold some of her wares and garnered as much information as she could. She returned to the Union camp not only with the information but with a beautiful horse from the Confederate camp, that she named Rebel. In the process of returning on this trip, Private Frank Thompson was wounded in the arm, but managed to stay in the saddle and elude the Confederates in the chase.

With the battle in Virginia slowing down, the Second Michigan was transferred to the Shenandoah Valley, in Virginia, to support the efforts of General Philip Sheridan. Private Thompson's reputation as a nurse and also as a spy preceded the transfer and Private Thompson soon found new territory for spying. On several occasions Emma went behind the Confederate lines as "Cuff," a fellow of whom Emma herself said, "I truly admire the little fellow—he's a plucky one; got his share of grit."

In August of 1862, Private Thompson again went behind enemy lines and this time Emma went as a black mammy complete with the black face and the bandanna. On this trip she became a laundress in the camp and while cleaning an officer's coat a packet of official papers fell out of his pocket. Emma quickly picked them up and decided it was time to return to the Union side with the packet. She did and the officers were delighted with the information she had garnered.

At the end of 1862, her unit was transferred and this time they were sent to the Ninth Corps, commanded by General Ambrose Burnside, near Louisville, Kentucky. As before, the reputation of Private Thompson preceded the transfer and his secret missions continued in the new area. Here he was asked to assume the role of a young man with Southern sympathies by the name of Charles Mayberry, and go to Louisville to assist in identifying the Southern spy network in the town. Once again, Private Thompson succeeded in his mission—this time just prior to the unit's transfer to the army of General Grant in preparation for the battle of Vicksburg.

Under General Grant, Private Thompson worked long hours in the military hospital until a real dilemma arose. She became ill with malaria and could not admit herself to the hospital where her true identity would be discovered. After much soul-searching Emma decided that she had to leave camp for awhile and recover in a private hospital. Arriving in Cairo, Illinois, she once again became a woman and checked herself into a hospital for treatment of malaria. Once recovered Emma planned to don her uniform and rejoin her unit—that is until she read the army bulletins posted in the window of the Cairo newspaper office. There on the list of deserters from the Union army was the name of Private Frank Thompson.

With the last of her funds, Emma Edmonds bought a train ticket to Washington where she worked as a nurse until the end of the war. There would be no more secret missions for Private Frank Thompson to add to the eleven successful missions in his career.

After the war Emma wrote her memoirs titled *Nurse and Spy in the Union Army,* which became a very popular book selling thousands of copies. Emma gave all of her profits from the book to the U.S. war relief fund. Once the book was completed Emma became homesick for her native Canada; when she returned there she found love. In 1867 Emma married Linus Seeyle and went back to the United States, initially to Cleveland, Ohio. The marriage was happy, and Emma raised three sons, one of whom enlisted in the army "just like Mama did."

While happy in her family life Emma continued to brood over being branded a deserter in the Civil War. With the encouragement of her friends she petitioned the War Department for a full review of her case. The case was debated and on March 28, 1884, the House of Representatives passed House Bill Number 5335 validating Mrs. Seelye's case. The House Bill includes the following statements:

Truth is ofttimes stranger than fiction, and now comes the sequel, Sarah E. Edmonds, now Sarah E. Seelye, alias Franklin Thompson, is now asking this Congress to grant her relief by way of a pension on account of fading health, which she avers had its incurrence and is the sequence of the days and nights she spent in the swamps of the Chickahominy in the days she spent soldiering.

That Franklin Thompson and Mrs. Sarah E.E. Seelye are one and the same person is established by abundance of proof and beyond a doubt. She submits a statement . . . and also the testamony of ten credible witnesses, men of intelligence, holding places of high honor and trust, who positively swear she is the identical Franklin Thompson. . . .

On 5 July 1884, a special act of Congress granted Emma Edmonds alias Frank Thompson an honorable discharge from the army, plus a bonus and a veteran's pension of twelve dollars a month.

The resulting Special Act of Congress read:

Be it enacted by the Senate and House of Representatives of the United States of America in Congress assembled, That the Secretary of Interior is hereby, authorized and directed to place on the pension-roll, the name of Sarah E.E. Seelye, alias Frank Thompson, who was late a private in Company E, Second Regiment of Michigan Infantry Volunteers, at the rate of twelve dollars per month.

Approved, July 5, 1884

Now satisfied Emma lived out the rest of her life in La Porte, Texas, where she died on September 5, 1889. She is buried in the military section of Washington Cemetery in Houston, Texas. In honor of her duty and devotion to her country she is the only female member of the organization formed after the Civil War by Union veterans—The Grand Army of the Republic (GAR).

In her own words Emma Edmonds said of her adventures:

I am naturally fond of adventure, a little ambitious, and a good deal romantic—but patriotism was the true secret of my success.

Elizabeth Van Lew, World Class Union Spy

The most successful spy, Union or Confederate, was also the most incongruous possible! She was a member of the Virginia aristocracy—very much the lady—who lived in Richmond and spied for the Union during the entire course of the war. Her name was Elizabeth Van Lew and she is ranked by knowledgeable experts in the field of espionage as one of the great female spies of all times! Which is very remarkable when one realizes that Miss Van Lew had absolutely no training as a spy and yet she developed a "tradecraft" that far excelled any of her contemporaries.

Miss Van Lew was born in 1818 to a very wealthy family in Richmond. She was sent North for her education which may account for her absolute hatred of slavery and all that it entailed. Before the Civil War Miss Van Lew's family had freed all of the family slaves and even sent some of them North for an education. The freed slaves were very loyal to the family and most stayed with her throughout the war and even into her later life. Her slaves knowingly became a very important part of her spy operation—especially by acting as couriers of information. They must have been well indoctrinated by Miss Van Lew as not a single one of her slaves was ever caught by the Confederacy for illicit activities or revealed Miss Van Lew's activities to the authorities.

With the commencement of the war, Miss Van Lew decided independently that she would keep the government in Washington informed of the events happening in the South—particularly in Richmond, the new Confederate capital. She did not know to whom she should correspond, so initially her correspondence went to the President. A little later she worked with the commander of Fort Monroe and finally when General Grant took over command in the East she sent her messages directly to General Sharpe, Grant's intelligence officer—in some cases she sent them to General Grant himself. Her messages were always well received and the importance of them can be estimated from this quote of General Sharpe:

> For a long, long time she represented all that was left of the power of the U.S. government in Richmond . . . The greater portion of our intelligence in 1864–65 in its collection and in good measure in its transmission we owed to the intelligence and devotion of Elizabeth Van Lew.

Miss Van Lew was not quiet about her feelings regarding slavery in Richmond—she spoke publicly on the subject as well as on her feelings about the war (i.e., she defiantly refused to help make shirts for the Confederate soldiers). However, she still managed to remain free throughout the war. How did she do it? First of all Miss Van Lew was a member of the old line Virginia aristocracy and therefore it was incomprehensible that such a person would ever dream of spying for the Union, and secondly without any special training she developed truly exceptional "spy tradecraft" which served her throughout the war. Some examples of what she did include:

• In order to allay suspicions of her activities she recruited her elderly mother to work with her—particularly in visiting the prisons. Her mother must have been cut out of the same cloth as she joined in willingly and became a very adept agent in her own right.
• She became known as "Crazy Bet" by the locals because she visited prisons and other unsavory places. She was known as a person who did not keep herself very "neat and tidy" and was assumed to be not in total control of her right senses. The feelings were so wide spread that one Richmond newspaper devoted an entire column to Miss Van Lew and her mother's shocking activities. The article talked of "two ladies, mother and daughter, living on Church Hill . . . who attracted public notice by their assiduous attention to Yankee prisoners." So what did Miss Van Lew do? She played on this reputation and became even more disheveled. The city of Richmond had given her excellent cover!
• Understanding the value of the messages she sent North and the misfortune that would befall her if they fell into the wrong hands, she always tore her messages into several parts and sent each part by a different courier and via a different route. If one section fell into enemy hands they had nothing but a piece of paper with a lot of "gibberish" on it. This technique is taught to this day!
• Miss Van Lew was well aware of the "time factor" involved with her message and she solved this problem better than any of the spymasters—either Union or Confederate. What she did was to establish five relay stations between her home in Richmond and the Union lines. Each relay station was manned by members of her house staff and they all knew what their mission was—to deliver the message to the Union lines as soon as possible. The system worked throughout the war and not one of her couriers were ever

caught. The system was so effective that she even had fresh flowers delivered to General Grant for his table—probably with a message inside.

• Unlike Belle Boyd who rarely used cipher, Miss Van Lew always enciphered her messages. She used a cipher that she herself had created and only she used. After her death in 1900 when the back of her watch was opened the key to her cipher was found. All of her messages were written in a colorless liquid which became visible with the application of milk. Her code consisted of a 5 by 6 matrix with letters and numbers in the cells. All of her communications were signed with the psuedonym of "Mr. Babcock."

• Frequently her couriers carried innocent looking letters exchanging family news between Miss Eliza Jones and her dear Uncle James Jones, who lived behind enemy lines in Norfolk. In reality, these letters were intended for General Butler at Fort Monroe. He knew that written between the lines of the letter was information about Confederate activities in Richmond, written in the invisible ink used by Miss Van Lew.

• She built a spy ring in Richmond that gleaned information for her and always kept her informed. In picking the members of her ring she carefully picked established citizens of Richmond and not the adverturist-types that some would have selected. Her ring included:

Philip Cashmeyer, detective for Gen. Winder (CSA) and agent for Miss Van Lew
Mrs. Graves (Green?), housewife
Martin M. Lipscomb, supplier of goods to CSA
Frederick W.E. Lohman, owner of a German restaurant
Robert Orrick, farmer
Charles Palmer, local merchant
"Quaker," identity known to Gen. Butler
Mrs. Lucy Rice, housewife
Walter S. Rowney, farmer
Samuel Ruth, manager of railroad
Franklin Steane, whiskey distiller
John G. Timberlake, associate of Mrs. Ruth

(It is also probable that Samuel Ruth and both Charles Phillips and his son John had connections to the Van Lew Ring as well as J.O. Kerbey and other members of the extensive Union Richmond Underground.)

It is interesting to note that while a spy for Miss Van Lew, Martin M. Lipscomb ran for mayor of Richmond and was almost elected—what a coup that would have been!

• Infiltration of the enemy camp is always an excellent way to glean intelligence and Miss Van Lew was very successful in this endeavor. She had sent a female servant of hers, Miss Mary Elizabeth Bowser, to the North to get an education. When the capital of the Confederacy moved to Richmond Miss Van Lew asked Miss Bowser to return to Richmond to do a task for her. What Miss Van Lew did was to get Miss Bowser hired as an employee in the presidential mansion where she worked as a nanny for the children and a waitress in the dining room. This provided Miss Van Lew with an excellent first hand source of information. It also tells you something about the loyalty of the servants to Miss Van Lew. The girl willingly left the security of the North to come South because Miss Van Lew needed her!

• Since in addition to their home in Richmond, the Van Lews owned a farm outside of Richmond, she brazenly went to the authorities and acquired military passes for her staff so they could go back and forth to the farm for produce and other errands. What the Confederates failed to realize was that this route was the first leg of a message's journey north. She employed baskets with false bottoms as well as hollow eggs that could contain a message.

All of the above are excellent examples of "spy tradecraft" and when one realizes that Miss Van Lew utilized all of them with no training or exposure to such a life style it is truly remarkable and the mark of a very talented and dedicated person.

Crazy Bet's visit to Libby Prison along with her mother were very frequent and profitable. They learned a great deal about future Confederate plans from the newly arrived prisoners as well as the escape plans of the prisoners in which they often assisted. One famous escape that was assisted by Miss Van Lew in company with Mrs. Rice and Mrs. Green was the escape of over 100 prisoners via a tunnel. Miss Van Lew hid several in her home and her partners helped to guide some of the escapees to freedom. To avoid any problems at the prison, when Miss Van Lew discovered that the newly arrived commander of Libby prison could not find a place to live, she offered him and his wife quarters in her home—which they gladly accepted.

Little did the man realize that the very house he was living in was a safe house for escaped prisoners! In her home Miss Van Lew had a room permanently ready to receive escaped Union prisoners. It had blankets over the windows and always had a gas heater going to keep it warm. She also had what she called the "End Room," which had a spring door that was hidden behind a book case. Neither room was ever discovered and they were frequently used. Near the end of the war when all horses were being confiscated for the war Miss Van Lew hid her last horse in one of these rooms, just in case it was needed to send a fast message north. Her diary contains this reference to the horse:

> He accepted at once his position and behaved as though he thoroughy understood matters, never stamping loud enough to be heard, nor neighing.

In early 1864, General Benjamin Butler of the Union army in Virginia planned a surprise attack on Richmond to free the Union prisoners held in the Old Libby Prison and possibly to kidnap President Jefferson Davis. On February 14, 1864, as he was in the final planning stages, he received a cipher message from Miss Van Lew which stated:

- The Confederacy was planning to move the Union prisoners away from Richmond to Georgia in the near future.
- Information regarding the number and locations of Southern troops around the city of Richmond.
- The city of Richmond could be taken easier than at any other time since the war began.

The attack, when launched, was quickly repulsed due to the fact that a Union deserter named William Boyle had informed the Confederate authorities about the impending raid.

While Miss Van Lew was never jailed or caught for her espionage activities, she did pay dearly. Just before the end of the war when a mob came to burn her house down, she stood on the porch and said words to the effect: "I know all of you and if you burn this house, as soon as the Union troops arrive, they will burn all of your houses down." With this the crowd dispersed.

When Richmond was set ablaze just prior to the Union entry into the city, it was reported that Miss Van Lew could be seen sifting through the ruins at the Confederate capitol looking for pieces of documents that would be of use to the United States government. One cannot say that she pulled her oars in before the war ended.

When General Godfrey Weitzel and the Union troops entered Richmond, one of his first acts was to implement an order given to him by General Grant. Grant realizing the potential of hostile feelings toward Miss Van Lew had ordered the assignment of a detail to protect Miss Van Lew and her property. She soon gave one of the first receptions in Richmond—and of course it was for a Yankee, Chief Justice Chase and his daughter. In her own words she describes her life after the war:

> I live here in the most perfect isolation. No one will walk with us on the streets, no one will go with us anywhere (Miss Van Lew and an invalid niece were all that were left of the family); and it grows worse and worse as the years roll on and those I love go to their long rest.

As her entire spy operation had been run with her own money, when the war was over "Crazy Bet" had very little money left. The family hardware business had fallen unto hard times with the death of her brother. When General Grant became President he named her the postmaster of Richmond—a position she held throughout the Grant administration. In 1877, Grant wrote to President Hayes on Miss Van Lew's behalf stating:

> Miss Van Lew was appointed by me as Postmaster of Richmond, Va., soon after my entrance (sic) from a knowledge of entire loyalty during the Rebellion and her service to the Cause. She has filled the office since then with capacity and fidelity, and is very deserving of continued confidence of a Republican administration. . . .

President Hayes chose not to re-appoint Miss Van Lew. President

Grant also proposed to Congress an outright gift of $15,000 for her services rendered. Congress never got around to enacting the gift and Miss Van Lew ended her years living in poverty. She was supported mainly by the loyal servants whom she had freed and donations from the Union prisoners she had helped to free.

Miss Elizabeth Van Lew died in 1900. She was still so detested in Richmond that no one from Richmond attended her funeral and the only mourners were the relatives of a Union soldier she had aided and her devoted servants. After her death, a group of admirers in Boston (the relatives of Colonel Paul Revere whom she had hidden in her secret room) had a gravestone placed in her burial site. The stone was a slab of Massachusetts granite with a bronze plaque that read:

She risked everything that is dear to man—friends, fortune, comfort, health, life itself, all for the one absorbing desire of her heart—that slavery might be abolished and the Union preserved.

The stone itself contains the following marker:

This Boulder

From the Capitol Hill in Boston, is a tribute from her Massachusetts friends.

On a scrap of paper in her diary Miss Van Lew had written what might be considered her own epitaph, which reads:

If I am entitled to the name of "spy" because I was in the Secret Service, I accept it willingly; but it will hereafter have to my mind a high and honorable signification. For my loyalty to my country I have two beautiful names—here I am called "Traitor," farther North a "Spy"— instead of the honored name of "Faithful."

The true value of Miss Van Lew's endeavors during the Civil War will never be known. In 1866, at her personal request, the War Department purged their files of all communications from Miss Van Lew. The papers were given to her personally and she immediately burned all of them. This action goes along with the personality of Miss Elizabeth Van Lew—but what a loss for the modern students of both history and espionage. She set a standard that has not been met by many of her counterparts—and she did it all out of love for her country and mankind!

A Sampling of the Lesser Known Union Female Spies

FRANCES ABEL: Mrs. Abel apparently lived in Baltimore, Maryland, and was utilized as a spy for the Union. From the pay voucher below, it appears that when she was on a spying mission she impersonated a man. Correspondence regarding her mission, found in files at the National Archives includes:

Headquarters, Middle Department
Office of Provost Marshal, 8th Army Corps
Balt. January 27, 1863

To Guards and Police:

The bearer, Mrs. Frances Abel, is employed by me on secret and important Service and as such is entitled to pass without molestation while in the performance of her duties.

William Fullicolt (?)
Provost Marshal.

Later on February 15, 1863, Mrs. Abel submitted a voucher to cover the cost for pants, coat and vest. (Obviously, when on her mission she wore men's clothing). The voucher contained her pay for the mission: $2 a day. It should be noted that the pass given to Mrs. Abel in order to pass freely is very explicit about her mission. Not a very good security measure.

HATTIE LAWTON—Mrs. Lawton was the wife of a Union Army captain. She was also a Pinkerton operative, who entered government service with her boss, Allan Pinkerton. She was particularly active during the initial part of the war. Mrs. Lawton traveled extensively in the Confederacy, often with the Negro operative John Scobell, as well as with Pinkerton's favorite agent, Timothy Webster.

She was arrested along with Timothy Webster in early 1862 and imprisoned. She continued to nurse the ailing Timothy Webster while in prison and was with him just prior to his execution. Mrs. Lawton was later exchanged in one of the regular prisoner exchanges.

Pinkerton credits Mrs. Lawton with the development of a great deal of intelligence during the early phase of the war. Due to her time away from the Union most of her intelligence would have been of a strategic nature and not of immediate value to the Union forces. If she uncovered intelligence of immediate value she often sent John Scobell back to the Union side with the specifics.

Little is known of Mrs. Lawton after her exchange. Her value as an infiltrator of the Confederacy was gone as her identity was known to Confederate officials.

JEANETTE LAURIMER MABRY—Mrs. Mabry was the wife of Colonel George W. Mabry, of the Confederate army. While the entire Mabry family, living in East Tennessee, was Confederate, Mrs. Mabry, a staunch Unionist, fed information to the Union throughout the entire war.

Mrs. Mabry according to one source "always had the latest news from the front." She was in constant contact with practically every guide, spy and envoy in her area from the Federal lines.

MRS. RICE AND MRS. GREEN—These two women lived in Richmond, Virginia, and worked with the Union agent, Elizabeth Van Lew. While it is not known if they actively spied for her, it is documented that they served as guides and points of contact for Union prisoners who escaped from Libby Prison in Richmond. They were both involved in the Libby Prison break when over 100 Union prisoners escaped.

DR. MARY E. WALKER—A contract surgeon with the Union army in the West, for the first three years of the war she served as a nurse/doctor. However, from March until August of 1864, during the Atlanta Campaign, Dr. Walker not only served as a doctor but also a spy. Assigned to the 52nd Ohio Infantry she would go ahead of the troops, ostensively to assist the civilian population and garner all the intelligence she could.

Dr. Walker is the only American woman to receive the Congressional Medal of Honor, and not for her medical skills but rather for her espionage skills. The medal was stripped from her in 1917 (along with over 900 other winners) and later restored to the family in 1975 by President Carter.

REBECCA WEST—A Quaker school teacher in Berkley County, West Virginia, she went about gathering information and reporting it to General Philip Sheridan prior to the Battle of Opequon in the Shenandoah Valley of Virginia. Her efforts are credited for General Sheridan's victory.

There are undoubtedly many other Union women who served their country in the intelligence area but they remain unknown and unheralded to this day. There is little doubt that the Union women did contribute to the intelligence efforts of the Union—and they did it willingly and without thought of their personal safety.

Chapter 13

Listing of Known Spies

The following list of both Union and Confederate spies constitutes all of the names that were uncovered in the process of doing the research for this book. Some of the names are addressed in the text while others appear only in the listing—that is all that is known of them. The list is in no way intended to be an all-inclusive listing of the people who operated as spies during the Civil War. It is intended only as an aid to the reader—hopefully there will be readers who can fill in some of the blanks about personnel on the listing, or add additional names.

It should be remembered that not all spies used their real names or in their accounts listed their fellow spies by their true names. What we have in the list are the names as they appear in the written texts used in the research. Names appearing within quotes are names known to be aliases.

The following abbreviations have been used in the listing:

CSA   Confederate States of America

DC   District of Columbia
KGC   Knights of the Golden Circle
NYC   New York City
ops   Operations
RR   Railroad
UK   United Kingdom
Valley   Shenandoah Valley
VP   Vice President

Alphabetical Listing of Spies

Abel, Mrs. Frank—Union spy who operated wearing men's clothing

Abraham, Thomas, Private—Union soldier executed as CSA spy

"Allen, E.J."—Alias used by Pinkerton when he traveled south as spy

Anderson, Ben, Col CSA—CSA agent who turned traitor

Anderson, Edward C., Col—CSA agent in UK with Bulloch

Anderson, Richard B., Sgt—CSA spy with C.E. Coleman

Andrews, J.J.—Union spy for General Buell, captured, hanged in Atlanta, 1862, for leading railroad raid.

Applegate, Samuel—Union soldier in employ of CSA agent, R. Greenhow

Aragon, Teodoso—CSA spy from Texas

Arnold, Samuel—Imprisoned in Lincoln plot

192

Listing of Known Spies

Ascot, William—Pinkerton agent

Ashbrook, Philip, Lt—CSA operative at NYC fire

Ashby, Turner, Col CSA—CSA spy who donned Union uniform and entered Union lines as a vet to treat the horses and gather data

Atzerodt, George—Hanged in Lincoln plot

Ayer, J. Winslow—Patent medicine salesman who spied for Union in prison camps (Camp Douglas) and in Sons of Liberty in Chicago

Babcock, John C. Mr.—With General Sharpe at Gettysburg—advised Meade to attack Lee on 4 July, also handler for Mr. Pole on trip to Richmond

Bailey, Josiah E.—CSA spy

Baker, Mrs. E. H.—Spy for Pinkerton who supplied Union with data on CSA underwater ships

Baker, Lafayette—Actual head of Union spy service in Washington after Pinkerton left

Bangs, George H.—Pinkerton field operative with Union military

"Barton, John"—Alias used by Mrs. McCarty when disguised as man and spying for CSA

Bates, David—Union cryptanalyst in DC

Battus, William—CSA spy in Valley

Beall, John Yates, Lt—CSA agent hanged in NYC

Beattie, Kate—CSA spy caught in Mo.

Beatty, "Tinker Dave"—Union spy in West

Benson, Berry Sgt—CSA spy

Bettersworth, J.J., Lt, CSA—Revealed Hines Chicago uprising plans to Union

Bissel, Jerry—CSA spy

Blackburn, Luke D. Dr—Developed idea for biological warfare for CSA

Blake, Henry—Union Negro spy

Bonfanti, F.J.—Associate of Mr. Lloyd; worked with him as spy for Union in CSA

Boone, Robert, Capt.—Relative of Daniel Boone who while in CSA army spied for Union using pseudo of "Charley Davis"

Booth, John Wilkes—Lincoln assassin, reported to have used the name "Renfrew" when spying

Botts, John M.—Member of Union underground in Richmond

Bowie, Walter—CSA spy in S. Maryland

Bowser, Mary Elizabeth—Van Lew spy placed in home of Jefferson Davis

Boyd, Miss Belle—Famous CSA spy in the Shenanodah Valley

Boyd, John E., Capt—Relative of Belle Boyd and CSA spy; hanged by Union on 12 Jan 1865

Boyd, Thomas H.S.—Employee of Mr. Lloyd—fellow spy in CSA for Union

Boyle, John H., Sgt—CSA spy

Brashear, Ella T.—Identified as "spy" from Frederick, Maryland

Listing of Known Spies

Braxley, Mrs—CSA spy arrested and held in Greenhow Prison and exchanged with Mrs. Greenhow

Bryant, Furney—Negro spy who controlled as many as 50 fellow Negro spies in North Carolina

Bridgeman, Sam—Pinkerton agent who worked with Pryce Lewis

Brown, Charles—CSA spy in Valley

Brown, Joshua—CSA spy worked with "Shaw"

"Brown, Kate"—Alias used by Mrs. Sarah Slater—"The French Woman" Confederate courier

Brown, Spencer Kellogg—Union spy in West

Bryan, E. Pliny—CSA spy in DC

Bryant, John R.—First CSA man to spy from a hot air balloon

Bulloch, James—CSA spy in England, got UK to build warships for CSA

"Bunker, General"—Codename for Union spy C.L. Ruggles

Burgess, William—CSA spy hanged Apr 20, 1863

Burging, Christian—German farmer and member of Union underground in Richmond

Burke, John, Colonel—Ace CSA spy

Burke, John—CSA spy (had glass eye) and Northern accent

Burley, Bennett R.—CSA agent in Toronto for Lake Erie ops

Callender, William—Union spy

Spies and Spymasters

Cameron, Stephen, Rev.—CSA agent in Montreal

Cammock, James—Union military scout/spy

Campbell, James—Sheridan operative in Valley

Campbell, Thomas W.—CSA spy

Campbell, William—Union spy, executed by CSA after railroad raid

Carlisle, Nick—Union spy in Valley

Carrington, Henry B., B Gen—Set up Union spy operation in Indiana against KGC

Carter, Charles—Courier for Mr. Ruth, Union spy. Provided by Gen Sharpe

Carter, Mrs.—Union spy

Carter, R. R., Lt—CSA naval agent in UK for Ironclads

Cashmeyer, Philip—Detective for CSA Gen. Winder in Richmond and Union agent for Miss Van Lew

Cassidy—Sheridan operative in Valley captured by CSA and hung

Castleman, John B. Capt—Hine's No. 2 in Canada ops

Caswood, Charles H.—CSA station crossing chief on Potomac

Catlin, Henry—Union spy for Gen. Butler in Virginia, used alias of "Harry S. Howard"

Chandler, Albert—Union cryptanalyst in DC

Chapman, George T.—Union spy in UK for Mr. Dudley (consul in Liverpool)

Listing of Known Spies

"Charley"—Union Negro spy

Cheatham, Ben F., Gen—CSA spymaster in Tennessee

Chewning, M.B.—CSA spy with C. Smith

"Chickasaw, Captain"—Alias for Union spy Noran working for Gen. Dodge

Clary, Frank, Maj—CSA spy in Baltimore

Cleveland, Henry W.—Union spy in North Carolina

Cockney, Charles—Ran a safe house in Baltimore for CSA agents

Coffin—Union spy in KGC saved by Stidger from execution

Cole, Charles—CSA agent in Toronto, arrested in Lake Erie expedition

Cole, Daniel—Gen. Sharpe's most trusted spy/scout

"Coleman, Captain"—Pseudo for CSA Agent Shaw

Compton, William B. Capt—Cousin of Belle Boyd and fellow CSA spy

"Conover, Stanford"—Pseudo used by Capt Maxwell CSA leader at City Point

Conrad, Thomas—Excellent CSA spy—mainly in DC

Cooper, Charles—CSA spy in Valley

"Cornelius"—Negro spy for Union in Virginia killed on a mission

Crenshaw, W. G.—CSA agent in UK to buy and ship supplies to CSA

"Cuff"—Assumed name for Union spy Emma Edmonds when in disguise of Blackman

Curran—CSA spy in KGC in Indiana

Curtis, C.P., Sgt—CSA spy for Gen. Lee

Curtis, George—Principal spy for Pinkerton in Richmond

Curtis, "Ike"—CSA spy with C. Smith

"Cushman, Pauline"—Union spy in West campaign arrested and sentenced to hang, rescued by Union troops just prior to execution. Real name was Harriet Wood

"Dabney"—Union Negro spy that used "clothes-line telegraph"

Dana, William—CSA spy in Valley

Davies, Harry—Pinkerton agent who used alias of Joe Howard

"Davis, Charlie"—Assumed name for Daniel Boone's great grandson who spied for Union

Davis, Harry—A top Pinkerton man, usually working in Baltimore

Davis, John—CSA spy in Tennessee

Davis, Sam—CSA courier for Coleman, hung when captured by Union

"Delcher, Edward"—Pseudo for Stringfellow, ace CSA agent in DC

Denny, John R., Lt Col—CSA agent who often served as Belle Boyd's contact

Dent, Stowton, Dr.—Doctor member of CSA doctor's line

Dickens, Francis A.—CSA spy

Listing of Known Spies

Dillard, Richard—CSA spy executed by Union

Dodd, David—CSA spy hanged by Union

Dodd, E. J.—CSA spy hanged by Union

Dodd, Henry W.—Union military scout/spy

Dodge, General Grenville—Commander of Union spies in West, had about 100 spies

Donnellon, George—Courier for Rose Greenhow in DC

Doolittle, Anson—Double agent probably in the employ of McClellan

Doughty, James—Union military scout/spy

Douglas, Alfred—CSA spy in Tennessee

Dunn, John—Sheridan operative in Valley

Duvall, Betty—Courier for Rose Greenhow, braided messages into hair

Eastin, George, Lt CSA—Hine's CSA operative

Edmondson, Belle—CSA spy in Memphis, Tenn

Edmonds, Miss E. Emma—Served in Union Army as Male Northern Nurse turned spy for Union

Edwards, Edwin S.—CSA spy in Baltimore

Ellsworth, George "Lightning"—CSA "wiretapper" for Morgan

Embert, John R. H.—Convicted CSA spy

Evans, Lemuel D.—Union spy in Texas & Mexico

Spies and Spymasters

Fannin, Dominic—Sheridan operative in Valley

Faulkner, Charles, Mrs.—CSA spy in Valley

Fay, William—Union spy in Richmond for General Sharpe

Featherstone, Jane—Dodge spy in West—important in battle of Vicksburg

Ferguson, Jane—CSA agent who worked disguised as Union soldier, caught and sentenced to hang but later sentence reversed

Ford, Antonia—Famous CSA spy for Mosby, worked with Rose Greenhow

Forster, William—Union "wiretapper"

"Fousha, William S."—Assumed name of CSA agent who informed Union of Johnson Island plot

Fowle, James—CSA agent in S. Maryland

French, Parker—CSA spy arrested by Baker in 1861

French, Peter—Union spy

Gardner, Alexander—Photographer spy for Union, worked with Pinkerton

Garfield, James A., Gen—First Union general to make effort to consolidate spy reports, later President of U.S.

Gaston, Charles—Tapped telegraph line between Grand and DC for two months for the Confederacy

Gibbons, Sam—Union spy in West, hanged by CSA in 1864

Glenn, James W. Capt.—Uncle of Belle Boyd and fellow CSA spy

Listing of Known Spies

Goodman, David—"Stuttering Dave," a Union spy

Gorman, W. P., Maj—CSA spy with Copperheads

Graves, Mrs.—Member of Union underground in Richmond

Greenhow, Mrs. Rose O'Neal—Famous CSA spy who operated in DC

Gregg, Alexander—CSA agent who continued to use C. E. Coleman to sign messages while Shaw in prison

Grenfel, George St Leger, Col—CSA spy imprisoned on Keys near Florida (escaped—never found)

Hale, Jonathan P., Dr.—Union spy, worked with Beatty

Handy, William—CSA spy in Baltimore

Hanna, Laura Ratcliffe—CSA agent for Mosby

Harpin, Thomas—CSA agent who Dr. Mudd introduced to John W. Boothe

Harris, Ike—Sheridan operative in Valley with Rowand—killed there

Harrison, Henry Thomas (?)—Possibly Harrison the CSA spy employed by Longstreet, important at Gettysburg

Harrison, James—Possibly Harrison the CSA spy employed by Longstreet, important at Gettysburg

Harrison, William—Leader of scouts for General Dodge

Hart, Nancy—CSA operative in Virginia

Hart, William Pvt—Union agent in Valley

Harwood—CSA spy

Hassler, Betty—Courier for Rose Greenhow in DC

Headley, John W. Lt—CSA operative at NYC fire & plot to kidnap the VP

Hearn, Samuel B.—Convicted CSA spy

Heidsick, Charles—Frenchman who spied for CSA

Henson, Colonel Philip—Union spy in West, very effective

Herad, David—Hanged in Lincoln plot

"Hewitt, Ada"—alias used by CSA agent Agusta Mason

Higgins, John—Member of Union underground in Richmond

Hines, Thomas H.—Main CSA spy in Toronto, Canada

Hinton, John—CSA spy

Hogan, Dick, Sgt—CSA spy with C. Smith

Holbut, W.H.—CSA spy in Tennessee

Holmes, A.B. Mr—Member of Union underground in Richmond

"Howard, Harry S."—Alias for Union spy Heny Catlin

Howard, James—Clerk in Provost Marshall's office in DC, was CSA spy, caught by Pinkerton early in war.

"Howard, Joe"—Alias for Harry Davies, an early Pinkerton man in Baltimore

Howell, Agustus (Gus)—CSA agent arrested at Surratt tavern

Listing of Known Spies

Humphreys, David, Lt—CSA spy in Valley

Huse, Caleb, Major—CSA agent in Europe to purchase weapons for CSA

Hutchinson, William, Lt—Co-leader of Vermont CSA raid

Hyams, Godfrey J.—Double agent who told Union about CSA NYC fire plan

Irving, John—Union military scout/spy

Jackson, William A.—Coachman for Jefferson Davis and Union spy

"Jem"—Negro who worked as spy for Pinkerton

Jobe, Dewitt Smith—CSA spy in Tennessee, hanged

Johnson, Adam R.—Spy/courier for Gen Forrest

Johnson, J. Stoddard—Ch. spy for Gen. Bragg, CSA

Johnson, Herschel V.—CSA spy in KGC

Jones, Francis—CSA operative in Canada, planned Maine raid that never happened

Jones, Thomas A.—Key link on Maryland side for CSA crossings of Potomac

Joplin, Thomas—CSA spy with C.E. Coleman

Jordan, Capt Thomas—Recruited R. Greenhow for CSA and established DC spy ring

Judd, Clara, Mrs.—CSA spy in Tennessee

"Kalieski, Count"—Alias used by Sobieski when in CSA spying for Union

Keefe, Tom—Union agent who shadowed Thomas Hines

Kennedy, Dolph—CSA spy

Kennedy, Robert, Capt—CSA spy hanged in NYC

Kent, Dr.—Union doctor who worked as courier on CSA "Doctor's Line"

Kerbey, J.O.—Union telegraphic spy in CSA

King, Charles, Private—Union soldier executed as CSA spy

King, Sterling—Double agent working in the Richmond area

Knight—Meade's chief operative

Knight, Judson—Miss Van Lew's favorite "guide"

Landegon, John—Union spy in Valley & with Sherman on his march to the sea

Langhorn, Maurice—Betrayed fellow CSA agents in Chicago plot

Langley, Charles E.—CSA spy executed by Union 6 April 1865

Lawson, James—Negro spy for Union in Virginia

Lawton, Mrs. Hattie—Spy for Pinkerton

Lee, W.L.—Union military scout/spy

Lewis, Pryce—Union spy from UK who identified Webster when caught

Lipscomb, Martin M.—Supplier to CS army, spy for Ms. Van Lew

Littlefield, Augustus K.—Pinkerton operative

Listing of Known Spies

Lloyd, William A.—Lincoln's personal spy in CSA

Lohman, Frederick W.E.—Collaborated with Mr. Ruth for Union in Richmond

Lomas, Mr.—CSA spy for Sheridan's staff

Lonegran—Union "wiretapper"

Longuemare, Capt—CSA operative at NYC fire

"Lopez, Carlos"—Alias used by Samuel Ward, brother of Julia Ward Howe when serving as Union spy

Low, John—CSA seaman agent in UK with Bulloch

Lowe, Thaddeus, Professor—Inventor of air balloon for Union Army and first aerial observer

"Lupo, DR."—Union spy from Italy, true name was Orazio Lugo de Antonzini

Lyon, Braxton—Convicted CSA spy

Lytle, A.D.—CSA photographer spy

Mabry, Mrs. Jeanette Laurimer—Union spy in Tennessee, husband a CSA officer

Mac Kall, Lillie—CSA courier for Mrs. Greenhow in Washington, DC

Maffett, Eugene—CSA seaman with Bulloch in UK

Mainard, Mary—Union spy for Gen. Dodge, captured 1863 and held for duration of war.

Malone, Molly—Dodge favorite spy in West, was illiterate

Marmaduke, Vincent, Col CSA—Testified against fellow CSA agent on Chicago op

Martin, Robert M., Col—CSA leader at NYC fire & plot to kidnap the vice president, used alias of Richard Montgomery, was a double agent throughout war

Martin, Thomas—CSA spy with C.E. Coleman

"Mason, Mrs."—Alias used by CSA agent Agusta Morris

Maughan, John P.—Canadian who worked with CSA Toronto operation & testified against Castleman

Maxwell, Capt—Used name of Sanford Conover, led CSA team in City Point, Va, blast

Mc Arthur, Lewis L.—Clerk who worked with CSA spy Rose Greenhow

Mc Cabe, Joseph E., Sgt—Union spy in Shenandoah Valley & in Gettysburg

Mc Cammon, Thomas—Union spy in Hagerstown, supplied information to Union prior to Battle of Gettysburg

Mc Carty, Mrs. L.A.—CSA spy who worked disguised as a man, used alias of "John Barton"

Mc Daniel, Jedekiah, Capt—Headed CSA Secret Service Unitformed in 1864

Mc Donald, Kate—Worked with CSA in NYC

Mc Entee, John—Spy for Gen Sharpe from 80th New York Infantry

Mc Laughlin, Michael—Imprisoned in Lincoln plot

Milburn, Charles—CSA spy in Maryland

Listing of Known Spies

Milburn, James—CSA spy in Maryland

Miller, Harly—Union spy

"Montgomery, Richard"—Alias used by CSA agent Robert Martin, double agent

Montgomery, Richard—Union spy who served as courier for CSA

Moon, Ginnie, Miss—CSA sister spy in West

Moon, Lottie, Miss—CSA sister spy in West

Morgan, George H.—Union spy in Tennessee

Morris, Mrs. Augusta—Came to DC and tried to sell CSA codes to Union, later arrested as CSA spy

Mudd, Samuel, Dr.—Imprisoned in Lincoln plot

Mullasky, Patrick—Union "wiretapper"

Newcombe, Louis—Boy spy/courier for Lincoln between farm in Va and DC

Noran, L.A.—Union spy with Gen Dodge, used alias of "Captain Chickasaw"

Norris, Major William—Head of CSA spy efforts in Richmond

Norris, William—Ran a safe house in Baltimore for CSA agents

North, James H., Lt—CSA naval agent in UK for ironclads

Norton, Edward—CSA double agent on Baker's staff, worked with Conrad

Orrick, Robert—Farmer in Richmond area who collaborated with Ms. Van Lew's Union spy ring in Richmond

"O 'Shea, Bridget"—assumed name for Union spy Emma Edmonds when disguised as Irish peddler

Overall, Mary—CSA sister spy team in Tenn

Overall, Sophia—CSA sister spy team in Tenn

"Paine, Lewis"—Alias for Lewis Powell, hanged in Lincoln plot

Palmer, Charles—Merchant in Richmond and spy for Ms. Van Lew

Passmore, Dr. William—Englishman who spied for Gen Lee

Patterson, Ann—CSA spy in Tennessee

Patterson Everand—CSA spy with Shaw

Patterson, Kate—CSA spy in Tennessee worked with sister-in-law Ann

Patterson, Samuel—CSA spy with Shaw

Peters, Walter G., Lt—CSA agent caught and hanged

Phillips, Charles—Son of John Y., served as Union courier and spy

Phillips, John Y.—Union spy in Richmond

Pike, Corporal—Union spy enlisted by Gen Sherman

Pinkerton, Allan—Union spy leader for McClellan

Pole, Mr.—Union spy from UK caught in Richmond

Pollock, Sallie Ms.—CSA spy in Cumberland, ran intelligence center

Powell, Charles Capt—CSA spy

Listing of Known Spies

Powell, Lewis—True name of Lewis Paine, hanged in Lincoln plot

"Quaker"—Member of Miss Van Lew's ring in Richmond, true name known to Gen. Butler

Quiggle, James W.—Consul in Antwerp, main figure in Garibaldi scheme

"Rayford, Thomas J."—Alias used by Captain Jordan while head of CSA intelligence efforts in DC

Regley, Henry, Private—Union soldier executed as CSA spy

"Renfrew"—Name probably used by John Wilkes Boothe when spying for CSA

Rennehan, F.—U.S. Govt clerk CSA spy for Rose Greenhow in DC

Rice, Lucy, Mrs.—Member of Union underground in Richmond

Richardson, William—CSA spy hung at Frederick

Richter, Hartman—Imprisoned in Lincoln plot

Riley, Jack—Sheridan operative in Valley

Robertson, Samuel, Pvt—Union spy executed by CSA as member of railroad raid

Ross, Marian, Sgt—Union spy executed by CSA for role in railroad raid

Rowand, Archibald H.—Union spy for Sheridan, awarded Medal of Honor

Rowley, Walter S.—Ran German restaurant in Richmond and spied for Ms. Van Lew

Ruggles, C.L.—Union Operative for Gen Leggett

Ruth, Samuel—Supervisor of Richmond/Fredericksburg RR, acted as Union spy and saboteur on RR line

Sanburn—General Dodge's spy in Miss

Sanford, Harry S.—US ambassador to Belgium & chief Union spymaster in Europe

Sanford—Dodge spy in Vicksburg, advised Dodge that Johnston would not aid Pemberton in an attack

Sanders, B.W.—Union spy who had infiltrated CSA government, passed info on supplies coming from Europe

Scobell, John—Famous Negro Union spy

Scott, Hugh Henderson—CSA spy with C. Smith

Scott, John, Sgt—Union spy executed by CSA for role in railroad raid

Scully, John—Union UK spy who identified Webster when caught by CSA

Seaford, John—Pinkerton man in Baltimore

Shadburne, George D., Sgt—CSA spy with C. Smith

Shadrach, Perry, Pvt—Union spy executed by CSA for role in railroad raid

Shanks, J.J.—CSA turncoat spy for Union who worked with Ayer to uncover plot at Camp Douglas

Shannon, Alexander M.—CSA spy

Sharpe, George H., Gen, USA—Head of intelligence for Grant in East

Listing of Known Spies

Shaw, Henry, Capt—CSA spy in west, went under name of "Coleman"

Shoolbred, Jack—CSA spy

Silver, Isaac—Worked with Mr. Ruth in Union ring in Richmond

Slater, Sarah—CSA spy suspect in Lincoln assassination, never found

Slavens, Sam, Pvt—Union spy executed by CSA for role in railroad raid

Smith, Channing—Ace CSA spy, worked with Stringfellow, Lee's favorite spy

Smith, H.B., Lt—Gen. Sharpe man in Maryland, Delaware and Virginia

Smithson, William T.—Banker & CSA spy for Rose Greenhow in Washington

Sobieski, John—Union spy from Poland, traveled under name of "Kalieski"

Spencer, George, Capt—Spied for General Dodge under "white flag" ruse

Spangler, Samuel—Imprisoned in Lincoln plot

Steane, Franklin—Whiskey distiller in Richmond, member of Union underground

Stearns, Alvin—Sheridan operative in Valley

Stidger, Felix—Union counter spy who infiltrated Copperheads

Straus, Levi—Union spy hanged by Jackson

"Streight, Colonel"—Codename used by General Sharpe with agents

Stringfellow, Private Frank—Head of a CSA ring in DC, used name of "Edward Delcher"

Strother, David H.—Union spy in Valley

Surratt, John Harrison, JR—Arrested in Lincoln plot

Surratt, Mary—Hanged in Lincoln plot

Sykes, Richard M, Dr.—Dentist in Alexandria, Va, worked with Stringfellow for CSA

Tanksley, Henry—CSA in Tennessee

Tatum, Mollie—CSA spy

Taylor, Walker—CSA spy in Tennessee

Tesser, E., Capt—CSA naval agent in France

Thadburne, George D., Sgt—CSA spy in Virginia

"The Toppers"—Union spies in Richmond for General Sharpe

Thomas, Richard, Col. CSA—Tried to make over steamer in Baltimore for CSA, disguised as woman

Thompson, Jacob—CSA spy in Canada

"Thompson, James"—Name used by Richard Montgomery the Union spy who couriered for CSA

"Thompson, Kate"—Alias used by Sarah Slater, the "French Woman" courier, for the Confederacy

Listing of Known Spies

Thompson, Michael (Col)—DC Socialite & CSA spy for Rose Greenhow in Washington

Tillman, William—Negro sailor who shangaied CSA ship *The Waring* and took it to New York

Timberlake, John G.—Worked with Mr. Ruth in Richmond spy ring

Tomlinson Frank—CSA spy

Touvestre, Mary—Negro spy who brought Union plans for remodeling the *Merrimac*

Trager, Louis—Immigrant who spied in CSA for General Grant

Trussel—Union agent with Kellogg Brown

Tubman, Harriet—Conductor on underground railroad and Union spy

Tucker, George Washington, Jr—Arrested in Baltimore in 1861 as CSA spy, later released, became chief courier for Gen A.P. Hill

Turnbull, David—Union spy in KGC in Indiana

"Uncle Gallus"—Union spy in South (Legal League)

"Urz"—CSA spy hanged by Union

Valequez, Madam—CSA spy held in Old Capitol Prison, exchanged along with Rose Greenhow

Van Camp, Aaron, Dr.—Dentist & CSA spy for Rose Greenhow in Washington

Van Lew, Elizabeth—Premier Union spy, operated in Richmond, Va

Van Valkenbergh, F.S.—Union "wiretapper"

Volck, Dr. Adalbert J.—Baltimore dentist & CSA courier, ran safe house in Baltimore for CSA agents

Voorhies, F.F.—CSA spy

Walker, Mary E., Dr—Contract union surgeon who spied for Sherman during the March to Atlanta, only female to receive the Congressional Medal of Honor

Walker, William—US Government clerk & CSA spy for Rose Greenhow in Washington, DC

Walworth, M.T.—CSA spy

Ward, Samuel—Brother of Julia Ward Howe who served as Union spy and used alias of "Carlos Lopez"

Wardwell, B.—Member of Union underground in Richmond

Waring, John—CSA spy in Maryland

Warne, Kate, Mrs—Early Pinkerton operative, assisted getting Lincoln through Baltimore

Webster, Timothy—Principal spy for Pinkerton, hanged in Richmond in 1861

"West, Brodie"—Alias used by CSA spy Belle Edmondson

West, Rebecca—Union spy in West Virginia

Weichman, Louis J.—Arrested in Lincoln plot

White, Jim—Sheridan operative in Valley

Williams, James—CSA spy in Missouri, executed by Union 5 April 1864

Williams, Philip—CSA in Valley

Williams, William O., Col—CSA agent caught and hanged in West

Wilson, George D.—Union spy executed by CSA for role in railroad raid

Winder, Gen. John Henry—CSA counterespionage chief in Richmond

Wood, Harriet—Real name of famous Union spy Pauline Cushman

Wood, William A.—Union secret agent who served as head of Old Capitol Prison

Woodruff, Robbie, Mrs—CSA spy Tennessee

Wright, Rebecca—Union spy in Valley

Wyvell, Doctor—Maryland doctor member of the "Doctor's Line"

Yonge, Clarence R.—CSA seaman with Bulloch in UK, became agent for Union in "Alabama" case

Yonley Sisters—CSA spies

Young, Bennett H., Lt—Led CSA bank raid in Vermont

Young, Harry H. Maj. USA—Sheridan's commander of secret service in Valley

Young, Ogilivie B.—CSA spy

Zeulzschek, C.J.—CSA spy in Nashville

Glossary
of
Civil War Spy Terms

The following glossary of terms is supplied for the reader's use. The terms included are those that appear in the text and may be unfamiliar to the reader. In addition to a definition of the terms an effort has been made, where applicable, to associate the term with a person or activity of the Civil War.

Agent—a person acting as a spy for another government or organization. The mission of the agent is to remain in a covert role throughout his mission. An agent normally works as a member of an organization, although in the Civil War many of the agents worked independently of any central organization.

Breaking a code or cipher—the ability to "de-cipher" or "decode" a message without prior knowledge of the system used to encode or encipher the original text. The Union had three young men, who although totally untrained, were able to read the highest level of Confederate messages: David Homer Bates, Charles A. Tinker and Albert B. Chandler.

217

Cipher—the basic unit of encipherment is the individual alphabetic letter, which is represented by another letter or cipher. For example the word *Lincoln* might be represented as *AJKEFQI* (same word length as original word). To avoid word length association, messages are often sent in "group length" format. AJKEFQI might appear as AJK EFQ IZF.

Code—consists of thousands of words, phrases, letters, any syllables with codewords, codenumbers, sometimes called code groups, that replace the plaintext elements. As possible examples:

Codenumbers: 3964 equates to "emplacing"
Codewords: ADAM equates to "President of the U.S."

Compromise—the act of making public knowledge information that is meant to be kept secret. For example in Civil War times, acquiring the enemy code/cipher without their knowledge, revealing military plans, or revealing the identity of an enemy agent such as Pauline Cushman, thereby rendering them ineffective for the future.

Counterespionage—efforts employed by a government to counter the efforts of enemy spies targeting government. The efforts may include the capturing of enemy spies, tightening of security to prevent intelligence leaks and releasing misinformation to deceive the other government. Allan Pinkerton and Layafette Baker for the Union and General Winder for the Confederacy represent good examples of counterespionage chiefs.

Counterintelligence—synonymous with *counterespionage*

Courier—a person, who may or may not be a spy, but is utilized to carry intelligence information to a designated person or organization. Their missions are usually covert and it is important to avoid capture by the enemy forces. If captured the information they carry gives the other side good intelligence of their enemy's spying capabilities as well as the interest area of their commanders. Couriers were very important during the Civil War as they represented the only way to communicate over a long distance. The telegraph was new and not a secure method of transmitting a covert message.

Cover—the assumption of a new identity, occupation or allegiance in order to hide the agent's real intent. If the cover is exposed, the agent is of little future use to his parent government.

Covert activity—an activity that is conducted secretly or more popularly known as "undercover."

Cryptanalysis—employing methods of breaking codes and ciphers. The Union was able to break the Confederacy's code used by senior government officials, while the Confederacy was never able to read the senior level Union code/cipher.

Handler—A person who manages a spy or spy operation. The handler provides intelligence requirements to be satisfied by the spy, renders payments and usually receives the results of the spy's activities. A Civil War example of a handler is General Sharpe who served in that capacity for Miss Van Lew's operation in Richmond.

Infiltration—in spydom, infiltration is the act of covertly becoming a member of an enemy organization without their knowledge. Timothy Webster is an excellent example of a Union spy who was successful in infiltrating the Confederate government.

Intelligence—information acquired that is of benefit to that person or government. The intelligence may be obtained either overtly or covertly. In Civil War times much intelligence was gained through newspapers, personal conversations, as well as through the use of covert spying and cryptanalysis.

Operative—synonymous with the word *spy*

Overt activity—an activity that is conducted in an open "above board" manner.

Penetration—synonymous with *infiltration*.

Safe house—located in hostile territory, a place known to spies as a location where they will be protected, fed and allowed to remain undetected by enemy government agents. The Surratt Tavern in southern Maryland is an excellent example of a Civil War safe house.

Scout—In Civil War terms a scout could be a person who advanced ahead of the troops and ascertained the presence of troops, the terrain and other information. He could also be utilized as a guide when troops advanced into unknown territory. The word *scout* was often used in the Civil War when describing a spy, and in fact some people, such as Henson for the Union, served as both a scout and a spy.

Spy—a person who works covertly to gather intelligence for a government. A spy may or may not work in a geographic area hostile to his government.

Spymaster—the person who is normally in charge of a group of spies. He is not necessarily the person to whom the spy reports his gathered intelligence. He is however the person who tasked the spy and is responsible for his "care and maintenance." Pinkerton, General Dodge and General Sharpe are all good examples of spymasters during the War of the Rebellion.

Spy ring—a group of spies operating for a common cause under the control of a senior operative. Miss Van Lew ran a spy ring in Richmond for the Union, and in the early days of the war Mrs. Greenhow ran a Confederate spy ring in Washington, D.C.

Strategic intelligence—intelligence that is of value for long range planning and not the day to day military operations. During the Civil War period this would have included long range government planning, morale of the troops, availability of food supplies, pending political/military appointments and foreign relations activities. Intelligence of this nature normally does not have the time-sensitive requirement of tactical intelligence. Miss Van Lew and Mrs. Greenhow are good examples of collectors of this type of information during the Civil War.

Tactical intelligence—intelligence of immediate use, particularly to military commanders. It would include such information as troop movements, time of attack, plan of attack, strength of attacking force and force commanders. Information of this nature was frequently derived but rarely delivered in a timely manner during the Civil War. Henson's information to the Union regarding Vicksburg, prior to the attack, is an example of tactical intelligence.

Time-sensitive intelligence—intelligence that has value only for the immediate future. Normally relates to military activities such as time of attack, points of attack and size of attacking forces. The lack of delivery of time-sensitive information was a major problem to field commanders throughout the Civil War.

Tradecraft—the actual techniques and methods used by a spy to achieve his mission, remain undiscovered by the enemy and successfully report the information back to the appropriate officials. In the Civil War, tradecraft was self-taught as no official training existed. Some, such as Miss Van Lew, quickly learned good tradecraft, others such as Belle Boyd never rose above the amatuer status.

BOOKS WRITTEN BY CIVIL WAR SPIES

Alexander, Edward Porter, *Military Memoirs of a Confederate.* New York: Charles Scribner's Sons, 1907.

Anderson, Edward Clifford, *Confederate Foreign Agent.* University of Alabama Press, 1976.

Ayer, J. Winslow, *The Great Northwest Conspiracy.* Chicago: U.S. Publishing Co., 1865.

Baker, Lafayette, *History of the U.S. Secret Service.* Philadelphia, 1868.

Baker, Lafayette, *Traitors and Conspirators of the Late Civil War.* Philadelphia, John E. Potter, 1894.

Baker, Lafayette, *The United States Secret Service in the Late War.* St. Louis: Halloway & Co 1889.

Spies and Spymasters

Bates, David Homer, *Lincoln in the Telegraph Office.* New York: Century, 1907.

Boyd, Belle, *Belle Boyd in Camp and Written by Herself.* South Brunswick, N.J.: Thomas Yoseloff, 1968.

Brown, Spencer Kellogg, *Spencer Kellogg Brown, His Life in Kansas and His Death as a Spy (1842–1863)* as disclosed in his diaries. New York: D. Appleton, 1903.

Bulloch, James D., *The Secret Service of the Confederate States in Europe OR How the Confederate Cruisers Were Equipped.* New York: G.P. Putnam's, 1884.

Castleman, J. M., "Active Service." Louisville, Ky: Courier-Journal Job Printing, 1917.

Conrad, Thomas N., *A Confederate Spy.* New York: S. J. Ogilvie, 1892; *The Rebel Spy.* Washington, D.C.: The National Publishing Co, 1904.

Edmonds Sarah Emma, *Nurse and Spy in the Union Army/ Comprising the Aventures and Experiences of a Woman in Hospitals, Camps and Battlefields.* Hartford, Ct.: W.S.Williams, 1865.

Ellis, Daniel, *The Thrilling Adventures of Daniel Ellis.* New York: Harpers and Brothers, 1861.

Greenhow, Rose, *My Imprisonment and the First Year of Abolition Rule in Washington.* London: Richard Bently, 1863.

Headley, John W., *Confederate Operations in Canada and the North.* New York: Neale Publishing, 1906.

Henson, Philip, *The Southern Union Spy.* St. Louis: Nixon Jones Printing Co., 1887.

Kerbey, J. O., *The Boy Spy, A Substantially True Record of the Secret*

Service During the War of the Rebellion. Chicago: American Mutual Library Association, 1889.

Newcombe, Louis, *Lincoln's Boy Spy.* New York: G.P. Putnam's & Sons, 1929.

Patrick, Marsena R., *Inside Lincoln's Army; The Diary of Marsena Patrick,* edited by David Sparks. New York: Thomas Yoseloff, 1964.

Pinkerton, Allen, *The Spy of the Rebellion.* New York: G.W.Carleton, 1883.

Richarson, Albert D. *Secret Service, The Field, The Dungeon and the Escape,* Chicago, IL.: American Publishing Company, 1865.

Ruggles, C. L., *The Great American Scout and Spy.* Olmstead & Co, 1870.

Stidger, Felix, *Treason History of the Sons of Liberty.* Chicago: 1903.

Thompson, J., *A Leaf from History,* Report of J. Thompson, Secret Agent of the Late Confederate Government, Stationed in Canada, for the Purpose of Organizing Insurrection in the Northern States and Burning Their Principal Cities. Washington, D.C.: Office of the Great Republic, 1868.

Velazquez, Loreta Janeta, *The Woman in Battle: A Narrative of the Exploits, Adventures, and Travels of Madame Loreta Janeta Velazquez, Otherwise Known as Lieutenant Harry T. Buford, Confederate States Army.* Hartford, Ct.: T. Belknap, 1876.

Bibliography

Books and Original Material

A Concise Encyclopaedia of the Civil War, compiled by Henry Simmons. New York: Bonanza Books, 1950.

Abraham Lincoln and the Fifth Column, G. F. Milton. The Vanguard Press, 1942.

Africa's Gift to America, J. A. Rogers. New York: 1959.

A Guide to the Archives of the Government of the Confederate States. Henry Putney Beers. Washington, D.C.: National Archives, 1986.

A Guide to the Federal Archives Relating to the Civil War, Henry Putney Beers and Kenneth W. Munden. Washington, D.C.: National Archives, 1986.

A Leaf from History, Report of J. Thompson, Secret Agent for the Late Confederate Government, stationed in Canada for the purpose of organizing insurrection in the Northern states and burning their principal cities. Washington D.C.: Office of the Great Republic, 1868.

A Rebel Spy in Yankeeland, The Thrilling Adventures of Major W.P. Gorman Who Was the Emissary of the Confederacy to the Copperheads of the North, 1861–1865, edited and introduced by W. Stanley Hoole. University of Alabama: Confederate Publishing Co., 1981.

A Short History of Espionage, Col. Allison Ind. David McKay Company, Inc, 1963.

Behind Enemy Lines, The Incredible Story of Emma Edmonds, Civil War Spy, Seymour Reit, Harcourt Brace Jovanovich, 1980.

Belle Boyd in Camp and, Written by Herself, Belle Boyd, Thomas Yoseloff. South Brunswick, NJ, 1968.

Between the Lines: Secret Service Stories Told Fifty Years After, H B. Smith. New York: Booz Brothers, 1911.

Black Americans and Their Contributions Toward Union Victory in the American Civil War (1861–1865), Joe H. Mays. Lanham, Maryland: University Press of America, 1894.

Black Writers and the American Civil War, Black Involvement and Participation in the War Between the States, edited by Richard A. Long. The Blue & Grey Press, 1988.

Brave Deeds of Confederate Soldiers, Philip A. Bruce. George W. Jacobs & Company, 1916.

Come Retribution, William Tidwell. University of Mississippi Press, 1988.

Confederate Foreign Agent: The European Diary of Major Edward C. Anderson, Edward C. Anderson. University of Alabama Press, 1976.

Confederate Purchasing Operations Abroad, Samuel B. Thompson. Chapel Hill, N.C.: University of North Carolina Press, 1935.

Confederate Spy, James D. Horan. Crown Publishers, Inc., 1954.

Bibliography

Confederate Spy Stories, Katherine and John Bakeless. New York: J.B. Lippincott Co., 1973.

Desperate Women, James D. Horan. N.Y.: Bonanza Books, 1952.

Disloyalty in the Confederacy, Georgia Lee Tatum. University of North Carolina Press, 1934.

Freedom, A Documentary History of Emancipation 1861–1867, Series II, The Black Military Experience, Ira Berlin, editor. Cambridge University Press, 1982.

Generals in Blue, Lives of the Union Generals, Ezra J. Warner. Louisiana State University Press, 1959.

Generals in Gray, Lives of the Confederate Generals, Ezra J. Warner. Louisiana State University Press, 1959.

Grenville M. Dodge, Stanley P. Hirshson. Indiana University Press, 1967.

History of the United States Secret Service, General L. C. Baker. Philadelphia: L. C. Baker, 1867.

Honorable Treachery, A History of U. S. Intelligence, Espionage, and Covert Action from the American Revolution to the CIA, G.T.A. O'Toole. New York: The Atlantic Monthly Press, 1991.

Jefferson Davis and His Generals, The Failure of Confederate Command in the West, Steven Woodworth. University Press of Kansas, 1990.

Ladies of Richmond, Katharine M. Jones. Bobbs-Merrill Co, Inc., 1962.

Lincoln's Boy Spy, Captain Louis N. Newcombe. G.P. Putnam & Sons, 1929.

Spies and Spymasters

Lincoln in the Telegraph Office, David H. Bates. New York: The Century Co., 1907.

Marching Toward Freedom, James M. McPherson. Facts on File, New York, 1991.

Memoirs of General William T. Sherman, William T. Sherman. The Library of America, 1990.

Military Intelligence 1861–1863, Edwin C. Fishel. CIA Studies in Intelligence (Summer 66).

On Hazardous Service: Scouts and Spies of the North and South, William G. Beyer. Harper & Bro, 1912.

Personal Memoirs of U. S. Grant, U. S. Grant. Da Capo Press, 1982.

Personal Memoirs of P.H. Sheridan, P.H. Sheridan. Jenkins & McCowan, 1888.

Photgraphic History of the Civil War, (Volumes Seven and Eight) Francis T. Miller. Thomas Yoseloff Publisher.

Rebel Rose, Ishbel Ross. Mockingbird Books, 1954.

Provost Marshall General File, Headquarters to Field Reports. National Archives, Washington, D.C.

Provost Marshall General File, Scouts, Guides, Spies and Detectives, National Archives, Washington, D.C.

Scouts, Spies, and Heroes of the Great Civil War, Linus P. Brockett. Jersey City Publishing Co, 1892.

Secret Missions of the Civil War, edited by Philip Van Doren Stern. Rand McNally & Co, 1959.

Secret Service, 33 Centuries of Espionage, Richard Wilmer Rown with Robert G. Deindorfer, 1967.

Bibliography

Secret Service, The Field, the Dungeon and the Escape, Albert D. Richardson. Hartford, Ct.: American Publishing Co., 1865.

Spencer Kellogg Brown, His Life in Kansas and His Death as a Spy, 1842–1863, as Disclosed in His Diary, Spencer K. Brown. New York: D. Appleton, 1903.

Spies and Spymasters, Jock Haswell. Thames & Hudson, 1977.

Spies for the Blue and Gray, Harnett T. Kane. Hanover House, 1954.

Spies of the Confederacy, John Bakeless, J. B. Lippincott Company, 1970.

Spies, Scouts and Raiders of the Civil War: Irregular Operations. Time Life Series, 1985.

Spies, Traitors, and Conspirators of the Late Civil War, Lafayette Baker. J. E. Potter & Company, 1894.

Spying for America, The Hidden History of U.S. Intelligence, Nathan Miller. Paragon House, 1989.

Stringfellow of the Fourth, R. Shepard Brown. Crown Publishers Inc, 1960.

The Battle of Atlanta and Other Campaigns, Addresses, etc, Major-General Grenville Dodge. Council Bluffs, Iowa: The Monarch Printing Company, 1910.

The Blue and the Gray, Thomas B. Allen. Washington, D.C.: The National Geographic Society, 1992.

The Boy Spy, J. O. Kerbey. Chicago: American Mutual Library Associates, 1889.

The Civil War Dictionary, Mark Maye Boatner, III. New York: David McKay, Inc, 1959.

231

Spies and Spymasters

The Civil War: Strange and Fascinating Facts, Burke Davis. Orlando, Florida: Holt, Rinehart and Winston Inc., 1982.

The Codebreakers, David Kahn. The MacMillan Company, 1967.

The Craft of Intelligence, Allen Dulles. Harper & Row, 1963.

The Great American Scout and Spy "General Bunker," C. L. Ruggles. Olmstead & Co, 1870.

The Messages and Papers of Jefferson Davis and the Confederacy, 1861– 1865, Volumes I and II, R. R. Bowker. Chelsea House-Robert Hector Publishers, 1966.

The Negro in the Civil War, Benjamin Quarles. Russell & Russell, 1968.

The Pinkertons: The Detectives Dynasty That Made History, James D. Horan. Crown Publishers, Inc., 1967.

The Secret Service of the Confederate States in Europe, Volumes I and II, James D. Bulloch. Thomas Yoseloff Press, 1959.

The Signal and Secret Service of the Confederate States, Dr. Thomas E. Taylor. Tooney Press, 1986.

The Southern Union Spy, Philip Henson, George S. Johns. St. Louis: Nikxon Jones Printing Co, 1887.

The Spy of the Rebellion, Allan Pinkerton. 1883.

The Story of the U.S. Army Signal Corps, edited by Lt. Col. Max L. Marshall, USA (Ret). Franklin Watts, Inc, 1965.

Turner/Baker papers. National Archives, Washington, D.C.

The War Between the Spies, A History of Espionage During the American Civil War, Alan Axelrod. New York: The Atlantic Monthly Press. 1992.

Trial of John Y. Beall, As a Spy and Guerrilla, New York: Military Commission, B. Appleton, 1865.

Undercover Washington, Pamela Kessler. EPM Publications, 1992.

War of the Rebellion. U. S. War Department, 1894.

Who Was Who in the Civil War, Stewart Sieakis. New York: Facts on File Publications, 1988.

Additional Information Supplied By:

Commissioners of Charles County Maryland
Congressional Research Service
International Museum of Photography
Iowa State Historical Society
Kentucky Military History Museum
Maryland Historical Society
Moorland-Spingarn Research Center, Howard University
Museum of the Confederacy
New York State Historical Society
State Archives of Iowa
Surratt House Museum
Texas Department of Criminal Justice
United States Army Military History Library
Virginia Historical Society

Magazines

Blue & Gray Magazine, October 1992, "The Deception of Braxton Bragg," pages 17–21.

Civil War, The Magazine of the Civil War, Nov–Dec 1990, "Behind the Lines" issue.

Civil War Chronicle, fall 1992, "The Most Extraordinary and Astounding Adventure of the Civil War," Stephen W. Sears, pages 25–37.

Civil War Times Illustrated, April 1971, "Catching Harry Gilmor," page 34.

Civil War Times Illustrated, April 1978, "The Great Gainsville Hanging," page 12.

Civil War Times Illustrated October 1992, "The Great Raid on Calais," page 40; and "Hill's Favorite Courier," page 42.

Maryland Historical Society, September 1946, Volume XLI, Number 3, "Mrs. Greenhow and the Rebel Spy Ring," pages 173–191.

The Gettysburg Magazine, July 1990, Nr 3, "The Signal Corps at Gettysburg" pages 9–15.

The Gettysburg Magazine, January 1991, Nr 4, "The Confederate Signals Corps at Gettysburg. Pages 110–112.

The Virginia Magazine of History and Biography, October 1955, Volume 63, Number 4, "Disloyalty on Confederate Railroads in Virginia."

The Virginia Magazine of History and Biography, January 1963, Volume 71, Number 1, Samuel Ruth and General Robert E. Lee: "Disloyalty and the Line of Supply to Fredericksburg," 1862–1863.

The Virginia Magazine of History and Biography, April 1964, Volume 72, Number 2, "Colonel Ulric Dahlgren and Richmond's Union Underground," April 1864.

The Virginia Magazine of History and Biography, July 1981, Volume 89, Number 3, "Of Spies with Borrowed Names: The Identity of Union Operatives in Richmond Known as the Phillipses: Discovered."

The Virginia Magazine of History and Biography, July 1982. Volume 90, Number 3, "Dr. Lugo, An Austro-Venetian Adventurer in Union Espionage" (pages 339–358).

Index

Gardner, Alexander, Union photographic spy, 34, 151

Garfield, James A., as intelligence chief in West, 124-126; successes, 125; future president, 126

Garibaldi, Guiseppe, 72

Gatson, C.A., Confederate wiretapper, 82

General Intelligence Office, CSA, 3

Georgetown University, as signal station, 80

Germ warfare, Confederate use of, 54

Gettysburg, Battle of 14-15, 43; Harrison at, 105

Gibbons, Sam, 92

Glossary of terms, 217-222

Gorman, W.P., with Copperheads,103; arrest and escape, 104; member of Michigan Legislature, 104

Grant, U.S., building military intelligence department, 7; member of Order of Heroes, 27; Confederate telegraph operator on staff, 81

Graves, Mrs., 182

Gray, Mr. W.F., volunteer spy for Union from Switzerland, 70

"Greek fire," use of, in St. Louis, 53; use in New York, 54

Green, Mrs., 182; 188

Greenhow, Rose O'Neal, use of couriers, 19-20; general 159-164; achievement prior to Bull Run, 160-161; spy ring, 160; arrest and exchange, 162-163; in Europe, 163; death, 163-164

Grimes, A.C., 93

Hale, Nathan, 147

Hamilton Landing Raid, 140-141

Hanna, Laura R., 168

Hardinge, S. Wylde, 157-158

Harper, M.D., 92

Harrison, 104-106; with Gen. Longstreet, 104; at Gettysburg, 105; dispute over identity, 105-106

Harrison, Henry Thomas, 106

Harrison, James, 105-106

Hart, Nancy, 168

Hassler, Betty, 160

Heidsick, John, Confederate spy from France, 70-71

Henson, "Colonel" Philip, general 126-130; in Vicksburg, 126-127; as double agent, 127-128; arrest, 128; on lecture circuit, 129; recognition from Gen. Dodge, 128-129

Herrad, David, 93

Hines, Thomas H., call to Richmond and assignment, 51; attempt to kidnap Vice President Johnson 54; general, 106-110; with Morgan's raiders, 107; capture and escape 107; with Copperheads, 107-109; espionage actions, 52-54, 107

Holcombe, James P., 51

Hot air balloons, general, 36-38; Union use, 37; Confederate use, 37-38

Howard, James 160

Hyams, Godfrey, Union double agent, New York plot, 54, 116

Illinois, planned actions, 53-54

Imprisonment, 85

Indian spies use by Gen. Dodge, 9; use by Gen. Sharpe, 13

Individual spies, general, 95-98

Ironclads, 58, 75-76

HIPPOCRENE MILITARY LIBRARY

TERRIBLE INNOCENCE:
GENERAL SHERMAN AT WAR
Mark Coburn

In a war of set piece battles, with rivers of blood, General
William Tecumseh Sherman was a striking exception. He
believed that "the time has come when we should attempt the
boldest moves, and my experience is that they are easier of
execution than more timid ones." A master of logistics, he was
most sparing of his men's lives: "night and day I labor to the end
that not a life shall be lost in vain."

He burnt cities, but he saved lives; the terror he inspired made
his victories less expensive in lives and more effective. Contrary
to rumors, Sherman permitted arson and pillage, but not wanton
killing and rape. His army lived off the land, to make continuing
offensives less dependent on uncertain supplies.

A great strategist with an uncanny memory and a feeling for
terrain, General Sherman was a fine writer as well. His orders
were dear and to the point, and his memoirs most readable and
accurate. Mark Coburn's account is as lively and vital as his
subject, and does justice to a general who in his focus on winning
and in his thinking was as modern as General Patton 80 years
later.

An escaped New Yorker, Coburn lives in Durango, Colorado,
and teaches English at Fort Lewis College. He has written many
articles on the American past.

MILITARY BOOK CLUB MAIN SELECTION

240 pages, 6 x 9, 16 illustrations, 6 maps
0-7818-0156-7 $22.50 cloth

HIPPOCRENE MILITARY LIBRARY

New in Paperback

KOREA: THE FIRST WAR WE LOST (3rd EDITION)
Revised with Epilogue
Bevin Alexander

The best book ever written on the subject—now in its third printing!

Praise for the hardcover edition:

"[A] well-researched and readable book." —The New York Times

"This is arguably the most reliable and fully-realized one-volume history of the Korean War since David Rees' *Korea.*" —Publishers Weekly

"Bevin Alexander does a superb job ... this respectable and fast-moving study is the first to be written by a professional army historian." —Library Journal

580 pages   6 x 9
index, 82 b/w photos, 13 maps
0-7818-0065-X $16.95pb

HIPPOCRENE MILITARY LIBRARY

Also by Don Lowry:

FATE OF THE COUNTRY
The Civl War from June to September 1864
Don Lowry
"An excellent account of the period ... recommended"—**Booklist**
"[Lowry's] frame-by-frame chronology succeeds in heightening the natural drama of the events." —**Library Journal**
555 pages, 6 x 9, index, 4 maps
0-7818-0064-1   *$27.50*

NO TURNING BACK
The End of the Civil War
May-June 1864
Don Lowry
576 pages, 6 x 9
0-87052-010-5   *$27.50*

Other Military Titles:

ANATOMY OF VICTORY
Battle Tactics 1689-1763
Brent Nosworthy
359 pages, 6 x 9, 22 formation diagrams
0-87052-014-8   *$16.95pb*

BATAAN
Our Last Ditch
Lt. Col. John Whitman
700 pages, 6 x 9, 16 b/w photos, maps
0-87052-877-7   *$29.95*

COLLECTOR'S GUIDE TO
THIRD REICH MILITARIA
Robin Lumsden
176 pages, 5 3/4 x 8 1/2, 150 b/w photos and illustrations
0-7101-723-9   *$19.95pb*

DETECTING THE FAKES
Robin Lumsden
144 pages, 5 3/4 x 8 1/2, 150 b/w photos and illustrations
0-87052-829-7   *$19.95pb*

ELEPHANT AND THE TIGER
The Full Story of the War in Vietnam
Wilbur H. Morrison
"A comprehensive, hardnosed exploration of the question, how did we win every battle yet lose the war?... Includes a full account of South Vietnamese military operations, an element of the war usually ignored."
—**Publishers Weekly**
Military Book Club Dual Selection
640 pages, 6 x 9, 16 b/w photos
0-87052-623-5   *$24.95*

IMPROVISED WAR
Michael Glover
232 pages
0-87052-456-9   *$29.50*

INTELLIGENCE OFFICERS
IN THE PENINSULAR WAR
Julia Page
255 pages
0-87052-310-4   *$22.95*

MILITARY MANUAL OF SELF-DEFENSE
Anthony B. Herbert
0-87052-977-3   *$9.95pb*
Harry Albright
320 pages, 6 x 9
0-87052-007-5   *$8.95pb*

PATTON'S THIRD ARMY
Charles Province
"This book forms an invaluable work of reference which contains a vast wealth of facts and figures. I'm sure it will be of great interest to both the professional and amateur historian alike." —**British Army Review**
"Had I been able to refer to such a complete work of reference for my *Patton's Third Army at War*, then my task would have been made immeasurably easier." —**George Forty, Tank Magazine**
336 pages, 6 x 9
0-87052-973-0   *$22.50*

PEARL HARBOR
Japan's Fatal Blunder
Harry Albright
378 pages, 6 x 9
0-87052-074-1   *$8.95pb*

RIVER AND THE ROCK
Fortress West Point
Dave R. Palmer
0-87052-992-7   *$69.50*

ROYAL MARINES COMMANDOES
John Watney
0-87052-715-0   *$9.95pb*

SCOTTISH REGIMENTS
A Pictorial History
P. Mileham
0-87052-361-9   *$70.00*

All prices subject to change.

Order directly from HIPPOCRENE BOOKS by sending a check or mail order for the price of the book, plus $4.00 shipping and handling for the first book, and $.50 for each additional book to: HIPPOCRENE BOOKS, 171 MADISON AVE., NEW YORK, NY 10016